BLOOM'S

HOW TO WRITE ABOUT

Ernest Hemingway

KIM E. BECNEL

Introduction by
HAROLD BLOOM

BLOOM'S
LITERARY CRITICISM
An imprint of Infobase Publishing

Bloom's How to Write about Ernest Hemingway

Copyright © 2009 by Kim E. Becnel

Bloom's Literary Criticism
An imprint of Infobase Publishing
132 West 31st Street
New York NY 10001

Library of Congress Cataloging-in-Publication Data

Bloom, Harold.
  Bloom's how to write about Ernest Hemingway / Harold Bloom.
    p. cm.—(Bloom's how to write about literature)
  Includes bibliographical references and index.
  ISBN 978-0-7910-9746-5 (hardcover)
  1. Hemingway, Ernest, 1899–1961—Criticism and interpretation. 2. Criticism—Authorship. 3. Report writing. I. Title. II. Title: How to write about Ernest Hemingway. III. Series.
  PS3515.E37Z58248 2008
  813'.52—dc22   2008002982

Bloom's Literary Criticism books are available at special discounts when purchased in bulk quantities for businesses, associations, institutions, or sales promotions. Please call our Special Sales Department in New York at (212) 967-8800 or (800) 322-8755.

You can find Bloom's Literary Criticism on the World Wide Web at http://www.chelseahouse.com

Text design by Annie O'Donnell
Cover design by Ben Peterson

Printed in the United States of America

Bang MSRF 10 9 8 7 6 5 4 3 2 1

This book is printed on acid-free paper.

CONTENTS

SERIES
INTRODUCTION

BLOOM's How to Write about Literature series is designed to inspire students to write fine essays on great writers and their works. Each volume in the series begins with an introduction by Harold Bloom, meditating on the challenges and rewards of writing about the volume's subject author. The first chapter then provides detailed instructions on how to write a good essay, including how to find a thesis; how to develop an outline; how to write a good introduction, body text, and conclusions; how to cite sources; and more. The second chapter provides a brief overview of the issues involved in writing about the subject author and then a number of suggestions for paper topics, with accompanying strategies for addressing each topic. Succeeding chapters cover the author's major works.

The paper topics suggested within this book are open ended, and the brief strategies provided are designed to give students a push forward on the writing process rather than a road map to success. The aim of the book is to pose questions, not answer them. Many different kinds of papers could result from each topic. As always, the success of each paper will depend completely on the writer's skill and imagination.

HOW TO WRITE ABOUT ERNEST HEMINGWAY: INTRODUCTION

by Harold Bloom

EMINGWAY WAS one of the Western world's supreme artists of the short story, comparable in eminence to Turgenev, Chekhov, Maupassant, Henry James, James Joyce, and Isaak Babel. As a novelist, essentially Hemingway failed, if judged by a standard embracing Dickens, Tolstoy, George Eliot, Balzac, Flaubert, Manzoni, and Proust. Only *The Sun Also Rises* has not yet wholly faded, and in time I expect it will prove another period piece.

Wallace Stevens, who knew Hemingway at Key West, considered him to have been essentially a poet. Read as poetry, the best Hemingway stories transcend the emotional limitations of his protagonists and demonstrate that his true precursor was Walt Whitman rather than Mark Twain, particularly in *Huckleberry Finn*, as the author of the Nick Adams stories asserted.

Like Whitman's, Hemingway's cadences are biblical, in the modes of the King James or Authorized Version. Neither Whitman, an Epicurean visionary, nor Hemingway, a Stoic storyteller, was a Christian except in the generic sense of what I have called the American Religion. Whitman, in his more ecstatic moments, is a kind of secular Kabbalist, as the great Jerusalem scholar Gershom Scholem loved to proclaim. Hemingway, more an incarnated mystique than a mystic, found his Christ in bullfighters and big-game hunters, men who "lived their lives all the way up." Courage, in Hemingway, is the prime theological virtue.

Jake Barnes, in *The Sun Also Rises*, suffers a nostalgia for Catholicism but cannot attain it. Hemingway's true surrogate is Nick Adams, boy and then young man, who in his manner of speaking inaugurates the Hemingway style: elliptical, terse and yet capacious, death haunted yet vitalizing, and surprisingly universal in its reticences and qualified affirmations.

Hemingway, like his exact American contemporary Hart Crane, was a natural, a poet who unfolded rather than developed. Both popular and elitist, Hemingway instantly intrigued the best writers of his time: James Joyce, D. H. Lawrence, Gertrude Stein, Ezra Pound, and many others. They found in him the original style of a masterly impressionist and a sensibility perfectly attuned to the spirit of the age, the twenties, a time haunted by the wake of World War I, prelude to catastrophes yet to come.

How to write about Hemingway? He has motivated oceans of commentary, most of it of little use. Begin then by recognizing how difficult he is to rationalize, analyze, or accept either on his own terms or those of the myriad critical schools, particularly the ones now fashionable. He is as evasive as Walt Whitman or his prime precursor, Joseph Conrad. What matters most in him is what Wallace Stevens beautifully called: "The hum of thoughts evaded in the mind." His difficulties, even for the trained deep reader, indeed are those of authentic poetry rather than prose.

I urge you then to start by selecting one of the major stories that find you and will not let you go. Read it aloud to yourself, which is the best way of reading poetry. You have to *hear* Hemingway as you hear Shakespeare or Wordsworth or Whitman, both with the outer and the inner ear.

A story I possess by memory is the four-page "God Rest You Merry, Gentlemen," about which I have written elsewhere in *How to Read and Why* (2000). I return to it now as a proof-text, after reciting it out loud to myself. The reader finds herself, in exotic Kansas City on Christmas Day, overhearing a conversation between two emergency-room surgeons, the bitterly wise Doc Fischer and the hapless, incompetent Doctor Wilcox. Their subject is a 16-year-old disturbed boy who, in his search for purity, has mutilated himself, probably fatally, after being refused when he begged castration. The dialogue between Fischer and Wilcox is classic:

> "Well, I wish you wouldn't ride me about it," Doctor Wilcox said. "There isn't any need to ride me."
>
> "Ride you, Doctor, on the day, the very anniversary, of our Savior's birth?"

"*Our* Savior? Ain't you a Jew?" Doctor Wilcox said.

"So I am. So I am. It always is slipping my mind. I've never given it its proper importance. So good of you to remind me. *Your* Savior. That's right. *Your* Savior, undoubtedly *your* Savior—and the ride of Palm Sunday."

"You're too damned smart," Doctor Wilcox said.

"An excellent diagnosis, Doctor. I was always too damned smart. Too damned smart on the coast certainly. Avoid it, Horace. You haven't much tendency but sometimes I see a gleam. But what a diagnosis—and without the book."

"The hell with you," Doctor Wilcox said.

"All in good time, Doctor," Doc Fischer said. "All in good time. If there is such a place I shall certainly visit it. I have even had a very small look into it. No more than a peek, really. I looked away almost at once. And do you know what the young man said, Horace, when the good Doctor here brought him in? He said, "Oh, I asked you to do it. I asked you so many times to do it.""

"On Christmas Day, too," Doctor Wilcox said.

"The significance of the particular day is not important," Doc Fischer said.

"Maybe not to you," said Doctor Wilcox.

"You hear him, Horace?" Doc Fischer said. "You hear him? Having discovered my vulnerable point, my Achilles tendon so to speak, the doctor pursues his advantage."

"You're too damned smart," Doctor Wilcox said.

Fischer, though he alludes to Shylock earlier in the story, has in him the mordant verbal energy of Marlowe's Barabas, the Jew of Malta, though actually the doctor is benign in his dark wit. What this marvelous dialogue performs is an educational challenge to any reader who wishes to comment upon it. That Doc Fischer speaks for something at Hemingway's curtailed own center is palpable, but how do we come to know that? Nihilism informs Fischer's rhetoric, but what sense of self-curtailed goodwill underlies it? Unlike Nathanael West's Shrike in *Miss Lonelyhearts*, who appalls us by his savage parodies, Fischer moves us to symphathize with his battered apprehension of the abyss of everyday life. How to write about Hemingway? Develop and maintain an awareness of the living resilience of his language, and of the indirect brilliance of his extraordinary skill of characterization.

HOW TO WRITE
A GOOD ESSAY
by Laurie A. Sterling and Kim E. Becnel

WHILE THERE are many ways to write about literature, most assignments for high school and college English classes call for analytical papers. In these assignments, you are presenting your interpretation of a text to your reader. Your objective is to interpret the text's meaning in order to enhance your reader's understanding and enjoyment of the work. Without exception, strong papers about the meaning of a literary work are built upon a careful, close reading of the text or texts. Careful, analytical reading should always be the first step in your writing process. This volume provides models of such close, analytical reading, and these should help you develop your own skills as a reader and as a writer.

As the examples throughout this book demonstrate, attentive reading entails thinking about and evaluating the formal (textual) aspects of the author's works: theme, character, form, and language. In addition, when writing about a work, many readers choose to move beyond the text itself to consider the work's cultural context. In these instances, writers might explore the historical circumstances of the time period in which the work was written. Alternatively, they might examine the philosophies and ideas that a work addresses. Even in cases where writers explore a work's cultural context, though, papers must still address the more formal aspects of the work itself. A good interpretative essay that evaluates Charles Dickens's use of the philosophy of utilitarianism in his novel *Hard Times*, for example, cannot adequately address the author's treatment of the philosophy without firmly grounding this discussion in the book itself. In other words, any analytical paper about a text, even one that seeks to evaluate the work's cultural context, must also have a firm handle on the work's themes, characters, and language. You must look for and evaluate these aspects of a work, then, as you read a text and as you prepare to write about it.

WRITING ABOUT THEMES

Literary themes are more than just topics or subjects treated in a work; they are attitudes or points about these topics that often structure other elements in a work. Writing about theme therefore requires that you not just identify a topic that a literary work addresses but also discuss what that work says about that topic. For example, if you were writing about the culture of the American South in William Faulkner's famous story "A Rose for Emily," you would need to discuss what Faulkner says, argues, or implies about that culture and its passing.

When you prepare to write about thematic concerns in a work of literature, you will probably discover that, like most works of literature, your text touches upon other themes in addition to its central theme. These secondary themes also provide rich ground for paper topics. A thematic paper on "A Rose for Emily" might consider gender or race in the story. While neither of these could be said to be the central theme of the story, they are clearly related to the passing of the "old South" and could provide plenty of good material for papers.

As you prepare to write about themes in literature, you might find a number of strategies helpful. After you identify a theme or themes in the story, you should begin by evaluating how other elements of the story—such as character, point of view, imagery, and symbolism—help develop the theme. You might ask yourself what your own responses are to the author's treatment of the subject matter. Do not neglect the obvious, either: What expectations does the title set up? How does the title help develop thematic concerns? Clearly, the title "A Rose for Emily" says something about the narrator's attitude toward the title character, Emily Grierson, and all she represents.

WRITING ABOUT CHARACTER

Generally, characters are essential components of fiction and drama. (This is not always the case, though; Ray Bradbury's "August 2026: There Will Come Soft Rains" is technically a story without characters, at least any human characters.) Often, you can discuss character in poetry, as in T. S. Eliot's "The Love Song of J. Alfred Prufrock" or Robert Browning's "My Last Duchess." Many writers find that analyzing character is one of the most interesting and engaging ways to work with a piece of literature and to shape a paper. After all, characters generally are human, and we all know something about being human and living in the world. While it is always important to remember that these figures are not real people but creations of the writer's imagination, it can be fruitful to begin evaluating them as you might evaluate a real person. Often you can start with your own response to a character. Did you like or dislike the character? Did you sympathize with the character? Why or why not?

Keep in mind, though, that emotional responses like these are just starting places. To truly explore and evaluate literary characters, you need to return to the formal aspects of the text and evaluate how the author has drawn these characters. The 20th-century writer E. M. Forster coined the terms *flat* characters and *round* characters. Flat characters are static, one-dimensional characters who frequently represent a particular concept or idea. In contrast, round characters are fully drawn and much more realistic characters who frequently change and develop over the course of a work. Are the characters you are studying flat or round? What elements of the characters lead you to this conclusion? Why might the author have drawn characters like this? How does their development affect the meaning of the work? Similarly, you should explore the techniques the author uses to develop characters. Do we hear a character's own words, or do we hear only other characters' assessments of him or her? Or, does the author use an omniscient or limited omniscient narrator to allow us access to the workings of the characters' minds? If so, how does that help develop the characterization? Often you can even evaluate the narrator as a character. How trustworthy are the opinions and assessments of the narrator? You should also think about characters' names. Do they mean anything? If you encounter a hero named Sophia or Sophie, you should probably think about her wisdom (or lack thereof), since *Sophia* means "wisdom" in Greek. Similarly, since the name *Sylvia* is derived from the word *sylvan,* meaning "of the wood," you might want to evaluate that character's relationship with nature. Once again, you might look to the title of the work. Does Herman Melville's "Bartleby, the Scrivener" signal anything about Bartleby himself? Is Bartleby adequately defined by his job as scrivener? Is this part of Melville's point? Pursuing questions like these can help you develop thorough papers about characters from psychological, sociological, or more formalistic perspectives.

WRITING ABOUT FORM AND GENRE

Genre, a word derived from French, means "type" or "class." Literary genres are distinctive classes or categories of literary composition. On the most general level, literary works can be divided into the genres of drama, poetry, fiction, and essays, yet within those genres there are classifications that are also referred to as genres. Tragedy and comedy, for example, are genres of drama. Epic, lyric, and pastoral are genres of poetry. *Form,* on the other hand, generally refers to the shape or structure of a work. There are many clearly defined forms of poetry that follow specific patterns of meter, rhyme, and stanza. Sonnets, for example, are poems that follow a fixed form of 14 lines. Sonnets generally follow one of two basic sonnet forms, each with its own distinct rhyme scheme. Haiku is another example of poetic form, traditionally consisting of three unrhymed lines of five, seven, and five syllables.

While you might think that writing about form or genre leaves little room for argument, many of these forms and genres are very fluid. Remember that literature is evolving and ever changing, and so are its forms. As you study poetry, you may find that poets, especially more modern poets, play with traditional poetic forms, bringing about new effects. Similarly, dramatic tragedy was once quite narrowly defined, but over the centuries playwrights have broadened and challenged traditional definitions, changing the shape of tragedy. When Arthur Miller wrote *Death of a Salesman,* many critics challenged the idea that tragic drama could encompass a common man like Willy Loman.

Evaluating how a work of literature fits into or challenges the boundaries of its form or genre can provide you with fruitful avenues of investigation. You might find it helpful to ask why the work does or does not fit into traditional categories. Why might Miller have thought it fitting to write a tragedy of the common man? Similarly, you might compare the content or theme of a work with its form. How well do they work together? Many of Emily Dickinson's poems, for instance, follow the meter of traditional hymns. While some of her poems seem to express traditional religious doctrines, many seem to challenge or strain against traditional conceptions of God and theology. What is the effect, then, of her use of traditional hymn meter?

WRITING ABOUT LANGUAGE, SYMBOLS, AND IMAGERY

No matter what the genre, writers use words as their most basic tool. Language is the most fundamental building block of literature. It is essential that you pay careful attention to the author's language and word choice as you read, reread, and analyze a text. Imagery is language that appeals to the senses. Most commonly, imagery appeals to our sense of vision, creating a mental picture, but authors also use language that appeals to our other senses. Images can be literal or figurative. Literal images use sensory language to describe an actual thing. In the broadest terms, figurative language uses one thing to speak about something else. For example, if I call my boss a snake, I am not saying that he is literally a reptile. Instead, I am using figurative language to communicate my opinions about him. Since we think of snakes as sneaky, slimy, and sinister, I am using the concrete image of a snake to communicate these abstract opinions and impressions.

The two most common figures of speech are similes and metaphors. Both are comparisons between two apparently dissimilar things. Similes are explicit comparisons using the words *like* or *as*; metaphors are implicit comparisons. To return to the previous example, if I say, "My boss, Bob, was waiting for me when I showed up to work five minutes late today—the snake!" I have constructed a metaphor.

Writing about his experiences fighting in World War I, Wilfred Owen begins his poem "Dulce et decorum est" with a string of similes: "Bent double, like old beggars under sacks, / Knock-kneed, coughing like hags, we cursed through sludge." Owen's goal was to undercut clichéd notions that war and dying in battle were glorious. Certainly, comparing soldiers to coughing hags and to beggars underscores his point.

"Fog," a short poem by Carl Sandburg, provides a clear example of a metaphor. Sandburg's poem reads:

> The fog comes
> on little cat feet.
> It sits looking
> over harbor and city
> on silent haunches
> and then moves on.

Notice how effectively Sandburg conveys surprising impressions of the fog by comparing two seemingly disparate things—the fog and a cat.

Symbols, by contrast, are things that stand for, or represent, other things. Often they represent something intangible, such as concepts or ideas. In everyday life we use and understand symbols easily. Babies at christenings and brides at weddings wear white to represent purity. Think, too, of a dollar bill. The paper itself has no value in and of itself. Instead, that paper bill is a symbol of something else, the precious metal in a nation's coffers. Symbols in literature work similarly. Authors use symbols to evoke more than a simple, straightforward, literal meaning. Characters, objects, and places can all function as symbols. Famous literary examples of symbols include Moby-Dick, the white whale of Herman Melville's novel, and the scarlet *A* of Nathaniel Hawthorne's *The Scarlet Letter.* As both of these symbols suggest, a literary symbol cannot be adequately defined or explained by any one meaning. Hester Prynne's Puritan community clearly intends her scarlet *A* as a symbol of her adultery, but as the novel progresses, even her own community reads the letter as representing not just adultery, but able, angel, and a host of other meanings.

Writing about imagery and symbols requires close attention to the author's language. To prepare a paper on symbolism or imagery in a work, identify and trace the images and symbols and then try to draw some conclusions about how they function. Ask yourself how any symbols or images help contribute to the themes or meanings of the work.

What connotations do they carry? How do they affect your reception of the work? Do they shed light on characters or settings? A strong paper on imagery or symbolism will thoroughly consider the use of figures in the text and will try to reach some conclusions about how or why the author uses them.

WRITING ABOUT HISTORY AND CONTEXT

As noted above, it is possible to write an analytical paper that also considers the work's context. After all, the text was not created in a vacuum. The author lived and wrote in a specific time period and in a specific cultural context and, like all of us, was shaped by that environment. Learning more about the historical and cultural circumstances that surround the author and the work can help illuminate a text and provide you with productive material for a paper. Remember, though, that when you write analytical papers, you should use the context to illuminate the text. Do not lose sight of your goal—to interpret the meaning of the literary work. Use historical or philosophical research as a tool to develop your textual evaluation.

Thoughtful readers often consider how history and culture affected the author's choice and treatment of his or her subject matter. Investigations into the history and context of a work could examine the work's relation to specific historical events, such as the Salem witch trials in 17th-century Massachusetts or the restoration of Charles to the British throne in 1660. Bear in mind that historical context is not limited to politics and world events. While knowing about the Vietnam War is certainly helpful in interpreting much of Tim O'Brien's fiction, and some knowledge of the French Revolution clearly illuminates the dynamics of Charles Dickens's *A Tale of Two Cities*, historical context also entails the fabric of daily life. Examining a text in light of gender roles, race relations, class boundaries, or working conditions can give rise to thoughtful and compelling papers. Exploring the conditions of the working class in 19th-century England, for example, can provide a particularly effective avenue for writing about Dickens's *Hard Times*.

You can begin thinking about these issues by asking broad questions at first. What do you know about the time period and about the author? What does the editorial apparatus in your text tell you? These might be starting places. Similarly, when specific historical events or dynamics are particularly important to understanding a work but might be somewhat obscure to modern readers, textbooks usually provide notes to explain historical background. These are a good place to start. With this information, ask yourself how these historical facts and circumstances might have affected the author, the presentation of theme, and the presentation of character. How does knowing more about the work's specific historical context illuminate the work? To take a well-known example, understanding the complex attitudes toward slavery during the time Mark Twain wrote *Adventures of Huckleberry Finn* should help you begin to examine issues of race in the text. Additionally, you might compare these attitudes to those of the time in which the novel was set. How might this comparison affect your interpretation of a work written after the abolition of slavery but set before the Civil War?

WRITING ABOUT PHILOSOPHY AND IDEAS

Philosophical concerns are closely related to both historical context and thematic issues. Like historical investigation, philosophical research can provide a useful tool as you analyze a text. For example, an investigation into the working class in Dickens's England might lead you to a topic on the philosophical doctrine of utilitarianism in *Hard Times.* Many other works explore philosophies and ideas quite explicitly. Mary Shelley's famous novel *Frankenstein,* for example, explores John Locke's tabula rasa theory of human knowledge as she portrays the intellectual and emotional development of Victor Frankenstein's creature. As this example indicates, philosophical issues are somewhat more abstract than investigations of theme or historical context. Some other examples of philosophical issues include human free will, the formation of human identity, the nature of sin, or questions of ethics.

Writing about philosophy and ideas might require some outside research, but usually the notes or other material in your text will provide you with basic information, and often footnotes and bibliographies suggest places you can go to read further about the subject. If you have identified a philosophical theme that runs through a text, you might ask yourself how the author develops this theme. Look at character development and the interactions of characters, for example. Similarly, you might examine whether the narrative voice in a work of fiction addresses the philosophical concerns of the text.

WRITING COMPARISON AND CONTRAST ESSAYS

Finally, you might find that comparing and contrasting the works or techniques of an author provides a useful tool for literary analysis. A comparison and contrast essay might compare two characters or themes in a single work, or it might compare the author's treatment of a theme in two works. It might also contrast methods of character development or analyze an author's differing treatment of a philosophical concern in two works. Writing comparison and contrast essays, though, requires some special consideration. While they generally provide you with plenty of material to use, they also come with a built-in trap: the laundry list. These papers often become mere lists of connections between the works. As this chapter will discuss, a strong thesis must make an assertion that you want to prove or validate. A strong comparison/contrast thesis, then, needs to comment on the significance of the similarities and differences you observe. It is not enough merely to assert that the works contain similarities and differences. You might, for example, assert why the similarities and differences are important and explain how they illuminate the works' treatment of theme. Remember, too, that a thesis should not be a statement of the obvious. A comparison/contrast paper that focuses only on very obvious similarities or differences does little to illuminate the connections between the works. Often, an effective method of shaping a strong thesis and argument is to begin your paper by noting the similarities between the works but then to develop a thesis that asserts how these apparently similar elements are different. If, for example, you observe that Emily Dickinson wrote a number of poems about spiders, you might analyze how she uses spider imagery differently in two poems. Similarly, many scholars have noted that Nathaniel Hawthorne created many "mad scientist" characters, men who are so devoted to their science or their art that they lose perspective on all else. A good thesis comparing two of these characters—Aylmer of "The Birth-Mark" and Dr. Rappaccini of "Rappaccini's Daughter," for example—might initially identify both characters as examples of Hawthorne's mad scientist type but then argue that their motivations for scientific experimentation differ. If you strive to analyze the similarities or differences, discuss significances, and move beyond the obvious, your paper should move beyond the laundry list trap.

PREPARING TO WRITE

Armed with a clear sense of your task—illuminating the text—and with an understanding of theme, character, language, history, and philosophy, you are ready to approach the writing process. Remember that good writing is grounded in good reading and that close reading takes time, attention, and more than one reading of your text. Read for comprehension first. As you go back and review the work, mark the text to chart the details of the work as well as your reactions. Highlight important passages, repeated words, and image patterns. "Converse" with the text through marginal notes. Mark turns in the plot, ask questions, and make observations about characters, themes, and language. If you are reading from a book that does not belong to you, keep a record of your reactions in a journal or notebook. If you have read a work of literature carefully, paying attention to both the text and the context of the work, you have a leg up on the writing process. Admittedly, at this point, your ideas are probably very broad and undefined, but you have taken an important first step toward writing a strong paper.

Your next step is to focus, to take a broad, perhaps fuzzy topic and define it more clearly. Even a topic provided by your instructor will need to be focused appropriately. Remember that good writers make the topic their own. There are a number of strategies—often called "invention"—that you can use to develop your own focus. In one such strategy, called freewriting, you spend 10 minutes or so just writing about your topic without referring to the text or your notes. Write whatever comes to mind; the important thing is that you just keep writing. Often this process allows you to develop fresh ideas or approaches to your subject matter. You could also try brainstorming: Write down your topic and then list all the related points or ideas you can think of. Include questions, comments, words, important passages or events, and anything else that comes to mind. Let one idea lead to another. In the related technique of clustering, or mapping, write your topic on a sheet of paper and write related ideas around it. Then list related subpoints under each of these main ideas. Many people then draw arrows to show connections between points. This technique helps you narrow your topic and can also help you organize your ideas. Similarly, asking journalistic questions—Who? What? Where? When? Why? and How?—can develop ideas for topic development.

Thesis Statements

Once you have developed a focused topic, you can begin to think about your thesis statement, the main point or purpose of your paper. It is imperative that you craft a strong thesis; otherwise, your paper will likely be little more than random, disorganized observations about the text. Think of your thesis statement as a kind of road map for your paper. It tells your reader where you are going and how you are going to get there.

To craft a good thesis, you must keep a number of things in mind. First, as the title of this subsection indicates, your paper's thesis should be a statement, an assertion about the text that you want to prove or validate. Beginning writers often formulate a question that they attempt to use as a thesis. For example, a writer exploring the theme of Nick's psychological development in Hemingway's "Indian Camp" might ask, What is Nick's father trying to teach him in this story, and is he successful? While posing questions like this is a good strategy to use in the invention process to help narrow your topic and find your thesis, it cannot serve as the thesis statement because it does not tell your reader what you want to assert about Nick's psychological development. You might shape this question into a thesis by proposing instead an answer to that question: In Hemingway's "Indian Camp," Dr. Adams attempts to cultivate in his son the stoic philosophy that he associates with mature masculinity and that he himself embodies. However, due to several mistakes on his father's part, Nick—who is supposed to be learning that he, along with his father and every other human being, must resign himself to the will of nature and learn to react to that will in a rational way—actually ends up with a reinforced notion of his father's omnipotence. Ultimately, then, not only does Dr. Adams fail to teach Nick the principles of stoicism; he also is in large part responsible for thwarting Nick's progression into maturity by preventing him from learning what every maturing child must discover: the limitations of his father's power. Notice that this thesis provides an initial plan or structure for the rest of the paper, and notice, too, that the thesis statement does not necessarily have to fit into one sentence. After explaining Dr. Adams's stoic philosophy, you could turn to examining the mistakes that Dr. Adams makes in trying to impart this philosophy to Nick and the effects of these errors on Nick's psyche. Finally, you could theorize about what the story is saying about stoicism as a philosophy, including its benefits and limitations.

Second, remember that a good thesis makes an assertion that you need to support. In other words, a good thesis does not state the obvious. If you tried to formulate a thesis about Nick's psychological development by simply saying, Nick changes in an important way in the course of the story "Indian Camp," you have done nothing but rephrase the obvious. Since the story is clearly centered on the psychological changes that Nick experiences during the course of his excursion with his father, there would be no point in spending three to five pages supporting that assertion. You might try to develop a thesis from that point by asking yourself some further questions: How exactly does Nick change in the course of the story? What prompts this change? Are the changes he undergoes necessarily for the better? What does Nick's father have to do with the changes that Nick has experienced? Such a line of questioning might lead you to a more viable thesis, such as the one in the preceding paragraph.

As the comparison with the road map also suggests, your thesis should appear near the beginning of the paper. In relatively short papers (three to six pages), the thesis almost always appears in the first paragraph. Some writers fall into the trap of saving their thesis for the end, trying to provide a surprise or a big moment of revelation, as if to say, for example, "TA-DA! I've just proved that "in 'Big Two-Hearted River,' the main character wants desperately to exert control over the natural world, and although he realizes that he does not have the power to accomplish this, he never stops believing that he will one day be courageous and strong enough to conquer and control nature." Placing a thesis at the end of an essay can seriously mar the essay's effectiveness. If you fail to define your essay's point and purpose clearly at the beginning, your reader will find it difficult to assess the clarity of your argument and understand the points you are making. When your argument comes as a surprise at the end, you force your reader to reread your essay in order to assess its logic and effectiveness.

Finally, you should avoid using the first person (*I*) as you present your thesis. Though it is not strictly wrong to write in the first person, it is difficult to do so gracefully. While writing in the first person, beginning writers often fall into the trap of writing self-reflexive prose (writing *about* their paper *in* their paper). Often this leads to the most dreaded of opening lines: "In this paper I am going to discuss . . ." Not only does this self-reflexive voice make for very awkward prose, it frequently allows writers to announce boldly a topic while completely avoiding a thesis statement. An example might be a paper that begins as follows: Hemingway's "Big Two-Hearted River" tells the story of Nick Adams's excursion into the wilderness. In this paper, I am going to try to determine the larger significance of Nick's excursion. The author of this paper has done little more than announce a general topic for the paper (the motive of Nick's trip into the wilderness). While the last sentence might be a thesis, the writer fails to present an opinion about the significance of Nick's excursion. To improve this "thesis," the writer would need to back up a couple of steps. The writer should examine the story and draw conclusions about Nick's motivations before crafting the thesis. After carefully examining key passages in the story, the writer might determine that Nick, having had some disturbing and traumatic experiences in the war, goes out alone into the wilderness in the hope of establishing some kind of control over his environment, and in so doing, of his psyche as well. The writer might then craft a thesis such as this: In "Big Two-Hearted River," Nick seeks out nature not to experience harmony and peace, as many critics have suggested, but rather to try to conquer his environment so that he might experience a greater feeling of control than he has experienced in the world of men. Although the control he achieves over the natural world is only an illusion, as Nick himself realizes, he never relinquishes the hope that some day he will be strong enough to confront and conquer it.

Outlines

While developing a strong, thoughtful thesis early in your writing process should help focus your paper, outlining provides an essential tool for logically shaping that paper. A good outline helps you see—and develop—the relationships among the points in your argument and assures you that your paper flows logically and coherently. Outlining not only helps place your points in a logical order but also helps you subordinate supporting points, weed out any irrelevant points, and decide if there are any necessary points that are missing from your argument. Most of us are familiar with formal outlines that use numerical and letter designations for each point. However, there are different types of outlines; you may find that an informal outline is a more useful tool for you. What is important, though, is that you spend the time to develop some sort of outline—formal or informal.

Remember that an outline is a tool to help you shape and write a strong paper. If you do not spend sufficient time planning your supporting points and shaping the arrangement of those points, you will most likely construct a vague, unfocused outline that provides little, if any, help with the writing of the paper. Consider the following example.

Thesis: In "Big Two-Hearted River," Nick seeks out nature not to experience harmony and peace, as many critics have suggested, but rather to try to conquer his environment so that he might experience a greater feeling of control than he has experienced in the world of men. Although the control he achieves over the natural world is only an illusion, as Nick himself realizes, he never relinquishes the hope that some day he will be strong enough to confront and conquer it.

    I. Introduction and thesis

   II. Indications in the story that Nick cannot really control nature
      A. The river is still there, while the man-made town that Nick expects to see has been destroyed by fire

  III. Nick tries to control his environment
      A. Shows power over life and death
      B. Alters the natural landscape to suit him

   IV. Nick's own realization that the power of nature is too great for him to control
      A. Nick senses the power of the natural world when he hooks the big trout
      B. Nick decides not to fish the swamp because it seems too threatening and mysterious

```
    C. Nick kills the mosquito bothering him in
       his tent

 V. Nick's relationship with Hopkins

 VI. Conclusion
```

This outline has a number of flaws. First, the major topics labeled with the Roman numerals are not arranged in a logical order. It makes more sense to start out with Nick's successful attempts to establish some control over his environment and then follow that with the evidence that the story undercuts the notion that Nick really has any control over nature. The writer should probably switch Roman numerals I and II. Second, the thesis makes no mention of Nick's relationship to Hopkins, yet the writer includes this as a major topic in the outline. While Nick's thoughts about Hopkins are an interesting aspect of the story, if they do not relate to the thesis, they should not appear in the outline or in the essay for that matter. Third, the writer includes "Nick kills the mosquitoes bothering him in his tent" under section IV: "Nick's own realization that the power of nature is too great for him to control." Letters A and B refer to instances in the story that reveal Nick's reminders that nature wields a power beyond his control. Letter C, however, refers to an instance in which Nick successfully attempts to control the natural world and so would better fit under section III, letter A. A fourth problem is the inclusion of letter A in section II. An outline should not include an A without a B, a 1 without a 2, and so forth. The final problem with this outline is the overall lack of detail. None of the sections provides much information about the content of the argument, and it seems likely that the writer has not given sufficient thought to the content of the paper.

A better start to this outline might be the following:

```
Thesis: In "Big Two-Hearted River," Nick seeks out
nature not to experience harmony and peace, as many
critics have suggested, but rather to try to conquer
his environment so that he might experience a greater
feeling of control than he has known in the world of
men. Although the control he achieves over the natural
```

world is only an illusion, as Nick himself realizes, he never relinquishes the hope that some day he will be strong enough to confront and conquer it.

    I. Introduction and thesis

   II. Nick's successful attempts to exhibit some control over his environment
      A. Exhibits power over life and death
      B. Nick's place out in the woods is only "good" after he makes a number of alterations to the natural landscape and erects himself a little protected area where "nothing could touch him" (139)

  III. Subtle indications in the story that Nick's belief that he can truly control or conquer nature is unfounded
      A. Power of nature demonstrated by the fact that the man-made town that Nick expected to find has been destroyed by a natural force, fire; the river, however, "is still there"
      B. The things that make him think he has control in the natural world—such as his ability to keep direction by the sun—are all actually evidence of Nick's dependence on the greater forces of the natural world

  IV. Nick's own realization that the power of nature is too great for him to control
      A. Nick senses the power of the natural world when he hooks a big trout
      B. Nick decides not to fish the swamp because it seems too threatening and mysterious
      C. Nick makes a point of killing his trout just after refusing to enter the swamp, as

```
    if to emphasize his own power and control
    in the face of the more powerful swamp
```

```
  V. Conclusion
```

This new outline would prove much more helpful when it came time to write the paper.

An outline like this could be shaped into an even more useful tool if the writer fleshed out the argument by providing specific examples from the text to support each point. Once you have listed your main point and your supporting ideas, develop this raw material by listing related supporting ideas and material under each of those main headings. From there, arrange the material in subsections and order the material logically.

For example, you might begin with one of the theses cited above: In Hemingway's "Indian Camp," Dr. Adams attempts to cultivate in his son the stoic philosophy that he associates with mature masculinity and that he himself embodies. However, due to several mistakes on his father's part, Nick—who is supposed to be learning that he, along with his father and every other human being, must resign himself to the will of nature and learn to react to that will in a rational way—actually ends up with a reinforced notion of his father's omnipotence. Ultimately, then, not only does Dr. Adams fail to teach Nick the principles of stoicism, he also is in large part responsible for thwarting Nick's progression into maturity by preventing him from learning what every maturing child must discover: the limitations of his father's power. As noted above, this thesis supplies a framework for how the discussion could be best organized. You might begin by noting what Dr. Adams tries to teach Nick and follow that with a discussion of what Nick actually learns. You might begin your outline, then, with topic headings such as these: (1) benefits of Dr. Adams's stoicism, (2) mistakes Dr. Adams makes teaching this stoicism to Nick, (3) the effects of these mistakes on Nick's psychological development, and (4) what Nick ends up learning instead of stoicism. Under each of those headings, you could list ideas that support the particular point. Be sure to include references to parts of the text that help build your case.

An informal outline might look like this:

```
Thesis: In "Indian Camp," Dr. Adams attempts to
indoctrinate his son into the stoic philosophy he
```

embraces and that he associates with mature masculinity. However, due to several mistakes on his father's part, Nick—who is supposed to be learning that he, along with his father and every other human being, must resign himself to the will of nature and learn to react to that will in a rational way—actually ends up with a reinforced notion of his father's omnipotence. Ultimately, then, not only does Dr. Adams fail to teach Nick the principles of stoicism; he is in large part responsible for thwarting Nick's progression into maturity by preventing him from learning what every maturing child must discover: the limitations of his father's power.

Introduction and thesis

1. Why stoics reject emotion
   - Unpredictable results
   - Examples of negative and positive consequences

2. Evidence of Dr. Adams's stoicism and its benefits
   - Evidence of Dr. Adams's stoicism:
     ○ His pragmatism—using whatever equipment is on hand for the procedure
     ○ His refusal to hear the woman's screams because they are "not important"
   - Positive results of the doctor's stoicism make it seem like a good model of masculinity
     ○ The Indian woman remains healthy
     ○ The baby is born alive

3. Dr. Adams's mistakes—caused at least in part by his stoicism, which makes him fail to account for emotion in others
   - Dr. Adams fails to note that Nick is not mature enough to handle witnessing the cesarean procedure

- Nick wants his father to give the woman something for pain: "Oh, Daddy, can't you give her something to make her stop screaming?" (16)
- Nick averts his eyes when his father sews up the incision
- Dr. Adams underestimates the danger to the Indian father
  - Dr. Adams makes light of the Indian father's experience—"Ought to have a look at the proud father. They're usually the worst sufferers in these little affairs" (18)—not realizing that the father's strong emotions might result in death
  - As a result of his father's pragmatic treatment of the woman and failure to recognize the plight of the Indian father, Nick sees the bloody body of the father after he has committed suicide

4. The effects of Dr. Adams's mistakes on Nick's psychological development—a belief in the omnipotence of his father
  - His father can stand things no one else can
    - Even Uncle George runs off
    - The Indian father kills himself
  - Dr. Adams seems to have the power over life and death—his father's operation saves the woman and the baby when no one else was able to help
  - Under his father's protection, Nick feels secure and even immortal: "In the early morning on the lake sitting in the stern of the boat with his father rowing, [Nick] felt quite sure that he would never die" (19)

5. This belief in the power of the father is not in accord with stoicism, and further, it evidences a regression into childhood instead of a progression into maturity

   - If Nick learned proper stoicism, he would come to know that every human being has to resign himself to the "will of nature" and trust that he can handle and adapt to that will in a rational way
   - Dr. Adams's mistakes result in Nick failing to gain any faith in his own ability to deal with the crises that the "will of nature" might throw at him
   - They also result in Nick's gaining an exaggerated estimation of his father's power, which is in direct contradiction to the idea that every human being is subject to the will of nature
   - Nick's experience in the Indian camp is supposed to be a rite of passage toward adulthood, yet it actually ends up reinforcing Nick's childish ideas regarding his father's supremacy. Whether we think of this situation in terms of stoicism, or simply in more general terms of a child progressing toward maturity, it seems that Nick has experienced a regression instead of a rite of passage

Conclusion

   - Nick fails to make any progress toward the model of masculinity his father wants for him
   - Had Nick's father not made the mistakes he did, perhaps Nick would have learned the lesson his father wanted him to learn
   - Nick's father's mistakes stem from the very philosophy he wants to teach Nick; Dr. Adams

is bound to make these kinds of mistakes, as would Nick if he were to adopt this philosophy as his own. This suggests that there are some significant problems that emerge when one lives according to a strict stoic philosophy

- Many critics argue that stoicism is an inherent trait of the Hemingway hero; "Indian Camp" gives us insight into the limitations of this philosophy and suggests that the typical Hemingway hero is fundamentally flawed

You would set about writing a formal outline through a similar process, though in the final stages, you would label the headings differently. A formal outline for a paper that argues the thesis about "Big Two-Hearted River" cited above—that Nick engages in a futile attempt to control the natural world in order to gain some psychological peace—might look like this:

Thesis: In "Big Two-Hearted River," Nick seeks out nature not to experience harmony and peace, as many critics have suggested, but rather to try to conquer his environment so that he might experience a greater feeling of control than he has experienced in the world of men. Although the control he achieves over the natural world is only an illusion, as Nick himself realizes, he never relinquishes the hope that some day he will be strong enough to confront and conquer it.

I. Introduction and thesis

II. Nick's successful attempts to exhibit some control over his environment
    A. Exhibits power over life and death
        1. Nick picks up a grasshopper and studies it, then says, "Go on, hopper . . . Fly away somewhere." He makes

a conscious decision to spare the
grasshopper's life

   2. Nick kills a mosquito in his tent
      with a match: "The mosquito made a
      satisfactory hiss" (142)

B. Nick's place out in the woods is "good"
   only after he makes a number of alterations
   to the natural landscape and erects a
   little protected area where "nothing
   could touch him" (139)

   1. Nick chops out tree roots to level
      the ground

   2. Nick "pulled all the sweet fern
      bushes by their roots" (138) to make
      a smooth spot on which to sleep

   3. Nick pitches his tent and uses
      cheesecloth to keep out the
      mosquitoes

III. Subtle indications in the story that Nick's
     belief that he can truly control or conquer
     nature is unfounded

A. Power of nature demonstrated by the fact
   that the man-made town that Nick expected
   to find has been destroyed by a natural
   force, fire; the river, however, "is still
   there"

B. The things that make him think he has
   control in the natural world—such as
   his ability to keep direction by the
   sun—are all actually evidence of Nick's
   dependence on the greater forces of the
   natural world

IV. Nick's own realization that the power of nature
    is too great for him to control

A. Nick senses the power of the natural world when he hooks a big trout
  1. "There was a heaviness, a power not to be held" (150)
  2. After he fails to bring the fish in, the narrator says of Nick: "The thrill had been too much. He felt, vaguely, a little sick" (150)
B. Nick decides not to fish the swamp because it seems too threatening and mysterious
  1. The density of the swamp overwhelms Nick
     a. "the swamp looked solid with cedar trees" (155)
     b. "It would not be possible to walk through a swamp like that" (155)
  2. He begins to wish for something to read when he is faced with entering the swamp, indicating a desire to retreat to the world of men and civilization
C. Nick makes a point of killing his trout just after refusing to enter the swamp, as if to emphasize his own power and control in the face of the more powerful swamp

V. Conclusion
  A. Although Nick, on some level, realizes that he cannot truly control nature, he does not relinquish the hope that one day he will be able to do so: "He was going back to camp. He looked back. The river just showed through the trees. There were plenty of days coming when he could fish the swamp" (156)

        B. Nick has set an impossible task for himself; he will never be strong enough truly to conquer nature

        C. Nick is never going to find the peace he seeks—he will bounce back and forth between civilization, which he knows makes him unhappy, and the natural world, which he will never satisfactorily conquer and which he will then have to retreat from, like a pinball bouncing between two bumpers but never going anywhere

As in the previous sample outline, the thesis here provides the seeds of a structure, and the writer has been careful to arrange the supporting points in a logical manner, showing the relationships among the ideas in the paper.

Body Paragraphs

Once your outline is complete, you can begin drafting your paper. Paragraphs, units of related sentences, are the building blocks of a good paper, and as you draft you should keep in mind both the function and the qualities of good paragraphs. Paragraphs help you chart and control the shape and content of your essay, and they help the reader see your organization and your logic. You should begin a new paragraph whenever you move from one major point to another. In longer, more complex essays you might use a group of related paragraphs to support major points. Remember that in addition to being adequately developed, a good paragraph is both unified and coherent.

Unified Paragraphs

Each paragraph must be centered on one idea or point, and a unified paragraph carefully focuses on and develops this central idea without including extraneous ideas or tangents. For beginning writers, the best way to ensure that you are constructing unified paragraphs is to include a topic sentence in each paragraph. This topic sentence should convey the main point of the paragraph, and every sentence in the paragraph should relate to that topic sentence. Any sentence that strays from the central topic does not belong in the paragraph and needs to be revised or deleted. Consider the following paragraph about Nick's belief in the power of his father. Notice how the paragraph veers away from the main point.

As a result of his exposure to the birth and death scenes, Nick develops an unhealthy belief in the omnipotence of his father, a belief wholly at odds with the tenets of stoicism that Dr. Adams is trying to impart to Nick. When Nick asks his father why the Indian killed himself, Dr. Adams says, "He couldn't stand things, I guess" (19). The father could not stand to witness the operation; Nick himself could not look, and by this point, even Uncle George has run off. Nick comes to believe that his father is the only one with the power to "stand things," to continue to behave rationally and practically no matter what the emotional context. This ability to "stand things" is apparently what enabled his father to do, with confidence and detachment, what no other person could perform, the operation that saved both the woman's life and the life of her baby boy. Although most readers believe that this baby is the child of the Indian man who commits suicide, some critics have argued that the baby is actually Uncle George's son. Readers who endorse this interpretation of the story cite as evidence for George's paternity the fact that Uncle George hands out cigars—something the father of a new baby traditionally does—and that the woman chooses Uncle George's arm to bite when she is having labor pains.

Although the paragraph begins solidly and the first sentence contains its central idea, the author goes on a tangent in the paragraph's last two sentences. While the theory of Uncle George's paternity is interesting, it has no place in a paragraph about Nick's belief in his father's power, and consequently, these sentences should be deleted.

Coherent Paragraphs

In addition to shaping unified paragraphs, you must also craft coherent paragraphs that develop their points logically with sentences that flow smoothly into one another. Coherence depends on the order of your sentences, but it is not the only factor that lends the paragraph coherence. You also need to craft your prose to help the reader see the relationship among the sentences.

Consider the following paragraph about Nick's increasing faith in the power of his father. Notice how the writer uses the same ideas as in the preceding paragraph yet fails to help the reader see the relationships among the points.

> Nick develops an unhealthy belief in the omnipotence of his father, a belief wholly at odds with the tenets of stoicism that Dr. Adams is trying to impart to Nick. When Nick asks his father why the Indian killed himself, Dr. Adams says, "He couldn't stand things, I guess" (19). The father could not stand to witness the operation; Nick himself could not look, and by this point, even Uncle George has run off. Nick comes to believe that his father is the only one with the power to "stand things." This is what enabled his father to do what no other person could do, perform the operation that saved both the woman's life and the life of her baby boy. Dr. Adams seems to be in control of everything, including life and death. Nick has gained so much confidence in his father's abilities that he feels invincible when in his father's care. Hemingway writes: "In the early morning on the lake sitting in the stern of the boat with his father rowing, [Nick] felt quite sure that he would never die" (19). The syntax of the sentence indicates that Nick is not revealing a blanket faith in his safety and security. His feelings must be put in their proper context; it is only when Nick is "sitting in the stern of the boat with his father rowing"—when he surrenders entirely to his father's control—that he feels immortal.

This paragraph demonstrates that unity alone does not guarantee paragraph effectiveness. The argument is hard to follow because the author fails both to show connections between the sentences and to indicate how they work to support the overall point.

A number of techniques are available to aid paragraph coherence. Careful use of transitional words and phrases is essential. You can use transitional flags to introduce an example or an illustration (*for example, for instance*), to amplify a point or add another phase of the same idea (*additionally, furthermore, next, similarly, finally, then*), to indicate a conclusion or a result (*therefore, as a result, thus, in other words*), to signal a contrast or a qualification (*on the other hand, nevertheless, despite this, on the contrary, still, however, conversely*), to signal a comparison (*likewise, in comparison, similarly*), and to indicate a movement in time (*afterward, earlier, eventually, finally, later, subsequently, until*).

In addition to transitional flags, careful use of pronouns aids coherence and flow. If you were writing about *The Wizard of Oz*, you would not want to keep repeating the phrase *the witch* or the name *Dorothy*. Careful substitution of the pronoun *she* in these instances can aid coherence. A word of warning, though: When you substitute pronouns for proper names, always be sure that your pronoun reference is clear. In a paragraph that discusses both Dorothy and the witch, substituting *she* could lead to confusion. Make sure that it is clear to whom the pronoun refers. Generally, the pronoun refers to the last proper noun you have used.

While repeating the same name over and over again can lead to awkward, boring prose, it is possible to use repetition to help your paragraph's coherence. Careful repetition of important words or phrases can lend coherence to your paragraph by reminding readers of your key points. Admittedly, it takes some practice to use this technique effectively. You may find that reading your prose aloud can help you develop an ear for the effective use of repetition.

To see how helpful transitional aids are, compare the paragraph below to the preceding one about the way Nick comes to perceive his father in "Indian Camp." Notice how the author works with the same ideas and quotations but shapes them into a much more coherent paragraph whose point is clearer and easier to follow.

As a result of his exposure to these bloody scenes, Nick develops an unhealthy belief in the omnipotence of his father, a belief wholly at odds with the tenets of stoicism that Dr. Adams is trying to impart to Nick. When Nick asks his father why the Indian killed himself, Dr. Adams says, "He couldn't stand things, I guess" (19). The father could not stand to witness the operation; Nick himself could not look, and by this point, even Uncle George has run off. As a result, Nick comes to believe that his father is the only one with the power to "stand things," to continue to behave rationally and practically no matter what the emotional context. This power to "stand things" is apparently what enabled his father to do, with confidence and detachment, what no other person could perform, the operation that saved both the woman's life and the life of her baby boy. To Nick, his father seems to be in control of everything, including life and death. Nick has gained so much confidence in his father's abilities that he feels invincible when in his father's care, as the following lines make clear: "In the early morning on the lake sitting in the stern of the boat with his father rowing, [Nick] felt quite sure that he would never die" (19). The syntax of the sentence indicates that Nick is not revealing a blanket faith in his safety and security. On the contrary, his feelings must be put in their proper context; it is only when Nick is "sitting in the stern of the boat with his father rowing"—when he surrenders entirely to his father's control—that he feels immortal.

Similarly, the following paragraph from a paper on Nick's relationship with the natural world in "Big Two-Hearted River" demonstrates both unity and coherence. In it, the author argues that Nick's desire to dominate the natural world is evident in his attempt to exhibit control over the life and death of insects and the alterations he must make to the natural world to feel comfortable there:

Hemingway makes clear that Nick's desire is not to coexist in harmony with nature but rather to exert control over the natural world. Near the beginning of his journey, Nick picks up a blackened grasshopper and studies it. After some consideration, he says out loud: "Go on, hopper . . . Fly away somewhere," making a conscious decision to spare the grasshopper's life (136). In contrast, when a mosquito buzzes around in his tent, Nick does not hesitate to kill it with a lighted match: "The mosquito made a satisfactory hiss" (142). The satisfaction Nick experiences in this power over the life and death of these insects reveals his desire to exert control over the natural world. Further, Nick does not simply go out and enjoy the wilderness on its own terms. In fact, he considers the woods a "good place" only after he makes a number of alterations to the natural landscape. First, Nick chops out tree roots to level the ground and "pull[s] all the sweet fern bushes by their roots" (138), clearly putting his own physical comfort ahead of the health of the woods' natural inhabitants. Not only does Nick need to smooth out the ground before he can sleep on it, he also finds it necessary to create for himself a little protected area where "[n]othing could touch him" (139). He puts up his tent and uses cheesecloth to keep out the mosquitoes. Nick's need to place barriers between himself and nature and his desire to exhibit control over the life and death of the woods' inhabitants are strong indications of his desire not to connect with nature but to control it.

Introductions

Introductions present particular challenges for writers. Generally, your introduction should do two things: capture your reader's attention and explain the main point of your essay. In other words, while your introduction should contain your thesis, it needs to do a bit more work than that. You are likely to find that starting that first paragraph is one of the most difficult parts of the paper. It is hard to face that blank page or screen, and as a result, many beginning writers, in desperation to start somewhere, start with overly broad, general statements. While it is often a good strategy to start with more general subject matter and narrow your focus, do not begin with broad sweeping statements such as Many people search for harmony with the natural world. Such sentences are nothing but filler. They begin to fill the blank page, but they do nothing to advance your argument. Instead, you should try to gain your readers' interest. Some writers like to begin with a pertinent quotation or with a relevant question. Or, you might begin with an introduction of the topic you will discuss. If you are writing about Hemingway's presentation of Nick's relationship with nature in "Big Two-Hearted River," for instance, you might begin by talking about the psychological reasons that people are drawn to spend time in the natural world. Another common trap to avoid is depending on your title to introduce the author and the text you are writing about. Always include the work's author and title in your opening paragraph.

Compare the effectiveness of the following introductions:

1. Even in our technologically advanced 21st-century society, many people are drawn to nature and find themselves hiking, camping, or simply visiting their local park in order to be in closer proximity to it. People have different reasons for wanting a closer relationship to the natural world. In this story, the main character, Nick, seeks out nature not to experience harmony and peace, as some people do, but rather to try to conquer his environment so that he might experience a greater feeling of control than he has experienced in the world of men. Although the control he achieves over the natural world is only an illusion, as Nick himself realizes, he never relinquishes the hope that some day he will be strong enough to confront and conquer it.

2. According to Edward O. Wilson's theory of "biophilia," all human beings have an instinctive attraction to and connection with all other forms

```
of life. This intense interrelationship hardwired
into humanity might help to account for the
desire many people feel to immerse themselves in
the wild world of nature; it is as if we need to
reacquaint ourselves with its rhythms and cycles
and deepen our connection to other forms of life.
In Hemingway's "Big Two-Hearted River," however,
Nick is drawn to the wilderness for a different
reason entirely. Nick seeks out nature not to
experience harmony and peace, as many critics
have suggested, but rather to try to conquer his
environment so that he might experience a greater
feeling of control than he has experienced in the
world of men. Although the control he achieves
over the natural world is only an illusion, as
Nick himself realizes, he never relinquishes the
hope that some day he will be strong enough to
confront and conquer it.
```

The first introduction begins with a vague, overly broad sentence; cites unclear, undeveloped examples; and then moves abruptly to the thesis. Notice, too, how a reader deprived of the paper's title does not know the title of the story that the paper will analyze. The second introduction works with the same material and thesis but provides more detail and is consequently much more interesting. It begins by discussing biophilia and the human need for connection to nature. The paragraph ends with the thesis, which includes both the author and the title of the work to be discussed.

The paragraph below provides another example of an opening strategy. It begins by introducing the author and the text it will analyze, and then it moves on to provide some necessary background information before introducing its thesis.

```
Hemingway's "Indian Camp" is clearly a story about a
father trying to pass his values on to his son. In this
case, it is the philosophy of stoicism that Dr. Adams
wants to impart to the young Nick. According to Graham F.
Wagstaff and Andrea M. Rowledge, "Followers of stoicism
. . . believed that virtue, which was considered to be
```

the highest good, consisted of a will that was exercised in accordance with Nature and hence uninfluenced by all mundane desire. Emotion, therefore was to be condemned and controlled" (181). Thus, those who adhere to a stoic philosophy are generally said to be rational, pragmatic, self-reliant, and calm. In Hemingway's "Indian Camp," Dr. Adams attempts to cultivate in his son this stoic philosophy that he associates with mature masculinity and that he embodies. However, due to several mistakes on his father's part, Nick—who is supposed to be learning that he, along with his father and every other human being, must resign himself to the will of nature and learn to react to that will in a rational way—actually winds up with a reinforced notion of his father's omnipotence. Ultimately, then, not only does Dr. Adams fail to teach Nick the principles of stoicism; he also is in large part responsible for thwarting Nick's progression into maturity by preventing him from learning what every maturing child must discover: the limitations of his father's power.

Conclusions

Conclusions present another series of challenges for writers. No doubt you have heard the old adage about writing papers: "Tell us what you are going to say, say it, and then tell us what you've said." While this formula does not necessarily result in bad papers, it does not often result in good ones, either. It will almost certainly result in boring papers (especially boring conclusions). If you have done a good job establishing your points in the body of the paper, the reader already knows and understands your argument. There is no need merely to reiterate. Do not just summarize your main points in your conclusion. A boring and mechanical conclusion does nothing to advance your argument or interest your reader. Consider the following conclusion to the paper about Nick's relationship with nature in "Big Two-Hearted River."

In conclusion, Hemingway's "Big Two-Hearted River" features a main character who tries to conquer and control the natural world in hopes of gaining control of his own psychological unrest. Unfortunately, there is no way that a human being can harness the enormous power of nature. Nick, therefore, is doomed to failure.

Besides starting with a mechanical transitional device, this conclusion does little more than summarize the main points of the outline (and it does not even touch on all of them). It is incomplete and uninteresting.

Instead, your conclusion should add something to your paper. A good tactic is to build upon the points you have been arguing. Asking "why?" often helps you draw further conclusions. You might also speculate on other directions in which to take your topic by tying it into larger issues. You might do this by envisioning your paper as just one section of a longer essay. For example, in the paper on "Big Two-Hearted River," you might attempt to explain the psychological motivations behind Nick's desire to control the natural world. Along those same lines, you might also consider whether Nick's behavior is peculiar to him, or whether it represents a larger human pattern, and if so, what the larger implications of such a pattern might be. In the following conclusion to the paper on "Big Two-Hearted River," the author discusses how Nick handles the realization that he cannot, in fact, control the natural world and considers the implications of his reaction.

Hemingway makes clear that, contrary to many critics' arguments that Nick goes out into the wilderness to reconnect with the natural world, Nick is actually motivated by a strong desire to conquer and control nature. Nick, of course, cannot successfully hold dominion over the natural world, and on some level, he comes to realize that. He never, however, relinquishes the hope that one day he will be strong and courageous enough to do so, as the final lines of the story demonstrate: "He was going back to camp. He looked back. The river just showed through the trees. There were plenty of days coming when he could fish the swamp" (156). In essence, Nick has set an impossible task for himself. He seems doomed to keep moving back and forth between civilization, which he knows makes him unhappy, and the natural world, which

he will never satisfactorily conquer, never finding the
psychological peace he seeks.

Similarly, in the following conclusion to a paper on stoicism in "Indian
Camp," the author comments on the implications about stoic philosophy
that can be drawn from Dr. Adams's failed attempt to pass this philosophy on to his young son.

> By story's end, Nick has failed to make any progress
> toward adopting his father's model of stoicism. It is
> reasonable to speculate that had Dr. Adams not made
> the mistakes he did, perhaps Nick would have learned
> the lesson his father wanted him to learn and that
> perhaps this would have been a desirable outcome, as
> Dr. Adams does bring a great deal of good to the Indian
> community by virtue of his stoic response. However, if
> we consider the fact since Dr. Adams's mistakes amount
> to an inability or refusal to account for the emotional
> response of others and that one of the principles of
> stoicism is to condemn emotion, it is evident that
> Dr. Adams's mistakes stem from the very philosophy he
> wants to teach Nick. Dr. Adams is bound to make these
> kinds of errors, as Nick would be as well if he were to
> adopt stoicism successfully as his own philosophy. Thus,
> "Indian Camp" gives us some valuable insight into the
> limitations of living one's life according to a strict
> stoic philosophy. And since many critics argue that
> stoicism is an inherent trait of the typical Hemingway
> hero, the story also prepares us to look for these
> limitations and flaws in Hemingway's other heroes as
> well.

Citations and Formatting
Using Primary Sources
As the examples included in this chapter indicate, strong papers on literary texts incorporate quotations from the text in order to support their
points. It is not enough for you to assert your interpretation without providing support or evidence from the text. Without well-chosen quotations

to support your argument, you are, in effect, saying to the reader, "Take my word for it." It is important to use quotations thoughtfully and selectively. Remember that the paper presents *your* argument, so choose quotations that support *your* assertions. Do not let the author's voice overwhelm your own. With that caution in mind, there are some guidelines you should follow to ensure that you use quotations clearly and effectively.

Integrate Quotations:

Quotations should always be integrated into your own prose. Do not just drop them into your paper without introduction or comment. Otherwise, it is unlikely that your reader will see their function. You can integrate textual support easily and clearly with identifying tags, short phrases that identify the speaker. For example:

> The narrator describes the grasshoppers as "all a sooty black in color."

While this tag appears before the quotation, you can also use tags after or in the middle of the quoted text, as the following examples demonstrate:

> "Go on, hopper," says Nick.

> "I'm terribly sorry I brought you along, Nickie," says Dr. Adams. "It was an awful mess to put you through."

You can also use a colon to introduce a quotation formally:

> Nick's anxiety about the woman's pain comes through clearly: "Oh, Daddy, can't you give her something to make her stop screaming?"

When you quote brief sections of poems (three lines or fewer), use slash marks to indicate the line breaks in the poem:

> As the poem ends, Dickinson speaks of the power of the imagination: "The revery alone will do, / If bees are few."

Longer quotations (more than four lines of prose or three lines of poetry) should be set off from the rest of your paper in a block quotation. Double-space before you begin the passage, indent it 10 spaces from your left-hand margin, and double-space the passage itself. Because the indentation signals the inclusion of a quotation, do not use quotation marks around the cited passage. Use a colon to introduce the passage.

The narrator describes the preparations Nick makes for his camp:

> Between two jack pines, the ground was quite level. He took the ax out of the pack and chopped out two projecting roots. That leveled a piece of ground large enough to sleep on. He smoothed out the sandy soil with his hand and pulled all the sweet fern bushes by their roots. His hand smelled good from the sweet fern. He smoothed the uprooted earth. He did not want anything making lumps under the blankets.

This description of Nick's actions demonstrates to what degree he must alter the natural landscape before he can feel comfortable in it.

The whole of Dickinson's poem speaks of the imagination:

> To make a prairie it takes a clover and one bee,
> One clover, and a bee,
> And revery.
> The revery alone will do,
> If bees are few.

Clearly, she argues for the creative power of the mind.

It is also important to interpret quotations after you introduce them and explain how they help advance your point. You cannot assume that your reader will interpret the quotations the same way that you do.

Quote Accurately:

Always quote accurately. Anything within quotations marks must be the author's exact words. There are, however, some rules to follow if you need to modify the quotation to fit into your prose.

1. Use brackets to indicate any material that might have been added to the author's exact wording. For example, if you need to add any words to the quotation or alter it grammatically to allow it to fit into your prose, indicate your changes in brackets:

   ```
   Just after Nick decides that he does not want
   to enter the swamp, he takes "out his knife,
   open[s] it and st[icks] it in the log."
   ```

2. Conversely, if you choose to omit any words from the quotation, use ellipses (three spaced periods) to indicate missing words or phrases:

   ```
   As Nick debates entering the swamp, he reflects:
   "In the fast deep water . . . the fishing would
   be tragic."
   ```

3. If you delete a sentence or more, use the ellipses after a period:

   ```
   After some deliberation, Nick decides that he
   does not have the courage or the strength to face
   his demons: "He was going back to camp. . . .
   There were plenty of days coming when he could
   fish the swamp."
   ```

4. If you omit a line or more of poetry, or more than one paragraph of prose, use a single line of spaced periods to indicate the omission:

   ```
   To make a prairie it takes a clover and
       one bee,

   . . . . . . . . . . . . . . . . . . .
   ```

```
And revery.
The revery alone will do,
If bees are few.
```

Punctuate Properly:

Punctuation of quotations often causes more trouble than it should. Once again, you just need to keep these simple rules in mind.

1. Periods and commas should be placed inside quotation marks, even if they are not part of the original quotation:

   ```
   Dr. Adams's remark about completing the cesarean
   demonstrates his confidence and pride: "That's
   one for the medical journal, George."
   ```

   The only exception to this rule is when the quotation is followed by a parenthetical reference. In this case, the period or comma goes after the citation (more on these later in this chapter):

   ```
   Dr. Adams's remark about completing the cesarean
   demonstrates his confidence and pride: "That's
   one for the medical journal, George" (18).
   ```

2. Other marks of punctuation—colons, semicolons, question marks, and exclamation points—go outside the quotation marks unless they are part of the original quotation:

   ```
   Why does the narrator point out that Nick's
   "curiosity had been gone for a long time"?
   ```

   ```
   Nick seeks help as he struggles to understand
   what he has witnessed: "Why did he kill himself,
   Daddy?"
   ```

Documenting Primary Sources:

Unless you are instructed otherwise, you should provide sufficient information for your reader to locate material you quote. Generally, literature papers follow the rules set forth by the Modern Language Association (MLA). These can be found in the *MLA Handbook for Writers of Research Papers* (sixth edition). You should be able to find this book in the reference section of your library. Additionally, its rules for citing both primary and secondary sources are widely available from reputable online sources. One of these is the Online Writing Lab (OWL) at Purdue University. OWL's guide to MLA style is available at http://owl.english.purdue. edu/owl/resource/557/01/. The Modern Language Association also offers answers to frequently asked questions about MLA style on this helpful Web page: http://www.mla.org/style_faq. Generally, when you are citing from literary works in papers, you should keep a few guidelines in mind.

Parenthetical Citations:

MLA asks for parenthetical references in your text after quotations. When you are working with prose (short stories, novels, or essays) include page numbers in the parentheses:

> Dr. Adams's remark about completing the cesarean demonstrates his confidence and pride: "That's one for the medical journal, George" (18).

When you are quoting poetry, include line numbers:

> Dickinson's speaker tells of the arrival of a fly: "There interposed a Fly— / With Blue—uncertain stumbling Buzz— / Between the light—and Me—" (12–14).

Works Cited Page:

These parenthetical citations are linked to a separate works cited page at the end of the paper. The works cited page lists works alphabetically by the author(s)' last names. An entry for the above reference to Hemingway's "Big Two-Hearted River" would read:

> Hemingway, Ernest. "Big Two-Hearted River." In Our Time. New York: Scribner's, 1986. 133–56.

The *MLA Handbook* includes a full listing of sample entries, as do many of the online explanations of MLA style.

Documenting Secondary Sources:

To ensure that your paper is built entirely upon your own ideas and analysis, instructors often ask that you write interpretative papers without any outside research. If, on the other hand, your paper requires research, you must document any secondary sources you use. You need to document direct quotations, summaries or paraphrases of others' ideas, and factual information that is not common knowledge. Follow the guidelines above for quoting primary sources when you use direct quotations from secondary sources. Keep in mind that MLA style also includes specific guidelines for citing electronic sources. OWL's Web site provides a good summary: http://owl.english.purdue.edu/owl/resource/557/09/.

Parenthetical Citations:

As with the documentation of primary sources, described above, MLA guidelines require in-text parenthetical references to your secondary sources. Unlike the research papers you might write for a history class, literary research papers following MLA style do not use footnotes as a means of documenting sources. Instead, after a quotation, you should cite the author's last name and the page number:

> "Followers of stoicism . . . believed that virtue, which was considered to be the highest good, consisted of a will that was exercised in accordance with Nature and hence uninfluenced by all mundane desire" (Wagstaff and Rowledge 181).

If you include the name of the author in your prose, then you would include only the page number in your citation. For example:

> According to Wagstaff and Rowledge, "Followers of stoicism . . . believed that virtue, which was considered to be the highest good, consisted of a will that was exercised in accordance with Nature and hence uninfluenced by all mundane desire" (181).

If you are including more than one work by the same author, the parenthetical citation should include a shortened yet identifiable version of the title in order to indicate which of the author's works you cite. For example:

> According to Jeffrey Meyers, "Hemingway—far from being the Dumb Ox—did not simply glorify the Indians but based his story on profound understanding, gained from experience and from books, of their behavior, customs, and religion" (Hemingway's 219).

Similarly, and just as important, if you summarize or paraphrase the particular ideas of your source, you must provide documentation:

> The realistic and complex portrayal of Native Americans in Hemingway's "Indian Camp" reveals the author's significant knowledge and understanding of Native American culture (Meyers, Hemingway's 219).

Works Cited Page:

Like the primary sources discussed above, the parenthetical references to secondary sources are keyed to a separate works cited page at the end of your paper. Here is an example of a works cited page that uses the examples cited above. Note that when two or more works by the same author are listed, you should use three hyphens followed by a period in the subsequent entries. You can find a complete list of sample entries in the *MLA Handbook* or from a reputable online summary of MLA style.

WORKS CITED

Meyers, Jeffrey. "Hemingway's Primitivism and 'Indian Camp.'" Twentieth Century Literature 34.2 (1988): 211–22.

——. "The Hemingways: An American Tragedy." Virginia Quarterly Review 75.5 (1999): 267–80.

Strong, Amy. "Screaming Through Silence: The Violence of Race in 'Indian Camp' and 'The Doctor and the Doctor's Wife.'" The Hemingway Review 16.1 (1996): 18–32.

Plagiarism

Failure to document carefully and thoroughly can leave you open to charges of stealing the ideas of others, which is known as plagiarism, and this is a very serious matter. Remember that it is important to include quotation marks when you use language from your source, even if you use just one or two words. For example, if you wrote, Followers of stoicism believed that virtue consisted of a will that was exercised in accordance with Nature and hence uninfluenced by all mundane desire, you would be guilty of plagiarism, since you used Wagstaff and Rowledge's distinct language without acknowledging them as the source. Instead, you should write something such as Stoic philosophy involves ignoring "mundane desire" and bending one's will "in accordance with Nature" (Wagstaff and Rowledge 181). In this case, you have properly credited Wagstaff and Rowledge.

Similarly, neither summarizing the ideas of an author nor changing or omitting just a few words means that you can omit a citation. B. J. Smith's article, entitled " 'Big Two-Hearted River': The Artist and the Art," contains the following passage about the story's major themes:

> There is no question that the "Big Two-Hearted River" on the barest psychological level is, as Phillip Young says, a story of recovery from the damage of war but Hemingway's comparison of the loss of his work to an amputation or war casualties and the actual omitted ending provide clues for another metaphoric level in the story. This other level is found by considering Nick's fishing trip as an attempt by Hemingway to write, perhaps for the first time, about the artist and process of his art.

Below are two examples of plagiarized passages of the above extract from Smith's article:

> Hemingway's "Big Two-Hearted River" has more than one level of meaning. While the story is fundamentally concerned with Nick's healing from the trauma he suffered

in the war, it also has a great deal to say about the artistic process.

Hemingway's "Big Two-Hearted River" is most obviously about recovery from the damage of war. However, this profound and complex story works on another level as well; it can also be read as a metaphor for the life of the artist and process of his art (Smith 130).

While the first passage does not use Smith's exact language, it does list the same ideas he proposes as the critical themes behind two stories without citing his work. Since this interpretation is Smith's distinct idea, this constitutes plagiarism. The second passage has shortened his passage, changed some wording, and included a citation, but some of the phrasing is Smith's. The first passage could be fixed with a parenthetical citation; however, because some of the wording in the second remains the same, it would require the use of quotation marks, in addition to a parenthetical citation. The passage below represents an honestly and adequately documented use of the original passage:

According to B. J. Smith, Hemingway's "Big Two-Hearted River" is a story that works on multiple levels. While it is certainly "a story of recovery from the damage of war," it can also be read in terms of "the artist and process of his art" (130).

This passage acknowledges that the interpretation is derived from Smith while appropriately using quotations to indicate his precise language.

While it is not necessary to document well-known facts, often referred to as "common knowledge," any ideas or language that you take from someone else must be properly documented. Common knowledge generally includes the birth and death dates of authors or other well-documented facts of their lives. An often-cited guideline is that if you can find the information in three sources, it is common knowledge. Despite this guideline, it is admittedly often difficult to know if the facts you uncover are common knowledge or not. When in doubt, document your source.

Sample Essay

Fred Appleton
Ms. Crawford
English II
October 15, 2007

THE FAILURE OF STOICISM IN HEMINGWAY'S "INDIAN CAMP"
Hemingway's "Indian Camp" is clearly a story about a
father trying to pass his values on to his son. In this
case, it is the philosophy of stoicism that Dr. Adams
wants to impart to the young Nick. According to Graham F.
Wagstaff and Andrea M. Rowledge, "Followers of stoicism
. . . believed that virtue, which was considered to be
the highest good, consisted of a will that was exercised
in accordance with Nature and hence uninfluenced by all
mundane desire. Emotion, therefore, was to be condemned
and controlled" (181). Thus, those who adhere to a stoic
philosophy are generally said to be rational, pragmatic,
self-reliant, and calm. In Hemingway's "Indian Camp,"
Dr. Adams attempts to cultivate in his son this stoic
philosophy, which he associates with mature masculinity
and which he himself embodies. However, due to several
mistakes on his father's part, Nick—who is supposed to
be learning that he, along with his father and every
other human being, must resign himself to the will of
nature and learn to react to that will in a rational
way—actually ends up with a reinforced notion of his
father's omnipotence. Ultimately, then, not only does
Dr. Adams fail to teach Nick the principles of stoicism,
he also is in large part responsible for thwarting
Nick's progression into maturity by preventing him from
learning what every maturing child must discover: the
limitations of his father's power.

The world of emotional response, against which stoicism
defines itself, is an unpredictable one. "Indian Camp"
provides a couple of examples of the unpredictability of
emotions. On one hand, Uncle George's angry outburst at
being bitten by the Indian mother provides comic relief not

only to the readers of the story but to the participants as well; the tension surrounding the dangerous birth is lightened by the woman's emotional attack and Uncle George's emotional response. On the other hand, however, emotion drives the surprising death in the story too. Obviously, no one expected the Indian father's suicide, which was an emotional response with grave consequences. The value of acting out of emotion, then, is hard to ascertain except in hindsight, and adherents to stoicism believe it is worth sacrificing the benefits of emotion to escape the negative consequences.

Dr. Adams's stoic philosophy is clear in the way he handles the Indian woman's case. Dr. Adams is certainly pragmatic. He does not let fear, worry, or despair at the conditions he discovers overwhelm him; he simply adjusts to the situation he faces, using a jackknife as an operating tool to perform a cesarean and "nine-foot tapered gut leaders" to sew up the incision (18). His reaction to the woman's screams is perhaps the most convincing evidence of his stoic philosophy; eschewing emotion and remaining entirely rational, he says, "her screams are not important. I don't hear them because they are not important" (16). Based on the outcome of the cesarean procedure, Dr. Adams's philosophy appears to be a sound one. Against the odds, both the Indian woman and her baby boy survive, while without Dr. Adams's help, they would likely both have died.

While Dr. Adams's stoicism clearly and significantly benefits the Indian woman and her child, it also causes him to make some errors that will interfere with Nick's ability to learn this philosophy from him. To begin with, Dr. Adams fails to notice that Nick is too young and too sensitive to witness the cesarean procedure. Nick cannot ignore the woman's screams like his father does; he says, "Oh, Daddy, can't you give her something to make her stop screaming?" (16). After the baby is born, Nick began to look "away so as not to see what his father was doing" (17). And when his father says that Nick "can watch . . . or not" as he sews up the incision, we are told that "Nick did not watch. His curiosity had been gone for a long time" (17). It is obvious from Nick's reactions that he is overwhelmed by what he is witnessing. Dr. Adams not only fails to account for Nick's sensibilities and emotions, he also underestimates those of the baby's father as well. Dr. Adams makes light of the father's situation, saying, "Ought to have a look at the proud father. They're usually the worst sufferers in these little affairs" (18), only to discover that the man has committed suicide. Thus, as a result of Dr. Adams's failure to take into account the emotional states of Nick and the Indian father, Nick, in one short afternoon, finds himself exposed to the overwhelmingly extreme examples of a birth by cesarean section and a death by suicide.

As a result of his exposure to these bloody scenes, Nick develops an unhealthy belief in the omnipotence of his father, a belief wholly at odds with the tenets of stoicism that Dr. Adams is trying to impart to Nick. When Nick asks his father why the Indian killed himself, Dr. Adams says, "He couldn't stand things, I guess" (19). The father could not stand to witness the operation, Nick himself could not look, and by this point, even Uncle George has run off. As a result, Nick comes to believe that his father is the only one with the power to "stand things," to continue to behave rationally and practically no matter what the emotional context. This power to "stand things" is apparently what enabled his father to do, with confidence and detachment, what no other person could do, perform the operation that saved both the woman's life and the life of her baby boy. To Nick, his father seems to be in control of everything, including life and death. In fact, Nick has gained so much confidence in his father's abilities that he feels invincible when in his father's care, as the following lines make clear: "In the early morning on the lake sitting in the stern of the boat with his father rowing,

[Nick] felt quite sure that he would never die" (19). The syntax of the sentence indicates that Nick is not revealing a blanket faith in his safety and security. On the contrary, his feelings must be put in their proper context; it is only when Nick is "sitting in the stern of the boat with his father rowing"—when he surrenders entirely to his father's control—that he feels immortal.

Had Nick properly learned the tenets of stoicism, he would have come to believe that every human being has to resign himself to the will of nature and trust that he can handle and adapt to that will in a rational way. But Nick has been too overwhelmed to learn that he can use pragmatism and reason to deal with any obstacles that come his way. He has not undergone a rite of passage and come out the stronger for it, as his father had intended. Even Dr. Adams realizes his mistake: "'I'm terribly sorry I brought you along, Nickie,' said his father, all his post-operative exhilaration gone. 'It was an awful mess to put you through'" (18). Worse than the fact that Nick has no increased faith in his own abilities, though, is that he has developed a much too grand idea of his father's abilities. Instead of seeing his father as a model of the man who successfully resigns himself to the will of nature and uses his reason to adapt to that will, Nick sees Dr. Adams as capable of confronting and even altering nature's will. Thus, while Nick's experience in the Indian camp is supposed to be a rite of passage toward adulthood, it actually causes Nick to regress into childish ideas of his father's supremacy. The story demonstrates in a powerful, symbolic way this lack of progression by showing Nick carried back across the same lake he crossed at the beginning of the story; literally and figuratively, at the story's close, Nick is right back where he started.

By story's end, Nick has failed to make any progress toward adopting his father's model of stoicism. It is reasonable to speculate that had Dr. Adams not made the mistakes he did, perhaps Nick would have learned the lesson his father wanted him to learn and that perhaps this would have been a desirable outcome, as Dr. Adams does bring a great deal of good to the Indian community by virtue of his stoic response. However, if we consider the fact that because Dr. Adams's mistakes amount to an inability or refusal to account for the emotional response of others and that one of the principles of stoicism is to condemn emotion, it is evident that Dr. Adams's mistakes stem from the very philosophy he wants to teach Nick. Dr. Adams is bound to make these kinds of errors, as Nick would be as well if he were to successfully adopt stoicism as his own philosophy. Thus, "Indian Camp" gives us some valuable insight into the limitations of living one's life according to a strict stoic philosophy. And since many critics argue that stoicism is an inherent trait of the typical Hemingway hero, the story also prepares us to look for these limitations and flaws in Hemingway's other heroes as well.

WORKS CITED

Hemingway, Ernest. "Indian Camp." In Our Time. New York: Scribner's, 1986. 13–19.

Kautz, Elizabeth Dolan. "Gynecologists, Power and Sexuality in Modernist Texts." Journal of Popular Culture 28.4 (1995): 81–91.

Wagstaff, Graham F., and Andrea M. Rowledge. "Stoicism: Its Relation to Gender, Attitudes Toward Poverty, and Reactions to Emotive Material." Journal of Social Psychology 135.2 (1995): 181–84.

HOW TO WRITE
ABOUT HEMINGWAY

THE STATUS of Ernest Hemingway (1899–1961) as one of America's best-known and most respected writers is not in doubt, especially when one considers his Pulitzer Prize for *The Old Man and the Sea* in 1953, his Nobel Prize in literature in 1954, and the fact that his works are widely read and studied throughout the world today. As a member of the expatriate community in Paris in the 1920s, the charismatic Hemingway developed a reputation as artist, wounded soldier, outdoorsman, heavy drinker, and womanizer. Hemingway enjoyed his image as a sort of macho rebel and did everything he could to encourage this vision of himself in the public eye. As a result, one of the toughest challenges in writing about Hemingway's life and his literary work is to distinguish the myth from the man and both of these entities from the fictional characters he created.

One of the pitfalls of Hemingway's habit of perpetuating these myths about himself is that readers tend to look for the characters in his works that most resemble this mythological figure and to read and interpret them as keys to understanding the author's psychology. These characters—Nick Adams, Robert Jordan, and Jake Barnes, for instance—might be more accurately compared to the iconic Hemingway image than to the real man. If you are planning to write about connections between events in Hemingway's life or Hemingway's psychology and his fictional characters, do not rely on what you think you know about who Hemingway was. You will need to do some biographical reading, and it is a good idea to peruse at least two biographies. You might start with Carlos Baker's *Ernest Hemingway: A Life Story* and Jeffrey Meyers's *Hemingway: A*

Biography. This type of research will help you internalize a more accurate and complex vision of Hemingway as more than an icon of American pop culture and therefore enable you to make more accurate and nuanced observations about the relationship between the real Hemingway and his fictional heroes.

A related pitfall concerns our tendency, once we identify Hemingway with a particular fictional character, to locate the moral center of the novel with that character, reasoning that if a particular character represents Hemingway, then the author must have intended for this character to be the one worthiest of emulation. It is helpful to keep in mind, however, that whether this character can be most usefully compared to the "mythic Hemingway" or the "real Hemingway," the author does not necessarily endorse the behavior and/or philosophy of that particular character. Self-reflective authors, Hemingway in particular, are not above criticizing and parodying their own personalities. Take the case of *The Sun Also Rises.* The novel centers on Jake Barnes, and much of the narration is filtered through Jake's sensibilities. Given this and the fact that Jake Barnes has a good deal in common with the Hemingway persona, we might find ourselves tempted to consider Jake as a reliable and unbiased source of information and to believe that his perspective on life and love is the one most endorsed by the author. However, if we put aside these assumptions and spend some time critically examining Jake, we might find him to be a scarred and fundamentally flawed character hiding behind a facade of bravado and nihilism.

Besides the macho image, Hemingway is perhaps most famous for his spare, straightforward style, which, like the image, can prove to be a challenge to the would-be essay writer. After all, the language is so simple and the plot so uninvolved. How can one find a "deeper meaning" or write a literary analysis of a piece of literature written in short, declarative sentences, with generous doses of dialogue and very little in the way of narrative explanation or expository prose to dissect? The first step is simply to realize the level of skill and craftsmanship that goes into prose as deceptively simple as Hemingway's. It is not easy to write this way, nor does this type of writing make the reader's job easy, although it may seem to at first glance. Hemingway's economy of language and lack of narrative commentary force the reader constantly to interpret and make meaning. Hemingway refuses simply to tell you what is important. You have to figure it out, and you do that by paying painstaking attention to detail. You have to consider Hemingway's exact word choice as well as the order of words, sentences, and paragraphs. You have to consider what Hemingway omitted as well as what he included. Is there information or a particular detail that you would expect to learn in the story that you do not? You must think about why Hemingway left this out.

Hemingway's careful use of symbols also enables him to keep the prose simple while dealing with complicated ideas. You would do well always to be on the lookout for symbols in Hemingway's work and be prepared to explore their many layers of meaning. Take *The Old Man and the Sea*, for example. On the surface, it is a story about an old man trying to catch a big fish. Although he beats the odds and manages to catch the fish, he cannot get it into the boat, and although he tries desperately to combat them, sharks devour his catch before he makes it to shore. The old man winds up with only a skeleton to show for his efforts. *The Old Man and the Sea* is an adventure story, for sure, and even at face value, it has a great deal to say about humankind's ambiguous relationship with the natural world and about destiny and free will as well. However, the story of Santiago and his fish has also been read as an allegory on writing, the old man's struggle to catch the fish representing the author's struggle to produce literature, and as a religious parable, with Santiago as a Christ figure. The story has even been successfully interpreted as a commentary on Taoism; this reading has Santiago not defeated at all but having learned an important lesson in yielding his own will to the larger force of nature. Clearly, remaining open to the possible multiple meanings of symbols in Hemingway's work can result in a much richer experience of the texts.

A final challenge faced by readers of Hemingway concerns form and intertextuality. Hemingway produced some innovative texts, such as *In Our Time*, which is comprised of a collection of short stories with vignettes, called "interchapters," between them. Should you consider the work as a whole a novel or a collection of short stories? If you were going to write about *In Our Time* or any of the stories published in this collection, you would want to come to your own understanding of the relationship between the stories and the interchapters. Can you really write about "Big Two-Hearted River" without considering the interchapter that is placed between parts 1 and 2 of the story in *In Our Time*, for example? On a related note, Hemingway published many stories featuring the same character, Nick Adams. If you decide to write about any of

Hemingway's works that include Nick, you will have to decide whether you will take into account information about Nick located in works other than the one you are focusing on. In other words, do you consider the Nick Adams that appears in each separate publication to be a separate entity, or do you assume that the Nick Adams that appears in various Hemingway works is the same character and so find it acceptable, for example, to trace the development of Nick from a young boy in "Indian Camp" to a young man in "Big Two-Hearted River"?

Your keys to coping with these challenges to writing about Hemingway are thorough background research and your own careful, critical thinking. It is imperative that you take the time to do some background reading on Hemingway's life and the historical period in which he lived and wrote and to consider what other scholars have had to say about the work you are planning to write about before you begin your first draft. When you have a good sense of historical context as well as a firm grasp on the critical conversation about the work you are studying, you are much less likely to make naive mistakes or to rehash arguments that have been made many times before, and you are much better prepared to enter the critical conversation in an interesting and useful way.

TOPICS AND STRATEGIES

The following pages will give you ideas about how you might approach writing an essay about Hemingway. Of course, you will need to select a certain work or works to focus on, as you will not be able to discuss Hemingway's entire oeuvre in one essay. The sample topics will give you suggestions regarding which texts you might use in conjunction with a particular topic, but the final decision is up to you. Remember to consider the anticipated length of your essay, the length of the works you are considering, and the number of works you want to examine as you plan your paper. You want to make sure that you have ample space to consider the work(s) you have selected in a meaningful way. It is also a good idea to provide a rationale for grouping the texts you do in your essay. While sometimes your basis for selection will be obvious—you have chosen stories that relate to a particular theme or include the same character—at other times, it is beneficial to explain your selection to your reader. You might indicate for your reader, for example, that you have chosen all early Hemingway works to explore how Hemingway thought about a particular issue at one stage of his career, or perhaps you have selected pieces that span Hemingway's writing life in order to chart a progression in his thinking. If you are sure in your own mind of your reasons for choosing certain texts and your essay makes those reasons clear to readers, then you can be assured that your selection will not wind up appearing random and weaken your argument as a result.

Themes

Many of Hemingway's works engage similar themes. You might study, f example, artistic expression, the nature of romantic love, the effects war on the individual, or the human being's relationship with nature almost any of Hemingway's literary works. The sample topics below c you suggestions as to which works you might focus on for a given t but the lists they provide are by no means exclusive. Feel free to in another work or substitute a work you find particularly interesti place of one suggested in the topic. Once you have selected the wor want to study, you will want to reread each of them carefully, payi cial attention to any passages that pertain to your topic, analyzir passages, and keeping careful notes. Then comes the really excit of crafting an essay. You will want to compare the notes you ha about each of the works you have selected and synthesize your in the hope of drawing fresh and insightful conclusions.

Sample Topics:

1. **Artistic expression:** How does Hemingway portray t and the artistic process in his work?

   Begin by selecting pieces that seem to you to have sor say about the artistic process. You might consider " of Kilimanjaro," *The Sun Also Rises, The Old Man c* and/or "Big Two-Hearted River." Both "The Snows jaro" and *The Sun Also Rises* feature characters wh Would you say that these writers are successful Why or why not? What do you know about thei cesses? Though *The Old Man and the Sea* and "Bi River" do not feature characters who are writers been read by many as allegories about writir which character would be the artist in each of what activities would represent writing. In each story, what are the artist's goals and motivations? What are the obstacles he faces? What qualities are necessary for him to succeed? How is he different from the rest of his community?

2. **Romantic love:** What does Hemingway's work ultimately have to say about the nature of romantic love?

For this essay, choose one or more Hemingway pieces that feature an interesting romance. You might examine Harry and Helen's relationship in "The Snows of Kilimanjaro," for example, studying in particular Harry's comments about love, such as his comment to Helen: "Love is a dunghill . . . And I'm the cock that gets on it to crow" (43). You might also look at Catherine and Frederic's relationship as it develops through the course of *A Farewell to Arms.* Early in this novel, Frederic Henry reflects: "I knew I did not love Catherine Barkley nor had any idea of loving her. This was a game, like bridge, in which you said things instead of playing cards for money or playing for some stakes" (30–31). Does Hemingway consistently portray love in such a negative way? Is it typically some sort of power struggle as these two quotations seem to suggest?

Besides "The Snows of Kilimanjaro" and *A Farewell to Arms,* you might also consider Robert and Maria from *For Whom the Bell Tolls* or Jake and Brett from *The Sun Also Rises.* What seems to attract these lovers to one another? Would you consider any of the relationships healthy or fulfilling? Which and why? Taken together, how does Hemingway's work portray romantic love?

3. **Nature:** Hemingway is well known for his detailed and lovingly rendered portrayals of the natural world. But how exactly does he perceive the relationship between that world and the world of human beings?

You might focus, for this topic, on any of the following novels: *For Whom the Bell Tolls, The Sun Also Rises,* or *A Farewell to Arms.* You might also consider the short stories "Big

Two-Hearted River" and "The Short Happy Life of Francis
Macomber." In any case, you will want to study the way that
Hemingway depicts the natural world and the way that the
characters interact with it. Are the characters respectful of
nature? What do they use the wilderness for? What do they
perceive as their obligations to it? Do the main characters seem
to think of themselves, and humanity in general, as a part of
the natural world or as separate from and superior to it?

Character

When you are planning to write about characters in more than one li†
ary work, you will probably want to identify a certain group or typ
character to study to make your essay more manageable and mear
ful. In the case of Hemingway, you might decide to explore chara
who are or have been soldiers and what they share in common. (
Hemingway has received a great deal of criticism for his portra
female characters, you might choose to focus on Hemingway's v
ascertaining for yourself whether this criticism is justified. Wh
type of character you choose, you will want to reread all of the w
plan to talk about, taking careful and copious notes on your ch
Then, compare and contrast the characters in the individual
order to draw conclusions. Based on your study of several sol
acters or female characters, what kind of argument can you
about Hemingway's perception of soldiers or women?

Sample Topics:

1. **Hemingway's soldiers:** Many of Hemingway's novel
   ries deal with war in one fashion or another. Taker
   how do these works portray the soldier? Is he a hero o
   ordinary human being put in a very extraordinary s

   You might choose to focus on *For Whom the Bell '*
   well to Arms, The Sun Also Rises, "Big Two-He
   "The Snows of Kilimanjaro," and/or "Soldier's P
   what you know about each soldier's life befoı
   combat, and upon return to civilian life. Afte
   is complete, how do these characters come to
   selves and their wartime experiences? How

the traumatic events they have witnessed and participated in? What do these characters have in common? What generalizations can you make about Hemingway's portrayal of the soldier based on your study of these works?

2. **Hemingway's women:** Hemingway is often criticized for portraying women either as domesticated and submissive or as sirens who use their sexual power to control men. Do you think this is an accurate and fair assessment, or has Hemingway created some female characters who do not fit either of these molds?

For this essay, you can select any Hemingway text and examine and evaluate its female characters. For an example of Hemingway's traditional, subservient female character, you might examine Maria in *For Whom the Bell Tolls*, and for an example of one of his "bitches," you can look at Brett Ashley in *The Sun Also Rises* or Margot of "The Short Happy Life of Francis Macomber." For characters a little harder to peg, you might study Pilar of *For Whom the Bell Tolls*, Catherine from *A Farewell to Arms*, or the female character referred to as "Jig" in "Hills Like White Elephants." Whichever female characters you choose to study, be sure to examine their dialogue and behavior, their thoughts if you are privy to them, and their relationships with other characters. How do they interact with others, particularly men? Do they have their own goals and motivations? Are they willing to compromise, or must they always get what they want?

History and Context

t certainly is not as culturally jarring for a 21st-century student to read lemingway as it is to read, say, Shakespeare or Milton. The language familiar; the style is straightforward. In fact, you might say that it deceptively easy for a 21st-century reader to approach Hemingway. cause the language and style do not necessarily signal to us that we are ding something written in a different era, we have a tendency simply carry our modern assumptions and ideas with us into the Hemingway verse, and this is not something we can do without consequences. If do not step outside our modern perspective, we will fail to take into unt early 20th-century notions of technology and science, war, psychology, gender roles, and America's relationship to the world at large. On the other hand, if we spend some time doing a bit of research, discovering what ideas held sway in the society in which Hemingway was a part, we are much more likely to pick up on nuances that we might otherwise have missed and to ascertain what Hemingway's position was on various issues in relation to the prevailing notions of his world.

Sample Topics:

1. **World War I:** What do Hemingway's works have to say about the psychological and emotional effects of war on returning soldiers?

   You might want to begin with some background reading on World War I and the psychological conditions of the soldiers who returned from battle. You might try *American Voices of World War I: Primary Source Documents, 1917–1920* by M. Marix Evans or *World War I and the Cultures of Modernity* by Douglas Peter Mackaman and Michael Mays. As for primary texts, "Soldier's Home" and *The Sun Also Rises* would make particularly good choices. How does wartime experience seem to have affected Krebs from "Soldier's Home" and Jake from *The Sun Also Rises?* Does either of them seem to be suffering from what we now call post-traumatic stress disorder? Based on the information you are provided in the text, how are these characters different after the war than they were before entering military service? According to Hemingway's work, what are the consequences of participation in war? What does a returning solider need in order to reintegrate into society? Ultimately, what kind of commentary do you think Hemingway is making about the psychological effects of war on returning soldiers? Is he mirroring contemporary thought on the subject, or is he presenting something new?

2. **Prohibition:** What message does Hemingway's work send about Prohibition and alcohol consumption?

   You might wish to begin with some background reading on Prohibition, such as *Prohibition: Thirteen Years That Changed America* by Edward Behr or *Deliver Us from Evil: An Interpretation of*

American Prohibition by Norma H. Clark. Then, read or reread "The Killers" and *The Sun Also Rises,* paying particular attention to what these works have to say about Prohibition and alcohol consumption.

Critic Jeffery Schwartz argues that *The Sun Also Rises* "signifies both communal enjoyment of life and its pleasures and a manner of rebelling against prohibition and its nationalist agendas" (196). Do you agree with Schwartz's argument that *The Sun Also Rises* is a sort of protest against Prohibition? Now consider "The Killers" and its portrayal of organized crime, which began to flourish in America during the Prohibition era. Would you say that this story, too, demonstrates a "rebel[ion] against prohibition"? If so, how is this rebellion similar to and different from that portrayed in *The Sun Also Rises*? Taken together, what do these works have to say about the American attitude toward Prohibition and its consequences?

Philosophy and Ideas

If you are setting out to write an essay about the philosophy and/or ideas that Hemingway's work engages, you might think first of *nada*, a philosophical concept often associated with Hemingway that he describes in the short story "A Clean, Well-Lighted Place." While a study of *nada* and its presence or absence—or perhaps modification—in other Hemingway works would certainly make for an interesting essay, you might also consider topics that are not so overtly philosophical. You might, for instance, consider how characters determine good from bad and right from wrong in times of war when typical laws and moral rules do not seem to make any sense. Or, you might write about how Hemingway constructs masculinity in his literary work. What does it mean, in the Hemingway universe, to be a "real man"?

Sample Topics:

1. **Nada:** What exactly is Hemingway's concept of *nada*, and how is it incorporated into his larger worldview?

   For this topic, you will want first to examine "A Clean, Well-Lighted Place," which includes several explicit references to *nada*. In the context of the story, what does *nada* signify? Once you have a handle on the concept, think about other Hemingway works that may contain references to *nada*, with or without actually using that term. Would you say that Hemingway's concept of *nada* and the nihilistic worldview with which it is associated permeates all or most of his work? Do any of his works present an alternative philosophy or offer a tempered version of *nada*?

2. **Ethics in war:** What kind of commentary does Hemingway make about ethics in wartime?

   Many of Hemingway's stories and novels would work for this topic. Particularly interesting choices would include *For Whom the Bell Tolls* and *A Farewell to Arms.* How do the characters in these two novels determine what is right and what is wrong? When does one follow one's own conscience, and when does one follow orders, for example? Examine the different code of ethics held by Pablo, Anselmo, and Robert Jordan of *For Whom the Bell Tolls* and Frederic Henry and Rinaldi of *A Farewell to Arms.* Does Hemingway suggest that any of these characters has developed a particularly good or bad set of ethical principles to deal with the wartime environment? Can you figure out, from comparing and contrasting these characters, what Hemingway would consider a viable ethical system in wartime, or does his work indicate that such a thing is not possible, that each solider must constantly wrestle with his conscience and constantly adjust to new conditions and questions?

3. **Masculinity:** Identify and evaluate the multiple models of masculinity that are presented in Hemingway's work.

   For this topic, you might focus on *The Sun Also Rises, For Whom the Bell Tolls, A Farewell to Arms,* "The Short Happy Life of Francis Macomber," "Soldier's Home," "Big Two-Hearted River," and/or "The Killers." Record all the details you can about the male characters in the works you have chosen to study. How do these characters assert their masculinity? How do they interact with each other? How do they interact with women? What do these male characters have in common? Would you say that violence is a common thread for many of these men? How about emotion and sensitivity? Based on the comparisons you have made, what kinds of generalization can you make about Hemingway's portrayal of masculinity? How does his idea of masculinity compare to our notions of what it means to be a man in the 21st century?

Form and Genre

When you are asked to consider "form" and "genre," you want to ask yourself how a literary work is put together and what kind of story it is. In the case of Hemingway, one significant element of form is narration. You want to examine how the story is told, who tells it, and why. While initially these factors seem to be outside of the story proper, they are in fact an integral part of the story itself. You always want to keep in mind that the author and the narrator are separate entities. You have Hemingway, the author, who is actually writing the story, and you have the narrator, a character that Hemingway creates to tell the story. If you remember to think of the narrator as a storyteller created by the author, you will often gain incredibly interesting insights into the themes and meanings of the work you are studying. On a related note, particularly in the case of Hemingway, readers tend to conflate the author not with the narrator but with the protagonist, for instance, reading Nick Adams as an "alter ego" of Hemingway's. It can certainly be fruitful to examine similarities between an author's life and the lives of his characters, but you must do it carefully and with purpose, not arguing that Hemingway and Nick are one and the same, but using what you know about each of them to help illuminate the other.

Sample Topics:

1. **Narration:** Examine the narration and its effects on our interpretation of selected texts.

   Studying the narration of the texts you read can be surprisingly illuminating. When you examine a narrator, you will want to note whether the narrator is a character in the story or merely an outside observer, what kinds of information your narrator is privy to, and what biases he or she might have. What, do you imagine, is your narrator's motivation for telling the particular story he or she is telling? How might this motivation affect the way the narrator presents the story and, consequently, the way a reader interprets it? You can study narration in any of Hemingway's works, but *The Sun Also Rises* and *A Farewell to Arms* would make for especially interesting cases, studied separately or compared against each other.

2. **Biographical connections:** Many of Hemingway's works have been interpreted as retellings of and commentaries on the author's personal experiences and struggles. *The Old Man and the Sea,* for example, is seen as a commentary on Hemingway's own personal struggles at the time in which he was writing that novel. Critics have also noted many connections between Hemingway and Krebs of "Soldier's Home" and Nick of "Big Two-Hearted River" and other Nick Adams stories. Identify and discuss other examples of biographical connections in Hemingway's work.

Read about Hemingway's childhood, his family, and his writing career in Carlos Baker's biography, *Ernest Hemingway: A Life Story,* or in Jeffrey Meyers's *Hemingway: A Biography.* Then compare what you know about Hemingway's life to the fictional lives of his many characters. Is there some connection that resonates powerfully for you? If so, explore this connection and how it might help you better understand the literary work and its creator.

Symbols, Imagery, and Language

One interesting way to approach Hemingway's particular use of symbols and imagery is to discuss his "iceberg principle." Hemingway explains the iceberg principle as follows: "I always try to write on the principle of the iceberg. There is seven-eighths of it underwater for every part that shows. Anything you know you can eliminate and it only strengthens your iceberg" (Mangum 1622). You might select any of Hemingway's works and examine it for evidence of Hemingway's "icebergs." You might discuss the effectiveness of such a technique, perhaps comparing Hemingway's style to another writer, such as William Faulkner, who often provides

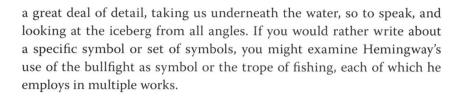

a great deal of detail, taking us underneath the water, so to speak, and looking at the iceberg from all angles. If you would rather write about a specific symbol or set of symbols, you might examine Hemingway's use of the bullfight as symbol or the trope of fishing, each of which he employs in multiple works.

Sample Topics:

1. **Hemingway's iceberg principle:** Many readers agree that Hemingway's use of understatement and symbolism contributes greatly to the success of his writing style. Hemingway himself called his technique the "principle of the iceberg." Analyze and evaluate Hemingway's use of the iceberg principle in one or more of his works.

   Reread "A Clean, Well-Lighted Place," which Hemingway considered to be one of the best examples of his use of the iceberg principle. How does the principle operate in this story? What does Hemingway keep beneath the surface? Do you agree that this technique makes the story more powerful? Why or why not? Choose one or two additional stories, such as "Hills Like White Elephants" and "The Killers," and evaluate Hemingway's use of the iceberg principle in these as well.

2. **Bullfighting:** How is bullfighting used symbolically in Hemingway's work?

   You might begin with some background reading, such as Carrie B. Douglas's *Bulls, Bullfighting, and Spanish Identities* or Hemingway's own *Death in the Afternoon*, as you prepare to write an essay on this topic. You will want to know what function bullfights traditionally serve in Spanish culture and what the different parts of the ritual represent.

   You will definitely want to look at *For Whom the Bell Tolls* and *The Sun Also Rises*. In *For Whom the Bell Tolls*, consider why Hemingway includes the long section about Pilar's lover who dies from a bull injury and Andrés's memories of bullbaiting. How are these sections thematically related to the rest of the novel? You will also want to think about why Hemingway has Jake, Brett, and the rest of their group attend the bullfights in *The Sun Also Rises.* How does the symbolism of the bullfight relate to the larger themes of this novel? Would you say that the bullfights serve the same symbolic function in *For Whom the Bell Tolls* and *The Sun Also Rises?* Why or why not?

3. **Fishing:** What does the act of fishing represent in Hemingway's work?

Look at several of Hemingway's works in which the main characters spend time fishing, such as "Big Two-Hearted River," *The Sun Also Rises,* and *The Old Man and the Sea.* Compare and contrast the fishing scenes in each of these works. What are the motivations of the fishermen? What are the obstacles they face? Are they ultimately successful? What does the act of fishing seem to represent in each of these works? What about the fish themselves?

Compare and Contrast Essays

The most important thing to remember when you are writing a comparison and contrast essay is that your essay should do a great deal more than merely point out similarities and differences among several literary works. It is your job to explain to your readers the significance of these similarities and differences, to turn your observations into an interesting interpretation or argument. This will be easier if you have a good reason for comparing the pieces you are discussing in the first place. For example, if you are comparing *A Farewell to Arms* with "Hills Like White Elephants" because they both deal with pregnancy, it is likely that your observations of the similarities between these two works will enable you to draw conclusions about Hemingway's portrayal of pregnancy and parenthood. Likewise, if you compare and contrast "Indian Camp" and "Big Two-Hearted River" because they both feature Nick Adams, as a young boy and a young man returning from war, respectively, then you will likely hone an argument regarding the development of Nick's character.

Sample Topics:

1. **Elements across Hemingway's works:** Compare and contrast an aspect of Hemingway's work, such as a type of character or a certain theme, across several of his works.

   You will want to start by choosing two or more texts that seem to you to have some significant connection. For example, you might be interested in the fact that *A Farewell to Arms* and "Hills Like White Elephants" both deal with a pregnancy. You might compare and contrast these two works, focusing on how the main characters seem to deal with the pregnancy. Do they welcome it? How does the pregnancy affect their relationship? In what terms do they think of the unborn child? Is there a difference in how the mother feels toward the child versus how the father feels? Once you have studied each of the texts separately, set them side by side to draw conclusions. Drawing on your analyses of these texts, how would you say Hemingway feels about children and parenthood? Alternatively, you might compare and contrast several stories that feature Nick Adams, noting whether the character changes over the course of the stories or remains relatively static. How is the Nick Adams that appears in "Indian Camp" different from the Nick Adams that appears in "Big Two-Hearted River," for example?

2. **Hemingway's work versus that of another author:** Compare and contrast Hemingway's work with that of another author working in the same time period.

   Begin by choosing two works with something in common. You might decide to compare and contrast Hemingway's "The Short Happy Life of Francis Macomber" with F. Scott Fitzgerald's *The Great Gatsby* or *Tender Is the Night,* for example, as they all feature rich Americans. You might begin by asking yourself what you know about these characters. How did they come by their fortunes? What do their priorities seem to be? How do they handle their money? Once you have made your observations and noted the similarities and differences among the characters, it is time to synthesize your findings and draw conclusions. In terms of this example, you might begin by asking yourself how you would characterize Hemingway's and Fitzgerald's perception of wealth and then compare and contrast these initial conclusions. If the similarities turn out to be more striking than the differences, you would focus on the former, using your paper to explain how two important American authors perceived wealth and status in a similar vein. On the other hand, if the differences seem more meaningful to you than the similarities, then your focus would be on describing the differences and drawing out their implications.

Bibliography and Online Resources

Baker, Carlos. *Ernest Hemingway: A Life Story.* New York: Scribner's, 1969.

———. *Hemingway: The Writer as Artist.* 4th ed. Princeton, NJ: Princeton UP, 1972.

Benson, Jackson J. *The Short Stories of Ernest Hemingway: Critical Essays.* Durham, NC: Duke UP, 1975.

Comley, Nancy R., and Robert Scholes. *Hemingway's Genders: Rereading the Hemingway Text.* New Haven, CT: Yale UP, 1994.

Mangum, Bryant. "Ernest Hemingway." *Critical Survey of Short Fiction.* Ed. Frank Magill. Vol. 4. Englewood Cliffs, NJ: Salem, 1982, 1,621–28.

Mandel, Miriam. *Reading Hemingway: The Facts in the Fictions.* Methuen, NJ: Scarecrow, 1995.

Meyers, Jeffrey. *Hemingway: A Biography.* New York: Harper & Row, 1985.

Nelson, Gerald B., and Glory Jones. *Hemingway: Life and Works.* New York: Facts On File, 1984.

Phillips, Larry W., ed. *Ernest Hemingway on Writing.* London: Grafton, 1986.

Reynolds, Michael S. *Hemingway: The Final Years.* New York: Norton, 1999.

———. *Hemingway: The Homecoming.* New York: Norton, 1999.

———. *Hemingway: The Paris Years.* New York: Norton, 1999.

———. *The Young Hemingway.* New York: Norton, 1998.

Scafella, Frank, ed. *Hemingway: Essays of Reassessment.* Oxford: Oxford UP, 1991.

Schwartz, Jeffrey. "'The Saloon Must Go, and I Will Take It With Me': American Prohibition, Nationalism, and Expatriation in *The Sun Also Rises.*" *Studies in the Novel* 33.2 (2001): 180–201.

Trogdon, Robert W., ed. *Ernest Hemingway: A Documentary Volume. Dictionary of Literary Biography.* Vol. 210. Detroit, MI: Gale, 1999.

Wagner, Linda Welshimer, ed. *Hemingway: Five Decades of Criticism.* East Lansing: Michigan State UP, 1974.

Wagner-Martin, Linda, ed. *A Historical Guide to Ernest Hemingway.* New York: Oxford UP, 2000.

Waldhorn, Arthur. *A Reader's Guide to Ernest Hemingway.* New York: Farrar, Straus, & Giroux, 1972.

Wilson, M. The Hemingway Resource Center. Updated 21 Dec. 2005. Retrieved 8 March 2008. <http://www.lostgeneration.com>.

Wylder, Delbert E. *Hemingway's Heroes.* Albuquerque: U of New Mexico P, 1969.

Young, Philip. *Ernest Hemingway.* New York: Rinehart, 1952.

FOR WHOM
THE BELL TOLLS

READING TO WRITE

Hemingway's *For Whom the Bell Tolls* (1940) presents the story of Robert Jordan, an American who volunteers to fight for the Loyalists in the Spanish civil war. Although the events of the novel take place over a stretch of only four days, we are provided with a great deal of insight into the psychology of a soldier through the interior monologues of Robert Jordan and with ample historical and cultural context through the use of flashbacks and storytelling. Thus, the novel provides a virtually limitless number of potential essay topics.

One technique you can use to identify a topic or to provide evidence for a claim you have already formulated is "close reading." When you close read a passage, you read it slowly multiple times, paying careful attention to the language. Ask yourself why Hemingway selected and arranged the words of this paragraph in the precise way that he did. Imagine how the sense of the passage would change if you replaced any of the words with a synonym or reordered the sentences. Choose a passage of interest to you, perhaps one of Robert Jordan's interior monologues, such as this one:

> Once you accept the idea of demolition as a problem it is only a problem. But there was plenty that was not so good that went with it although God knows you took it easily enough. There was the constant attempt to approximate the conditions of successful assassination that accompanied demolition. Did big words make it more defensible? Did they make killing any more palatable? You took it a little too readily if you ask me, he told himself. And what you will be like or just exactly what you will

be suited for when you leave the service of the Republic is, to me, he thought, extremely doubtful. But my guess is you will get rid of all that by writing about it, he said. Once you write it down it is all gone. It will be a good book if you can write it. Much better than the other (165).

The references in this passage to language and writing make it a particularly interesting one to analyze. As Robert Jordan thinks about his job, demolition, he reflects on the "constant attempt to approximate the conditions of successful assassination that accompanied demolition." As he is thinking about this, Robert Jordan seems to realize that perhaps he, or his superiors, or humankind in general, speaks about the war with "big words" in a valiant but ultimately futile attempt to make destruction "more defensible" and killing "more palatable." Stopping to remind himself of the meanings behind the words used to describe his job, Robert Jordan faults himself for falling into this trap of disguising violence and destruction beneath formal and technical language. This brings up many questions that you could address in an essay, most broadly, what does the novel have to say about the relationship of language to truth and reality? Does it ultimately serve to disguise primal human behaviors as something more sophisticated or noble? Does language have other, more virtuous, functions in the novel? The passage itself suggests that it does.

Robert Jordan believes that he will need to "get rid" of his wartime experiences in order to resume a normal civilian life. He imagines that he will accomplish this by "writing about it," expressing a belief that writing something, putting experiences into recorded language, can remove them from the psyche. This idea suggests that writing is healing. Is this notion supported elsewhere in the novel? Does it as a whole suggest that putting our damaging experiences into language allows us to move on? Reflecting on these questions, you might think about the sexual trauma suffered by Maria. Is she encouraged to talk about her experiences in order to recover? Why do you think Pilar gives the advice that once Maria is with a man of her own choosing, it will then be like the assaults never happened? Does Maria in this case have not only to write, or tell, her history but "rewrite" it as well? What is the significance of this? And finally, what do you make of the fact that Robert and Maria imagine that healing from their traumatic experiences requires an obliteration of them? Maria thinks she can make it as though the assaults never happened by having sex with Robert Jordan, and he thinks that he can "get rid" of—not deal with or process—his experiences by writing them down. According to the novel, is this type of recovery possible? Is it healthy?

As you can see, a close reading of one passage can generate ideas for several essays. If you have analyzed a passage and generated many questions and ideas, you should then identify other passages that you think will lead you toward some answers or help you to refine your thoughts. Analyze these subsequent passages as you did the first, and continue the process until you feel as though you have reached a conclusion that might function as a claim upon which you can base your essay.

TOPICS AND STRATEGIES

The following topics and essay ideas are only suggestions. Rather than limit or constrict you, they should spark your imagination. On a related note, do not approach these essay topics as a series of questions to be answered in sequence. Instead, use the questions to help generate ideas about a given topic. Once you have recorded your ideas and analyzed relevant passages in the novel, you should formulate your claim, the argument you want your essay to make. Then, you will go back to your notes and begin to marshal the evidence for your claim, organizing and arranging your thoughts into a persuasive essay.

Themes

When you think about a novel's theme, you are attempting to determine what major ideas or issues it is concerned with. Many works will share the same themes, as there are central questions that human beings try to grapple with through literature. Each work will have its own unique perspective on the themes with which it deals, and it is your job as a reader-writer to discover and articulate this perspective in your essay. *For Whom the Bell Tolls* deals with such themes as love, death, and war. By isolating the most significant passages pertaining to one of these themes and then reading them closely with an aim toward analyzing their language, you can discover what the novel is saying about that particular issue, and in so doing, you will have created a claim upon which to base your essay.

Sample Topics:

1. **Love:** What is the novel's message about romantic love in the context of war? Can they exist together?

Analyze the scenes between Robert Jordan and Maria. What does their relationship seem to be based on? What does it provide them? How does Robert Jordan's relationship with Maria affect his ideas about the war and his thoughts about the future? Does the novel see these changes in Robert as positive or as distracting him from more noble or altruistic goals?

2. **Death:** What kind of commentary is the novel making about death and its various forms? Is there such a thing as a "good" death?

According to the novel, is death just a common human denominator, or are some kinds of deaths more meaningful than others? Locate the passages in which Robert Jordan thinks about his father's suicide. How does he view suicide? How does he feel about the deaths of Sordo and his men? Analyze the final scene in which Robert Jordan must come to terms with his own imminent death. How does he feel about the possibility of taking his own life? Compare Robert Jordan's perception of death with other characters', such as Pablo's, for example. Do their views have anything in common? Did Hemingway mean for readers to perceive one view as superior to or truer than the other? How do you know?

3. **Power:** According to the novel, how should power be shared among the citizens of a country? Put another way, what form of government is fair?

Reread the novel, paying careful attention to discussions of power and individual rights and responsibilities. What do the communists and the fascists believe? According to each side, what should the relationship between government and its subjects be like? Does Hemingway portray either side of the conflict—fascist or communist—as the "right" side? Analyze Robert Jordan's politics. Why does he fight on the communist side? What philosophy of government does he believe in? At one point, Robert Jordan says to Maria, "I love thee as I love liberty and dignity and the rights of all men to work and not to be hungry. I love thee as I love Madrid that we have defended and as I love all my comrades that have died" (348). At another, he says to himself: "You're not a real Marxist and you know it. You believe in Liberty, Equality and Fraternity. You believe in Life, Liberty and the Pursuit of Happiness" (305). Based on these passages and others that you have identified in the novel, what are Robert Jordan's true political beliefs? Are we to assume that Robert Jordan's political beliefs are the ones endorsed by the author? How do you know?

4. **Nature:** What does *For Whom the Bell Tolls* have to say about human beings' relationship with the natural world?

Robert Martin writes: "Through abundant, actually pervasive and detailed descriptions of nature, especially of the pine trees, Hemingway suggests that man is not merely an interloper or casual observer of nature, but rather, he is an integral part of the wild, an active participant. He must, therefore, if he is to grow and mature, be not only a participant in nature, but also a pupil of it as well" (56). Locate and analyze several of these "detailed descriptions of nature." What do the pine trees, in particular, symbolize?

Does Robert Jordan seem to be a participant in and a student of the natural world? What does he learn from it? Locate some of the passages in which tanks, planes, or machine guns are described in detail. How does wartime technology fit into the novel's message about humans' relationship to nature?

Character

Analysis of a novel's characters can often provide insights that can help you interpret the piece's themes and meanings. In *For Whom the Bell Tolls,* we are presented with a number of interesting characters who warrant thorough analysis. When you perform such an analysis, you want to reread the text, highlighting any passages that seem to offer insight into your chosen character. Pay attention to any inner dialogue as well as dialogue with other characters. What are the character's motives, priorities, and values? Notice whether the character you've selected has changed in any way through the course of the novel and determine both the cause of this change and whether the novel portrays it in a positive or negative light. You might focus on Pablo, for example, and use your analysis to determine how the novel ultimately perceives him. Is he a hero or a villain? You might examine a certain category of character, women, for example, studying Pilar and Maria in order to comment on Hemingway's depiction of female characters. Additionally, you can often make a convincing argument about the novel's take on a particular idea through an analysis of one or more characters. You might investigate what the novel has to say about war, suicide, or love through an analysis of the main character, Robert Jordan, for instance.

Sample Topics:

1. **Robert Jordan:** Analyze the character of Robert Jordan. Does he develop throughout the course of the novel? If so, is this development positive or negative?

The novel covers only the span of a few days, but we are provided with extremely detailed information about Robert Jordan's thoughts and emotions during this time period. Robert Jordan feels that he has been ignorant but has begun to learn a lot since he has been assigned to blow the bridge. He says, "You've had as good a life as any one because of these last days. You do not want to complain when you have been so lucky. I wish there was some way to pass on what I've learned, though. Christ, I was learning fast there at the end" (467). Is it simply the knowledge that he will soon die that makes Robert Jordan think he has gained wisdom, or is he truly a wiser person? What is it that he feels he has learned? Do you think he has, in fact, been lucky? Why or why not?

You might also analyze the choices Jordan makes to blow the bridge despite the danger to himself and others and to stay behind once he has been injured by the fall of his horse. What do these decisions tell us about Jordan's priorities? What do they reveal about his character?

2. **Pablo:** Analyze and evaluate the character of Pablo.

Pablo is definitely one of the more intriguing characters in *For Whom the Bell Tolls*. Begin by recording everything you know about him. How do other characters react to him? Is there more to him than meets the eye? Why does he behave the way he does? By the novel's end, what does Robert Jordan think of Pablo? Does the novel imagine him as a hero, a villain, or something in between? Based on what?

3. **Pilar and Maria:** Hemingway has been accused by many critics of endorsing a gender hierarchy by portraying female characters as weak and submissive. Does *For Whom the Bell Tolls* fit this pattern? Analyze the two female characters in the work, Maria and Pilar, and use them to evaluate Hemingway's portrayal of women in this novel.

   Locate and analyze the passages that best describe these two characters. Do they have strong, independent personalities, or are they submissive to the men they are connected to? What do they have in common? What accounts for any significant differences in their characters? Using all of this analysis, draw some conclusions about Hemingway's portrayal of women in *For Whom the Bell Tolls.*

4. **Gypsies/Roma:** Analyze and evaluate their portrayal in the novel.

   Locate the passages in the novel that concern Gypsies, more correctly called the Roma or Romany. How is this group of people represented? What connections are made between Gypsies and superstitions? Gypsies and the supernatural? According to the novel, what is the relationship of the Gypsies to Spain? To the war? Analyze the character Rafael. What kind of a person is he? What are his positive and negative attributes? Are these directly linked to his status as a Gypsy? Do some background research on the Roma, such as David M. Crowe's *A History of the Gypsies of Eastern Europe and Russia*, to help you evaluate Hemingway's portrayal of them.

5. **Anselmo:** Analyze the character of Anselmo and the role he plays in the novel as a whole.

Record everything you know about Anselmo. What makes him different from the other soldiers? How would you describe his ideology? At one point, Anselmo expresses a wish "[t]hat we should win this war and shoot nobody. . . . That we should govern justly and that all should participate in the benefits according as they have striven for them. And that those who have fought against us should be educated to see their error" (285). Locate other passages that reveal Anselmo's desires and motivations, and analyze them. Do any of the other characters share his philosophy? Why or why not? Why do you think Hemingway includes a character like this in the novel? Is Anselmo supposed to be a kind of foil for Robert Jordan? How does this work?

History and Context

Although its characters and their actions are fictitious, *For Whom the Bell Tolls* takes place during a very particular moment in a particular place in the midst of an actual historical conflict. In order to understand what motivates the characters and what drives the action, then, it is vitally important to understand the novel's historical and social context. Some background knowledge on the Spanish civil war and the communist and fascist ideologies involved will help you come to a greater understanding of the plot and characters as well as to appreciate more fully the novel's subtler nuances.

Sample Topics:

1. **Hemingway's sympathies in the Spanish civil war:** What kind of commentary is the novel making about the Spanish civil war?

Hemingway began writing *For Whom the Bell Tolls* once the Spanish civil war was over, shortly after the fascist (Nationalist, Falangist) army took control of Spain in 1939. During the conflict, Hemingway himself had supported the Loyalists. Do some background reading on the Spanish civil war and Hemingway's role in it. You might begin with Patrick Turnbull's *The Spanish Civil War, 1936–39* and a biography of Hemingway, such as those by Jeffrey Meyers or Carlos Baker. Armed with this new knowledge, reevaluate the novel. Are Hemingway's sympathies evident? In what way? Does he foreshadow or suggest reasons for the ultimate defeat of the Loyalists?

2. **Guerrilla fighters:** What kind of commentary is the novel making about guerrilla soldiers?

Do some background reading on the Spanish civil war, specifically on guerrilla fighters. Then, reread the novel with this information in mind and use it to help you come to a greater understanding of Pablo, Sordo, and their bands. What determined who would be a member of the army and who fought in their own bands of guerrilla soldiers? How were these groups of people different from each other? Did they share the same goals? Techniques? Reasons for fighting? What kind of impression does the novel give of guerrilla fighters. Are they more or less honorable and useful than more traditional soliders?

3. **Foreign intervention in the Spanish civil war:** What does the novel have to say about the role of foreigners in the Spanish civil war?

To what degree were other nations and citizens of other countries involved in the conflict? For some help with this, turn to a source such as Andrew Forrest's *The Spanish Civil War*. Additionally, you might do some background reading on Hemingway's involvement in the Spanish civil war, beginning with a biography such as Jeffrey Meyer's *Hemingway: A Biography* or Carlos Baker's *Ernest Hemingway: A Life Story*. What were his motives? His contributions? Now, turn back to the novel, and reconsider Robert Jordan in the light of this historical context. According to the novel, what are Robert Jordan's motives? How would he be received if he were to return to America after the war? Using all of this information and analysis, formulate a claim about Hemingway's perception of the role of foreigners in the Spanish civil war.

Philosophy and Ideas

For Whom the Bell Tolls is a novel in which philosophy and ideas play a central role. Indeed, it deals with a wide spectrum of them, including fate and destiny, wartime ethics, and the relationship of government to its subjects. To write an essay on one of these topics, it is a good idea to reread the novel with this issue in mind and to identify characters who are associated with your topic and passages that seem to give insight into the novel's take on your selected issue. You will then want to analyze the characters and the passages you have identified in order to arrive at a claim to make in your essay. To discuss ethics in war, for example, you might look closely at Pablo and Anselmo and study their different ideas about the necessity and morality of killing in war. Then, evaluate the novel's take on these two characters. What are their fates? With which character are we more sympathetic? After performing your analysis and considering these questions, you might arrive at a claim such as the following: In *For Whom the Bell Tolls*, Hemingway demonstrates through the fates of Anselmo and Pablo the necessity of a wartime ethics that is decidedly different from those we embrace in everyday life. Anselmo, who clings to idealism and a strict moral code that condemns violence, spends his time agonizing over killing enemy soldiers and is ultimately killed, while Pablo, who is flexible and practical and believes that whatever behavior is necessary to ensure his own survival is acceptable, lives to lead his little band off to make another camp at the end of the novel. Alternatively, your analysis might lead you to a conclusion more like this: Through the characters Anselmo and Pablo, Hemingway demonstrates that an ethical code is just as necessary in wartime as it is in everyday life. Pablo, who seems either to enjoy or to take as a matter of course the many violent acts he commits, is painted as a villain, whereas Anselmo, who also kills in the context of war yet continuously agonizes over the morality of his actions, is depicted as one of the novel's heroes.

Sample Topics:

1. **Destiny/fate:** Does the novel suggest that our destinies have been predetermined, that we have free will, or some combination of these two ideas?

   Look at the scene in which Pilar reads Robert Jordan's palm as well as the subsequent references to this reading. What does

Pilar see in Jordan's future? Does her vision come true? Jordan himself says, "Seeing bad signs, one, with fear, imagines an end for himself and one thinks that imagining comes by divination . . . I believe there is nothing more to it than that" (250). Is this a true indication of his beliefs? According to the novel, which character's perception of fortune-telling is closer to the truth?

Think also about Andrés's mission to deliver Robert Jordan's letter to General Golz telling him to call off the attack, as the fascists are prepared for it. Consider the way Hemingway presents these events—Andrés's journey as well as Robert Jordan's preparations to blow the bridge in case the letter does not get through in time or Golz ignores his plea. Does Hemingway's presentation suggest that the end result is preordained, or does he give us the sense that in each moment individuals are making choices that will affect the outcome?

2. **Ethics in war:** What kind of commentary does the novel make about ethics in wartime?

How do the characters decide what is ethical or acceptable in an environment so detached from normal civilized society? Choose several characters, and study the way in which they determine wrong from right. How do Robert Jordan, Pablo, and Anselmo approach killing, for instance? Does the novel seem to suggest that one of these is the proper, ethical approach? Does it condemn any of these characters' ethics? Or does it suggest that each individual must develop his or her own code according to his or her conscience?

3. **Sexual trauma:** What kind of commentary does the novel make about sexual trauma and recovery?

Review what happens to Maria when the fascists capture her town. How does she handle it? Look closely at the relationship between Maria and Robert Jordan. Maria explains to him that Pilar had told her that "nothing is done to oneself that one does not accept and that if I loved someone it would take it all away" (73). She is in a hurry to consummate the relationship between them, saying, "And now let us do quickly what it is we do so that the other is all gone" (73). Does Maria's relationship with Robert Jordan in fact "take it all away"? How do you know? What does this indicate about the way that Hemingway understood sexual trauma? Research sexual trauma to help evaluate how realistically Hemingway has depicted the psychology and the behavior of a survivor and those close to her. One place to begin such research is the online library of the National Sexual Violence Resource Center (http://www.nsvrc.org).

4. **Following orders versus making independent decisions:** According to the novel, in the context of war, should an individual always follow orders or should he, on occasion, make independent decisions, even if they are contrary to previously given orders?

Look at Robert Jordan's own thinking on this topic as he considers the fact that many will likely die if he follows his orders to blow the bridge:

> The orders do not come from you. They come from Golz. And who is Golz? A good general. The best you've ever served under. But should a man carry out impossible orders knowing what they lead to? Even though they come from Golz, who is the party as well as the army? Yes. He should carry them out because it is only in the performing of them that they can prove to be impossible. How do you know they are impossible until you have tried them? (162)

According to this passage, what are Robert Jordan's reasons for following orders even if they seem impossible? Do these reasons seem adequate? Are they adequate for Robert Jordan? Locate other instances in the novel in which there is tension between an individual's will and his orders, and analyze these as well.

Form and Genre

It can often be fruitful to examine a piece of literature as a constructed work of art, paying close attention to features of the work such as narration, point of view, and organizational scheme. You should ask yourself why the author made the choices he did when constructing the work, and how the work would be different if he had made other choices. When studying *For Whom the Bell Tolls,* you might explore the structure of the novel and eventually use your essay to explain why the novel contains within it many other stories. Or you might focus on Hemingway's decision to use an epigraph and use your essay to examine how the stanza from John Donne's poem affects the meaning of the novel as a whole.

Sample Topics:

1. **Stories within the novel:** According to Michael Reynolds, "Without drawing undue attention to his artistry, Hemingway has written a collection of short stories embedded in a framing novel" (par. 30). Assuming that Reynolds's evaluation is true, what purpose does such a structure serve?

   Look again at the stories that Robert Jordan, Maria, Pilar, and Rafael tell. Imagine what the novel would be like without these stories. Are they necessary to the novel as a whole? In what way? Do they simply provide context and background, or are they serving some other purpose? You might also think about what the novel has to say about storytelling. To whom do these characters tell their stories? Why do they tell them when and where they do? Does the telling of their stories benefit the teller or the listener in some way, or does it burden them further?

2. **"For whom the bell tolls":** What is the significance of the title and the epigraph?

   The epigraph of the novel, from which the title of the novel comes, is a quotation from John Donne's "Meditation XVII" of *Devotions Upon Emergent Occasions*:

   > No man is an *Iland,* intire of it selfe; every man is a peece of
   > the *Continent,* a part of the *maine*; if a *Clod* bee washed away
   > by the *Sea, Europe* is the lesse, as well as if a *Promontorie* were,

as well as if a *Mannor* of they *friends* or of *thine owne* were;
any mans *death* diminishes *me,* because I am involved in *Man-
kinde;* And therefore never send to know for whom the *bell*
tolls; It tolls for *thee.*

First, analyze the meaning of this passage. Then, think about how
it might apply to the themes of the novel. What does the novel
have to say about the relationship between an individual and the
rest of humanity? You might think about why Robert Jordan is
involved in the Spanish civil war to help you answer this question.
Why do you think Hemingway picked "for whom the bell tolls" to
be the novel's title? Why this particular piece of the passage?

Language, Symbols, and Imagery

An analysis of the language, symbols, and imagery in a piece of literature
can result in new insights, which can help you come to a new interpretation of the text. Keep your eye out for lengthy descriptions of particular
scenes or items, especially ones that appear repeatedly. Also, as you are
reading, be sure to mark passages that seem to have a special resonance,
perhaps those that do not serve to further the plot so much as to reflect
on an important issue, event, or character. Among the many symbols
and images you might elect to focus on in *For Whom the Bell Tolls* are
food and bullfighting. In your essay, you will want to provide a new interpretation of the novel based on your analysis of these symbols. You might
argue, for example, that through the use of food and drink imagery in the
novel, Hemingway communicates that although he has been there only
a short time, Robert Jordan is a more integral part of the peasant community than is Pablo, who had once been their leader.

Sample Topics:

1. **Dialogue:** What does the language of the dialogue tell us about
   the novel's themes and meanings?

   Examine the dialogue in the novel. Notice the way that
   Hemingway often presents the English as a transliteration of
   the Spanish as well as his use of archaic English as in the case
   of the pronouns *thee* and *thou.* Why do you think he chooses
   to do this? What effect does it have on our perception of

the characters and their exchanges? Look at the words and phrases that Hemingway presents in Spanish. Does he offer translations? Why do you think he made the linguistic choices that he did in regard to the characters' dialogue? How do they affect you as a reader and your relationship to the characters?

To help you figure out what the novel has to say about language, identify and analyze any passages in the novel that directly comment on language and dialect. Specifically, you might look at the passage in which Robert Jordan reflects that his knowledge of the Spanish language caused Spaniards to trust him:

> He was lucky that he had lived parts of ten years in Spain before the war. They trusted you on the language, principally. They trusted you on understanding the language completely and speaking it idiomatically and having a knowing of the different places. . . . He never felt like a foreigner in Spanish and they did not really treat him like a foreigner most of the time; only when they turned on you. (135)

2. **Bullfighting:** What does the bullfight signify in the novel?

Analyze the discussion of bullfighters and bullfighting in the novel. You might do some background reading, for example, Carrie B. Douglas's *Bulls, Bullfighting, and Spanish Identities* or Hemingway's own *Death in the Afternoon,* as you prepare to write your essay. What function did the bullfight traditionally serve in Spanish culture? What does the ritual represent? Why do you think Hemingway includes the long section about Pilar's lover, who dies from a bull injury? What about Andrés's memories of bullbaiting? Are there any other scenes of ritualized violence in the novel? Can these scenes be usefully compared to the bullfight?

3. **Conspicuous absence of obscenities and expletives:** What is the effect of Hemingway's decision not to use objectionable language in this wartime novel?

In an article titled "Money and Marriage: Hemingway's Self-Censorship in *For Whom the Bell Tolls,*" Robert Trogdon notes that while Hemingway typically fought for the right to include objectionable language, particularly sexual references, in his works, he did not include them even in the manuscript of *For Whom the Bell Tolls.* Trogdon suggests that Hemingway employed this strategy so that the book might be serialized and chosen as a Book of the Month selection because he was in need of supplemental income. The novel did indeed turn out to be Hemingway's biggest commercial success. Trogdon argues that Hemingway's self-censorship in no way diminishes the power of the novel. Do you agree? Study the dialogue of *For Whom the Bell Tolls.* How does Hemingway avoid using objectionable language or expletives? What is the effect, if any, of this choice on the novel's themes and power?

4. **Food:** What do the scenes of eating and drinking signify in the novel?

Linda Underhill and Jeanne Nakjavani assert that in Hemingway's work, "food becomes a code which signifies the prevailing mood of the adventure" (qtd. in de Koster 115). Look carefully at the scenes of eating and drinking in *For Whom the Bell Tolls.* What can these scenes tell us about the characters, their relationships, and their psychological states? What kind of food is eaten? How is it served? Look particularly at Robert Jordan's behavior in these scenes. Do his eating and drinking behaviors signal that he is part of the group or outside it?

Compare and Contrast Essays

Comparing and contrasting similar elements within and across novels often serves to sharpen our focus, enabling us to notice features that we might otherwise have neglected to observe. You might, for instance, compare and contrast Pablo and Anselmo in order to determine what the novel has to say about courage, or Robert Jordan and his grandfather to illustrate what it takes to live a meaningful life. Comparisons and contrasts also allow us to make statements about the evolution of a particular theme across the span of an author's career. In this vein, you might compare and contrast the female characters of several of Hemingway's books in order to argue that his portrayal of women developed in a particular way. There are really endless options when it comes to compare and contrast essays. The key is not to compare and contrast simply for the sake of comparing and contrasting. Be sure to use your observations and analysis to make an argument that offers a unique and interesting interpretation of the text.

Sample Topics:

1. **Robert Jordan and his grandfather:** Compare and contrast Robert Jordan and his grandfather.

   What do you know about Robert Jordan's grandfather? How was he similar to Robert Jordan? Why does Robert Jordan feel such a powerful connection with his grandfather as opposed to his father? What significant differences are there between Robert Jordan and his grandfather? From your analysis of the novel's hero, Robert Jordan, and his idol, his grandfather, what generalizations can you make about the novel's depiction of success? What makes a good man? What constitutes a good life?

2. **Anselmo and Pablo:** Compare and contrast these two characters, particularly in regard to courage.

   You will first need to define what it means to have courage in the context of war. Then, pick out and analyze those passages that reveal the inner workings of Pablo and Anselmo. What do Anselmo and Pablo have in common? In what ways are they different? How does each character view the war? How about violence? How does each imagine his own role in the war? Drawing on this information, which of these two would you argue is the more courageous? Would you identify either, or perhaps both of them, as a coward?

3. **Maria and Catherine of *A Farewell to Arms* and/or Brett of *The Sun Also Rises*:** Comparing Maria to leading female characters of Hemingway's earlier novels, what can you say about the evolution of Hemingway's portrayal of women?

Compare and contrast Maria in *For Whom the Bell Tolls* (1940) with the main female characters in some of Hemingway's most famous novels, such as Catherine in *A Farewell to Arms* (1929) and Brett in *The Sun Also Rises* (1928). What do Maria, Catherine, and Brett have in common? How are they different? You might have a look at how Catherine and Brett, heroines of Hemingway's earlier fiction, are different from Maria, who appears in a much later novel, in order to make a claim regarding the evolution, or static nature, of Hemingway's perception and portrayal of women.

Bibliography and Online Resources for *For Whom the Bell Tolls*

Baker, Carlos. *Hemingway: The Writer as Artist.* 4th ed. Princeton, NJ: Princeton UP, 1972.

Crowe, David M. *A History of the Gypsies of Eastern Europe and Russia.* New York: Palgrave Macmillan, 1996.

de Koster, Katie, ed. *Ernest Hemingway.* Greenhaven Press Literary Companion to American Authors Series. San Diego, CA: Greenhaven, 1997.

Forrest, Andrew. *The Spanish Civil War.* New York: Routledge, 2000.

"*For Whom the Bell Tolls.*" *Novels for Students.* Vol. 14. Smith, Jennifer, ed. Famington Hills, MI: Gale, 2002. 22–39.

Hemingway, Ernest. *For Whom the Bell Tolls.* New York: Scribner, 2003.

Martin, Robert A. "Robert Jordan and the Spanish Country: Learning to Live in It 'Truly and Well.'" *Hemingway Review* 17.1 (1997): 49–57.

Meyers, Jeffrey. "*For Whom the Bell Tolls* as Contemporary History." *The Spanish Civil War in Literature.* Ed. Janet Perez and Wendell Aycock. Lubbock: Texas Tech UP, 1990. 85–107.

———. *Hemingway: A Biography.* Cambridge, MA: Da Capo, 1999.

Preston, Paul. *The Spanish Civil War: An Illustrated Chronicle, 1936–39.* New York: Grove, 1986.

Reynolds, Michael. "Ringing the Changes: Hemingway's Bell Tolls Fifty." *Virginia Quarterly Review* 67.1 (1991): 1–18. EBSCOhost. Retrieved 18 May 2007. <http://www.vqronline.org/articles/1991/winter/reynolds-ringing-changes/>

Trogdon, Robert W. "Money and Marriage: Hemingway's Self-Censorship in *For Whom the Bell Tolls.*" *Hemingway Review* 22.2 (2003): 6–19.

Turnbull, Patrick. *The Spanish Civil War, 1936–39.* New York: Osprey, 1977.

A FAREWELL
TO ARMS

READING TO WRITE

OFTEN REGARDED among the premier war novels of all times, *A Fare-well to Arms* draws heavily on Hemingway's personal experiences as an ambulance driver during World War I. Since its publication in 1929, first as a serial in *Scribner's* magazine then as a novel, a plethora of critics have discussed its meaning and debated what it has to say in regard to love, war, and self-discovery. So much has been written about this novel that you may initially find yourself overwhelmed at the prospect of finding your own voice in the debates. Rather than trying to read and assimilate all of the existing criticism, however, begin much more simply. As you think about adding your own voice to this conversation, start by selecting a particularly striking or intriguing passage or two to close read in order to spur your thinking. Let us take as an example the following conversation between Frederic Henry and the Priest. The Priest says to Frederic:

> "You understand but you do not love God."
> "No."
> "You do not love Him at all?" he asked.
> "I am afraid of Him in the night sometimes."
> "You should love Him."
> "I don't love much."
> "Yes," he said. "You do. What you tell me about in the nights. That is not love. That is only passion and lust. When you love you wish to do things for. You wish to sacrifice for. You wish to serve."
> "I don't love." (70)

The first thing you will likely notice about this conversation is the definition of love being offered by the Priest. He seeks to differentiate between lust and love, insisting that you wish to serve and sacrifice for the things you love. He offers this definition to demonstrate to Frederic that despite his protests, he does indeed love. What is the Priest referring to? What does he think Frederic loves? What, in the Priest's mind, does Frederic wish to serve and sacrifice in the name of? When Frederic persists, replying "I don't love," is he indicating that he is not as committed to the Italian army and its fight as he once was or should be?

Why do you think Frederic, who can state unequivocally that he does not love God, says also that he is "afraid of Him in the night sometimes"? What does this indicate about Frederic and his spiritual state? Can you find other passages in the novel that further elaborate on Frederic's belief in or fear of God? Frederic's conversation with the Priest moves from a discussion of loving God to sexual love and then possibly to romantic love or devotion to a cause or group. Are these types of love interchangeable? Can one feel more than one type of love at a time? Over the course of the novel, it seems that Frederic ultimately has to choose between devotion to the army and to Catherine. Also, he refers to love as his "religion" later in the novel. Is Hemingway saying that a person can have only one great love and that Frederic chose romantic love for Catherine over his other options?

Considering the questions you have generated thus far, you might decide to use your essay to investigate the different types of love present in the text and the interplay among them. Which is most powerful? Most fulfilling? Most potentially destructive? Alternatively, you might decide to evaluate Catherine and Frederic's connection in light of this discussion of love; many critics celebrate the two characters' devotion to each other. What do you think of their relationship? Is their love based on "passion and lust," or is it a selfless love as that described by the Priest? Do Catherine and Frederic feel the same kind of love for each other? Are they equally willing to serve and sacrifice for each other? Is the definition of love given by the Priest even applicable to a romantic relationship?

This single passage has provided us with much to think about and several possible essay ideas. If you were to select one of the topics suggested above, you would use your notes to help you identify other relevant passages to analyze, and these would lead you to still other relevant passages. After you have identified and analyzed all the passages pertinent to your topic, you would then synthesize your findings and use them to help you develop a thesis—the argument or interpretation of the text that your essay will present.

TOPICS AND STRATEGIES

In the pages that follow, you will find a wide variety of approaches that you might take as you begin to think about writing your essay on *A Farewell to Arms.* You may decide to select one of the suggested topics and to construct an essay in response to it, or you may find that the list of suggested topics inspires you to create a topic of your own. Other options are to combine two of the suggested topics or to modify one of them. When you do decide on a topic, remember to spend some time generating ideas and close reading relevant passages. Only after a great deal of thinking time will you be ready to construct your thesis sentence, which states the argument that you will make in your essay. Once you have decided on your thesis sentence, or claim, you can begin writing the body of your essay, in which you will present the evidence that supports your claim. Keep in mind that not all of the notes and preliminary analysis you do will wind up in your essay. Much of it will be discarded as you refine your thinking and develop your argument.

Themes

When you begin to think about the themes of a piece of literature, you want to ask yourself what major issues or subjects the work concerns itself with. Certainly, you will find that *A Farewell to Arms* contains many themes, as it is a rich and complicated artistic work. Those listed in the sample questions below are just the tip of the iceberg; there are many others that you might identify and write about.

When selecting a theme to focus on in your essay, choose one about which you think the novel has something unique or important to say. It is not necessary to know exactly what the novel is saying about, for example, marriage, when you select it as your topic. It is enough to have a general sense that the novel has something interesting to say about marriage. You will figure out exactly what when you identify relevant passages, analyze them, and synthesize your findings.

Sample Topics:

1. **Individual happiness versus duty:** What kind of commentary does the novel ultimately make about Frederic's decision to desert the army and move to Switzerland with Catherine? Is it acceptable or even preferable for him to focus on and pursue his individual happiness rather than participate in the cause he had previously committed to?

   As you think about this question, consider passages such as this one, in which Frederic reasons with himself in regard to his desertion:

   > You had lost your cars and your men as a floorwalker loses the stock of his department in a fire. There was, however, no insurance. You were out of it now. You had no more obligation. If they shot floorwalkers after a fire in the department store because they spoke with an accent and always had, then certainly the floorwalkers would not be expected to return when the store opened again for business. They might seek other employment. . . . (232)

   According to the novel, are Frederic's reasons for deserting valid? Are they sufficient? Under the terms of the novel, does one even need reasons or excuses for deciding to focus on his or her own desires instead of on a larger social cause, even one to which he or she has previously committed? Look carefully at Frederic and Catherine's discussions and thoughts about leaving the war behind as well as the responses of other characters to the couple's situation. From your analysis, what does the novel present as more important—pursuing individual happiness or fulfilling obligations that entail personal sacrifice?

2. **Love:** Analyze Catherine and Frederic's relationship and the role it plays in the novel. What does the novel have to say about love?

   You might begin by thinking about how love is defined in the novel. According to the Priest, "What you tell me about in the nights. That is not love. That is only passion and lust. When you love you wish to do things for. You wish to sacrifice for. You wish to serve" (72). Is this the prevailing notion of love in the novel? If not, what is? Once you have established this, you will want to examine Catherine and Frederic's relationship. Is it truly based on love as defined by the novel?

To decide, you will want to trace Catherine and Frederic's relationship as it develops through the course of the novel. What brings them together? What do they find attractive in each other? Early in the novel, Frederic Henry reflects: "I knew I did not love Catherine Barkley nor had any idea of loving her. This was a game, like bridge, in which you said things instead of playing cards for money or playing for some stakes" (30–31). When does their relationship stop being a kind of "game"? Or does it ever? Look at their actions and thoughts when they are apart, and compare them to their actions and thoughts when they are together. How does their togetherness change them? At one point, Catherine says, "I don't take any interest in anything else any more. I'm so very happy married to you" (154). Is this tendency to focus on only each other portrayed in the novel as healthy or symptomatic of other problems? Overall, would you say that their relationship is a positive or negative force in each of their lives?

3. **Marriage:** What does the novel have to say about the institution of marriage and conforming to social norms?

Reread the novel, paying careful attention to all discussions of marriage and of observing the rules of social propriety. Analyze Catherine and Frederic's feelings about marriage. At one point, when Frederic suggests that the two ought to marry, Catherine says, "Don't talk as though you had to make an honest woman of me, darling. I'm a very honest woman. You can't be ashamed of something if you're only happy and proud of it" (116). In what sense is the word *honest* being used here? What does this conversation tell you about Catherine's attitude toward society's rules of conduct? If she is not bothered by her relationship with Frederic, why do you think she feels "like a whore" when they get a hotel room the night before Frederic leaves for the front (152)?

Additionally, you will want to consider the ways in which Frederic and Catherine's thoughts evolve with the impending birth of their baby. At one point, Catherine says to Frederic, "I suppose if we really have this child we ought to get married," to which Frederic replies, "Let's get married now." Why does the coming of a baby change the way they feel about getting married? Why do you think, even with this change, Catherine refuses? She says to Frederic, "It's too embarrassing now. I show too plainly. I won't go before anyone and be married in this state" (293). When Frederic answers, "I wish we had gotten married," Catherine reassures him that they will get married once she is thin again and that she is really his wife already. "You're a lovely wife," he agrees. "Then don't be too technical, darling," she answers (294). Catherine never seems to be embarrassed about anything; in fact, this tendency is something she is proud of. Why, then, do you think she would be too embarrassed to be married while obviously pregnant? What does she mean when she tells Frederic not to be "too technical"? Does she really think of marriage as a technicality? Does Frederic?

4. **Parenthood:** How do Catherine and Frederic perceive parenthood, and what does this perception say about them as a couple?

How do Catherine and Frederic feel about their impending parenthood? Locate passages in which they discuss the pregnancy and the coming child, and analyze their feelings about it. Pay particular attention to the scenes in which Catherine is in labor and the baby is born. At one point, for example, Catherine says to Frederic, "I want to be a good wife and have this child without any foolishness. Please go and get some breakfast, darling, and then come back" (315). What does this kind of rhetoric tell us about Catherine's idea of being a wife and mother? How does Frederic feel about the child? Analyze in particular his reaction to the child's death. Once you have established the couple's feelings about childbirth and parenthood, think about what these feelings say about them as individuals and as a couple. Why, for example, do the two seem to feel as though the baby is an unwelcome intrusion into their lives? Is this a legitimate response to an unplanned pregnancy, or does it signify that there is something unhealthy about their relationship? If possible, locate other instances of parenthood in the novel against which to contrast Frederic and Catherine's ideas.

Character

Often, one of the most interesting ways to approach an analysis of a literary text is to select one or more of its characters to evaluate. In the case of *A Farewell to Arms,* an analysis of either of the main characters, Catherine Barkley or Frederic Henry, would certainly make for an interesting essay. When you perform such an analysis, you want to record everything you know about your character as well as the source of that knowledge so that you can evaluate its reliability. Additionally, you will want to consider whether the text provides access to your character's thoughts, or do you only get his or her spoken words? How do your character's thoughts and words compare? Does he always say what he thinks? How do other characters respond to your character? What do they think of him or her? Also, you will want to decide whether your character changes in a meaningful way during the course of the story and how the narrative treats that development. Is it portrayed as positive or negative? Finally, you will want to use your analysis to draw conclusions about the larger themes and meanings of the text. From the thinking you have done about your character, how do you understand the novel differently? For example, if you decide to write an essay about Frederic Henry, and your analysis has led you to conclude that he regrets having abandoned the war for a life with Catherine, you might wind up with a thesis sentence that says something like: While many readers consider *A Farewell to Arms* a love story at its core, an analysis of Frederic Henry's character reveals that the book is really about the danger of forgoing one's commitments to a cause when the going gets difficult.

Sample Topics:

1. **Catherine Barkley:** Analyze and evaluate the character of Catherine Barkley.

   Critics are divided in their estimation of Catherine Barkley. Many have condemned her as a poorly realized character, another of Hemingway's depthless, submissive women. To make their case, they point to comments such as, "I want what you want. There isn't any me any more. Just what you want" (106), and when she tells Frederic about the baby, "I'll try and not make trouble for you. I know I've made trouble now. But haven't I been a good girl until now? You never knew it, did you?" (138). Ernest Lockridge, however, takes a different stance on Catherine. He writes:

   > Hemingway does not have Catherine abnegate herself to Frederic Henry; rather, she abnegates herself, when she does so, to an idea in her head. Motivated by the agonizing grief and loss that she still feels after a year of mourning, Catherine Barkley is acting out through the narrator a one-sided, therapeutic game of "pretend." ... Through willed, deliberate projection upon the narrator, Frederic Henry, Catherine has temporarily resurrected her fiancé of eight years, blown "all to bits" on the Somme. (173–74)

   Perform your own analysis of Catherine's character. Do you agree with Lockridge that Catherine is acting out a "therapeutic game of 'pretend'" with Frederic? What evidence can you find to support the notion that Catherine is "resurrecting" her dead fiancé through her relationship with Frederic? If you think she is in fact doing this, do you agree with Lockridge that this pretending is therapeutic for Catherine? Does such a reading of the novel make you view Catherine in a different way? Write an essay in which you analyze Catherine's character; you might support, modify, or argue against Lockridge's claims.

2. **Frederic Henry:** Analyze and evaluate the character of Frederic Henry.

Reread the novel, focusing on the development of Frederic's character. How does he change over the course of the novel? Identify passages that seem to represent him at various stages of this evolution. You will definitely want to think about the ways in which Frederic's opinions about the war and his role in it change. What causes these changes? Look specifically at the scenes in which he discusses the war with others, particularly the Priest, for clues. After he decides to move to Switzerland with Catherine, Frederic thinks to himself: "I had the paper but I did not read it because I did not want to read about the war. I was going to forget the war. I had made a separate peace" (243). This seems to indicate that Frederic is content with his choices. A little later, however, we find him thinking: "Then I realized it was over for me. But I did not have the feeling that it was really over. I had the feeling of a boy who thinks of what is happening at a certain hour at the schoolhouse from which he has played truant" (245). What do passages such as this one tell us about Frederic's development? Is he satisfied with the decisions he has made?

3. **Count Greffi:** Analyze and evaluate the character of Count Greffi.

Review the passages in which Count Greffi plays a role (chapter 35). Why do you think Hemingway includes this character in the novel? Record everything you know about him and examine closely his interactions with Frederic. How are he and Frederic similar and different? Does Frederic have anything to learn from the older man?

4. **Rinaldi:** Analyze and evaluate the character of Rinaldi.

Record what you know about Rinaldi. Describe his relationship with Frederic. Compare and contrast the development of Frederic with the development of Rinaldi. Why do you think Hemingway included this character in the novel? Does he serve as a foil to Frederic? What can we learn about Frederic and his decisions by comparing them with Rinaldi's?

Philosophy and Ideas

A Farewell to Arms grapples with many important social and philosophical ideas. To write an essay, you must first narrow in on one idea or philosophy to examine. You might, for example, wish to consider what the novel has to say about self-knowledge, power, perspective in crisis, or war. To do so, it is a good idea to begin with some background reading, particularly if you have chosen an idea or philosophy with which you are not already very familiar. Once you have done a bit of preliminary research, return to the text, identifying and analyzing passages that concern the topic you have chosen. Think about whether there is a particular character associated with the idea or philosophy you are working with. If so, an analysis of that character will also be invaluable to the idea-generating phase of your essay.

Sample Topics:

1. **Self-knowledge:** What does *A Farewell to Arms* have to say about self-knowledge?

   According to John Beversluis, *A Farewell to Arms* is not primarily about the romantic relationship between Catherine and Frederic; it is instead most fundamentally concerned with Frederic Henry's quest for self-knowledge. Beversluis writes: "Dramatically penetrating and psychologically unsettling, Hemingway's treatment of the problem reveals that, for some people at least, self-knowledge comes hard and can be achieved only on the condition that they are prepared to reassess their lives at a bedrock level. Frederic Henry is such a person" (18). Beversluis argues that what Frederic finally learns is that he always fails to do what he really wants to do. The ultimate manifestation of this is when Frederic gives up the war for a relationship with Catherine when "it was at odds with almost everything else that he subsequently thought and felt" (24).

   As you begin to think about this question, you may wish to read the entirety of Beversluis's article, entitled "Dispelling the Romantic Myth: A Study of *A Farewell to Arms*." Then, return to the novel with his provocative arguments in mind. What evidence can you find that Frederic does not truly want to be with Catherine or that he regrets leaving the war? Write an essay in which you support Beversluis's argument with evidence of your own or modify it in some way. You might, for example, agree with Beversluis that the book is really about Frederic coming to self-knowledge, but you might have a different idea about what that knowledge turns out to be. Finally, you might write an essay arguing that the novel demonstrates how self-knowledge is inextricably linked to relationships with others.

2. **Power:** What does the novel have to say about power, particularly in times of war?

The Priest associates officers with those "who would make war" and notes that there "are other people who would not make war" (71). Frederic Henry responds, "But the first ones make them do it" (71). Reread the novel focusing your attention on this kind of power dynamic. Who wants to make war? Who does not? What source of power enables one group to force another group into risking their very lives? What happens to those who refuse to take part in the fighting?

In another conversation with Frederic, the Priest refers again to the soldiers: "They were beaten to start with. They were beaten when they took them from their farms and put them in the army. That is why the peasant has wisdom, because he is defeated from the start. Put him in power and see how wise he is" (179). Thinking along these lines, look again at the scene in which Frederic Henry is pulled out of the retreat and almost executed. What is he being accused of? Does this scene signal a shift in power dynamics away from officers? What might such a shift signify?

3. **Perspective in crisis:** What does the novel ultimately have to say about the way human beings' perceptions change in times of crisis.

Think about the following scene to get you started: When Catherine tells Frederic that she will somehow arrange to go with him on his convalescent leave, even though that might be difficult considering her nursing duties, she reveals a belief that "[l]ife isn't hard to manage when you've nothing to lose" and thinks about "how small obstacles seemed that once were so big" (137). What is Catherine talking about here? Why does she say she has "nothing to lose"? Are there other instances in the novel in which things that would seem very important or troubling in an ordinary environment seem trivial because of the wartime context? Analyze these scenes in order to determine what the novel is saying about this phenomenon. Is it presented as positive or negative? How so?

4. **War:** What does the novel have to say about the complex phenomenon of war? Would you argue that *A Farewell to Arms* is a realistic war novel or a protest novel?

Begin by examining what the characters think of the war. Trace the evolution of their opinion through the course of the novel. Look at Frederic and Catherine's estimation of the war's duration, for example. Frederic thinks to himself, "Perhaps wars weren't won any more. Maybe they went on forever. Maybe it was another Hundred Years' War" (118). Later, Catherine tells Frederic: "For three years I looked forward very childishly to the war ending at Christmas. But now I look forward till when our son will be a lieutenant commander" (141). What is the significance of these comments? What do they tell us about the perceptions of those participating in the war efforts? How has Frederic's opinion of the war, in particular, evolved through the course of the novel? Look also at characters such as Rinaldi, Count Greffi, the Priest, and other minor characters who express opinions about the war. Identify the scenes that seem to you to represent the essence of the wartime experience.

Once you have identified and analyzed the relevant passages, try to figure out what Hemingway is saying about the war. Is he presenting a realistic war novel that depicts the actual conditions and struggles of war, or does he go beyond that, creating a novel that objects to and protests against war, presenting, as critic William Dow has put it, "a world of suffering and absurdity in which natural events and humanity's irrational actions collide" (82)?

Form and Genre

One interesting way to approach a piece of literature is by examining its craftsmanship. Keep in mind how many choices the author had to make as he was constructing this piece of literature. How is the story organized and presented? What familiar literary patterns does it replicate or modify? To aid you in your thinking, try to imagine what the piece would be like if the author had made different decisions. When writing about *A Farewell to Arms,* you might write about its structure, analyzing the way that Hemingway organized the piece, or about its narration, evaluating the manner in which Hemingway decided to have the story told. Or you might compare the novel to tragedies in the more traditional Aristotelian sense and elaborate on the significance of the similarities and differences you locate.

Sample Topics:

1. **Tragedy:** Is *A Farewell to Arms* a tragedy in the traditional sense or a new kind of literary tragedy?

   Robert Merrill argues that while *A Farewell to Arms* does not fit the classical definition of a tragedy, it can be considered a new twist on the tragic form. He writes:

   > Since Aristotle it has been thought necessary to tragedy that the doom of the hero issue from his own acts. The hero may be flawed in knowledge or character . . . but his downfall must derive from this "flaw." Whereas the tragic catastrophe is supposed to result from the hero's mistaken actions, tragedy in *A Farewell to Arms* depends on Frederic Henry doing the one thing we most desire him to do and most respect him for doing—committing himself in love to Catherine Barkley. (571–72)

   What do you think of Merrill's argument? Do you agree that Frederic's doom springs from his most noble act? If not—if you believe, for example, that Frederic made a mistake by deserting the war effort—you might write an essay in which you argue that *A Farewell to Arms* is, in fact, a tragedy in the traditional Aristotelian sense because his downfall does stem from his failure to remain true to his commitments and obligations. Or you might write an essay in which you agree with Merrill's premise that *A Farewell to Arms* represents a new kind of literary tragedy and use your essay to define that new form and discuss its implications.

2. **Structure:** Analyze the structure of the novel and discuss the significance of that structure to your interpretation of the text.

Look carefully at the way the novel is divided into books and chapters. Chart out what happens in each section of the novel. Think about the organization of the work as a deliberate artistic decision. Why do you think Hemingway structured this novel as he did? How would it be different if it were divided into three books instead of five, or if each chapter was given a title instead of a chapter number? Write an essay in which you analyze the structure of the novel, using this analysis to help you elaborate on a fresh, interesting interpretation of the text.

3. **Narration:** What insight into *A Farewell to Arms* can be gained through a study of its narration?

In *A Farewell to Arms,* Frederic Henry narrates the story of his life, and according to Mary Prescott, he "obviously revises and recreates as he narrates" (51). Can you distinguish between the Frederic in the past—the character in the tale—and the Frederic who is telling the story? Locate some passages and scenes in which you can distinguish one from the other, and analyze these carefully. How does Frederic shape the story as he tells it? What do you think is his motivation for telling it? Why do you think Hemingway has Frederic tell his own story after the events have transpired? What effects does this strategy create? Does this decision indicate something meaningful about the novel's themes and purpose?

Language, Symbols, and Imagery

Words are the very fabric out of which a literary text is built. Talented and experienced writers like Hemingway use language in precise and sometimes surprising ways, redefining them and creating linguistic symbols that represent ideas or emotions. Also, they often use their skill with language to comment on the nature of language and communication as Hemingway certainly does in *A Farewell to Arms*. Not surprisingly, careful attention to the language of a piece can be incredibly rewarding in terms of new insights into the meaning of the text as a whole. Considering what a piece of literature like *A Farewell to Arms* has to say about language and communication can also reward you with an interesting and insightful essay.

Sample Topics:

1. **Rain:** How does Hemingway symbolically use rain in *A Farewell to Arms?*

   While Hemingway biographer Philip Young notes that Hemingway uses rain to signal disaster in this novel, literary critic John Killinger suggests a more complex meaning behind Hemingway's use of the rain: "I believe that the rain is a symbol of fertility. . . . To Hemingway death means rebirth for the existentialist hero in its presence, and therefore the rain, as an omen of death, at the same time predicts rebirth" (48). Locate and analyze the scenes in which rain figures predominantly. In your estimation, does the rain spell only disaster or is rebirth implied, as Killinger argues? You will want to examine the end of chapter 9 in which Catherine reveals to Frederic her fear of the rain (126) to help you make this determination.

2. **Communication and misunderstanding:** What kind of commentary does the novel make about communication and misunderstanding?

   Begin thinking about this topic with an analysis of the following passage. Catherine says to Frederic: "We really are the same one and we mustn't misunderstand on purpose . . . [like] people do. They love each other and they misunderstand on purpose and they fight and then suddenly they aren't the same one" (139). What is the context for this remark? What exactly does Catherine mean here? Can you locate other instances of miscommunication, intentional or otherwise, in the novel? From your analysis of these scenes, draw some conclusions about Hemingway's portrayal of the powers and the dangers of language in *A Farewell to Arms*.

3. **The sacred:** What does the novel have to say about the nature of the "sacred," particularly in the context of war?

Begin by thinking about the concept of the "sacred" and how it applies in today's world and in your own life. How is this word typically used? Then, refocus your attention on the novel, locating and analyzing all references to *sacred* in the text. You will want to look carefully at the following passage in which Frederic ruminates on the nature of the sacred in wartime:

> I was always embarrassed by the words sacred, glorious, and sacrifice and the expression in vain. We hear them, sometimes standing in the rain almost out of earshot, so that only the shouted words came through, and had read them, on proclamations that were slapped up by billposters over other proclamations, now for a long time, and I had seen nothing sacred, and the things that were glorious had no glory and the sacrifices were like the stockyards at Chicago if nothing was done with the meat except to bury it. There were many words that you could not stand to hear and finally only the names of places had dignity. Certain numbers were the same way and certain dates and these with the names of the places were all you could say and have them mean anything. Abstract words such as glory, honor, courage, or hallow were obscene beside the concrete names of villages, the numbers of roads, the names of rivers, the numbers of regiments and the dates. (185)

Why is Frederic "embarrassed" by words such as *sacred?* How are they used in war? Frederic seems to be saying that, at least for some soldiers, new things become sacred in the context of war. How and why does this happen?

Consider also Rinaldi and Frederic's discussion of Catherine. When Rinaldi begins to speak in a vulgar way about her, Frederic says to him: "Please shut up. If you want to be my friend, shut up" (169). Rinaldi finally understands: "All my life I encounter sacred subjects. But very few with you. I suppose you must have them too" (169). What does this conversation tell us about Rinaldi and Frederic? What does it say about Frederic's relationship with Catherine? About the nature of the sacred in wartime?

4. **Night and day:** What do night and day symbolize in the novel? How does understanding this symbolism help us to interpret the text in a new way?

Locate the passages in the novel that discuss the difference between night and day. You might begin with an analysis of the conversation in which Frederic explains to the Priest why he did not visit the Priest's hometown. He describes

> nights in bed, drunk, when you knew that that was all there was, and the strange excitement of waking and not knowing who it was with you, and the world all unreal in the dark and so exciting that you must resume again unknowing and not caring in the night, sure that this was all and all and all and not caring. Suddenly to care very much and to sleep to wake with it sometimes morning and all that had been there gone and everything sharp and hard and clear and sometimes a dispute and the cost. Sometimes still pleasant and fond and warm and breakfast and lunch. Sometimes all the niceness gone and glad to get out on the street but always another day starting and then another night. I tried to tell about the night and the difference between the night and the day and how the night was better unless the day was very clean and cool and I could not tell it. (13)

Review the context of this passage and take a close look at its language. What do night and day represent here? What does the night provide for Frederic that the day does not? Why would a "very clean and cool" day be just as good as a night? You will also want to consider Frederic's comments about night and day that occur later in the novel, once he and Catherine are living together in Switzerland:

> I know that the night is not the same as the day: that all things are different, that the things of the night cannot be explained in the day, because they do not then exist, and the night can be a dreadful time for lonely people once their loneliness has started. But with Catherine there was almost no difference in the night except that it was an even better time. (249)

According to these two passages, how is Frederic's life different with Catherine than it was before this relationship? What do Frederic's comments about night and day reveal to us about his psychological and emotional health? Do they give us a sense of how he is handling the war?

Compare and Contrast Essays

It can prove quite productive to compare and contrast different works of literature. Setting two novels side by side can throw important details into sharp relief. You might, for example, compare and contrast the two Hemingway novels *A Farewell to Arms* and *For Whom the Bell Tolls.* While you might begin by comparing and contrasting the novels in general, you would eventually want to narrow your focus, selecting a particular aspect of these novels to compare. You might choose, for example, to compare and contrast the romantic relationships in the two novels in order to build your essay around a claim concerning Hemingway's portrayal of love. Similarly, you might focus on the psychological effects of war as presented in these two novels. In either case, you might use your analysis to generalize about Hemingway's writing, or you might use it to highlight important differences in the two works and discuss their significance. Of course, you are not restricted to comparing and contrasting works by the same author. You might choose to compare a work with another piece of literature penned in the same period, one with similar themes or one the piece itself seems to allude to.

Sample Topics:

1. *A Farewell to Arms* and *Wuthering Heights:* What fresh insights can be gained when you compare and contrast these two novels?

Critic Lisa Tyler writes: "The correspondences between these two novels are not between characters, but between emotions and themes. I am not arguing that Frederic is Heathcliff or that Catherine is Heathcliff; I am arguing that the lovers in Hemingway's novel experience the same passion and grief as do those in Bronte's" (82). Tyler indicates that the intensity of these relationships, "coupled with the lack of faith in a conventional afterlife, virtually guarantees that any separation, let alone death, will create grief so intense that it threatens sanity" (86). Reread *A Farewell to Arms* and *Wuthering Heights* with Tyler's observations in mind. You may want to read in its entirety Tyler's article, entitled "Passion and Grief in *A Farewell to Arms*: Ernest Hemingway's Retelling of *Wuthering Heights*," to get a sense of her full argument. Do you agree with her assessment? What other parallels can you trace? What are the most significant differences in the two works? Can comparing and contrasting these two novels provide you with a fresh interpretation of *A Farewell to Arms*?

2. **Love in *A Farewell to Arms* and *For Whom the Bell Tolls*:** Compare and contrast the relationships between Catherine and Frederic and Maria and Robert Jordan. Based on these two relationships, what conclusions can you draw about Hemingway's perception of romantic love?

In *A Farewell to Arms*, Catherine says to Frederic, "There isn't any me. I'm you. Don't make up a separate me" (115), and "there's only us two and in the world there's all the rest of them. If anything comes between us we're gone and then they have us" (139). After they have moved to Switzerland, Catherine talks about having her hair cut: "Then we'd both be alike. Oh, darling, I want you so much I want to be you too." Frederic answers: "You are. We're the same one" (299). Read *For Whom the Bell Tolls*, keeping your eyes peeled for similar sentiments. How is Maria and Robert Jordan's relationship similar to Catherine and Frederic's? How is it different? Using your analysis, write an essay that demonstrates and evaluates the way that Hemingway's characters conceive of love and relationships.

Bibliography for *A Farewell to Arms*

Beversluis, John. "Dispelling the Romantic Myth: A Study of *A Farewell to Arms.*" *Hemingway Review* 9.1 (1989): 18–25.

Bloom, Harold, ed. *Ernest Hemingway's* A Farewell to Arms. Contemporary Literary Views Series. New York: Chelsea House, 1996.

Cirino, Mar. "'You Don't Know the Italian Language Well Enough': The Bilingual Dialogue of *A Farewell to Arms.*" *Hemingway Review* 25.1 (2005): 43–62.

Dow, William. "*A Farewell to Arms* and Hemingway's Protest Stance: To Tell the Truth Without Screaming." *Hemingway Review* 15.1 (1995): 72–86.

Hemingway, Ernest. *A Farewell to Arms.* New York: Simon & Schuster, 1995.

Hewson, Marc. "'The Real Story of Ernest Hemingway': Cixous, Gender, and *A Farewell to Arms.*" *Hemingway Review* 22.2 (2003): 51–63.

Killinger, John. "The Existential Hero." *Hemingway and the Dead Gods.* Lexington: UP of Kentucky, 1960.

Lockridge, Ernest. "Faithful in Her Fashion: Catherine Barkley, the Invisible Hemingway Heroine." *Journal of Narrative Techniques* 18 (1988): 170–78.

Merrill, Robert. "Tragic Form in *A Farewell to Arms.*" *American Literature* 45.4 (1974): 571–80.

Prescott, Mary. "*A Farewell to Arms*: Memory and the Perpetual Now." *College Literature* 17.1 (1990): 41–53.

Solotaroff, Robert. "Sexual Identity in *A Farewell to Arms.*" *Hemingway Review* 9.1 (1989): 2–17.

Tyler, Lisa. "Passion and Grief in *A Farewell to Arms*: Ernest Hemingway's Retelling of *Wuthering Heights.*" *Hemingway Review* 14.2 (1995): 79–96.

Young, Philip. *Ernest Hemingway.* New York: Rinehart, 1952.

THE SUN ALSO RISES

READING TO WRITE

PUBLISHED IN 1926, *The Sun Also Rises* tells the story of a group of expatriates mired in postwar disillusionment and despair. The story centers on the narrator, Jake Barnes, and his love interest, Lady Brett Ashley, with whom he is unable to sustain a romantic relationship due to a war injury that has rendered him impotent. Jake watches as Brett flits from man to man, embarking on relationships with his good friend Robert Cohn and a promising young bullfighter named Pedro Romero while engaged to yet another man. According to W. M. Frohock, "Jake's physical disability is in large part a symbol for the general feeling of frustration and pointlessness of life," and thus, "if Jake were physically qualified to possess Brett it would make very little difference" (171). Indeed, it does not seem to have made a difference for Mike Campbell, who is Brett's fiancé. Mike, who is aware of Robert Cohn's affair with Brett, finally confronts Cohn openly; a close reading of Mike's verbal attack reveals his continued frustration as well as the tension and competition that is usually suppressed in the group of friends:

> "Breeding be damned. Who has any breeding, anyway, except the bulls? Aren't the bulls lovely? Don't you like them, Bill? Why don't you say something, Robert? Don't sit there looking like a bloody funeral. What if Brett did sleep with you? She's slept with lots better people than you."
>
> "Shut up," Cohn said. He stood up. "Shut up, Mike."
>
> "Oh, don't stand up and act as though you were going to hit me. That won't make any difference to me. Tell me, Robert. Why do you follow Brett around like a poor bloody steer? Don't you know you're not wanted? I know when I'm not wanted. Why don't you know when you're not wanted? You

came down to San Sebastian where you weren't wanted, and followed Brett around like a bloody steer. Do you think that's right?" (146).

The most obvious place to begin with this passage is Mike's comparison of men with bulls and steers. To get a real sense of the implied meaning here, we have to know the difference between these animals. Both start out as bull calves, but bulls are allowed to grow normally, while steers are castrated. In his remarks, Mike makes an association between the bulls and Brett's suitors—the other men she has slept with who are "lots better" than Robert Cohn—and condemns Cohn as impotent by calling him a steer.

Despite the implication made by Mike's labeling him a steer, it does not seem to be physical prowess that Cohn lacks; presumably, he and Brett consummated their relationship in San Sebastian. It is not, then, impotence that makes Robert a "steer." What distinguishes Robert from the other men in Brett's life is his desire to have sole claim to her. This desire, oddly enough, is what renders him impotent in the chase for Brett.

Because steers are used in bullfighting to stop the bulls from hurting each other, it is ironic that it is Cohn, the "steer," who ultimately commits violence upon his competitors, Jake, Mike, and Pedro. However, as Mike warns in the passage above, saying to Cohn, "Oh, don't stand up and act as though you were going to hit me. That won't make any difference to me," this violence will not deter any of the other suitors or endear him to Brett.

Thus, a close reading of this passage reveals some important features of masculinity as defined by this expatriate crowd. While Robert Cohn's desire to possess Brett entirely and his willingness to use violence to subdue his competition might be considered traditionally masculine characteristics, they actually detract from his masculine potency in the eyes of his compatriots, particularly Mike. This brings up some questions you might pursue further. How exactly is masculinity defined in *The Sun Also Rises?* What kinds of qualities, according to Mike, would a good man, a "bull," possess? Is Mike's point of view shared by all of the other men in the group besides Cohn? How does this outburst reflect on Jake, who himself is literally impotent? Does he share Mike's point of view? What version of masculinity does it seem to endorse? How can you tell?

You might identify other passages in the novel that seem to you to speak about this issue of masculinity and analyze them as we have done the passage above. More than likely, your analyses will lead you to further questions before they begin to present definitive answers. Once you have made your way to a conclusion—once you have found something interesting that you want to share with others about the presentation of masculinity in *The Sun Also Rises*—you have arrived at your claim and are ready to begin drafting your essay.

TOPICS AND STRATEGIES

The topics suggested below are designed to help you develop an approach as you consider writing about *The Sun Also Rises*. They are by no means exhaustive, and so it is very possible that you will devise a topic of your own once you have looked at some examples. If you decide to use one of the sample topics listed here, be sure to use it in your brainstorming, idea-generating, and planning stages. You will want to consider the subquestions listed in topics and analyze the passages that the topic points you to, but you will need to go further than that. You will develop other questions of your own and identify other passages to analyze as your understanding of the topic deepens. Ideally, you will continue this process until you feel you have reached some kind of conclusion that you want to present to the readers of your essay. This conclusion will become your thesis, and you will select the best evidence for your thesis from among your notes and analyses to present in the main body of your essay.

Themes

Romantic love, questions of value, the natural world, and the nature of masculinity are clearly at the heart of this novel, and any of these would make a good starting point for an essay on theme in *The Sun Also Rises*. Perhaps the trickiest element of writing an essay on theme is refraining from having the essay simply establish that the work does, indeed, deal with questions about romantic love, or the nature of masculinity, for example. Your essay needs to make a point not readily observable; it needs to explain precisely what the novel has to say about romantic love or masculinity. After careful analysis, you might argue, for example, that *The Sun Also Rises* indicates that healthy romantic relationships are impossible in this society because the war has made people too self-centered to focus on the needs of another person and too preoccupied with their own psychology to spend time nurturing a relationship. Depending on where your own thinking and analysis of the text take you, you might argue instead that the novel, far from illustrating the futility of romance, actually shows that true love breaks all boundaries and rules, that the relationship shared by Brett and Jake is, while nontraditional, still an example of devoted partnership functioning in the best way it can. In any case, you want your essay to tell your reader exactly what you think the novel's take on your topic is, in this case, romantic love.

Sample Topics:

1. **Romantic love:** While much of *The Sun Also Rises* revolves around male friendships, those friendships seem frequently to be threatened when one or more of the men become interested in a particular woman, often Brett. And the central romantic relationship in the novel—that between Brett and Jake—rests on the fact that it can never be consummated. Taking into account these complexities and tensions, what do you think the novel has to say about romantic love?

   Record and analyze each of the romantic relationships depicted in the novel. How would you characterize each? You will want to look in particular at Jake and Brett's relationship. What is it that holds them together? What is it that prevents them from becoming a committed couple? Examine the last lines of the novel for clues as to the nature of their relationship:

   > "Oh, Jake," Brett said, "we could have had such a damned good time together."
   > Ahead was a mounted policeman in khaki directing traffic. He raised his baton. The car slowed suddenly pressing Brett against me.
   > "Yes," I said. "Isn't it pretty to think so?" (251)

   Are there any positive examples of romantic love in the novel? What, according to the novel, might a healthy romantic partnership look like? Is such a thing possible?

2. **Nature:** What does *The Sun Also Rises* ultimately have to say about the relationship between humankind and the natural world?

According to literary scholar David Savola:

> *The Sun Also Rises* is profoundly concerned with ecological considerations, as the passage of Ecclesiastes echoed in its title would suggest. The novel presents the main characters as aimless, displaced persons without a secure sense of meaning or value and suggests that the characters could find that meaning and value in cultivating a more intimate connection with the natural environment. The novel criticizes conventional depictions of nature, and calls for a literature that offers a more complex picture of the connection between humanity and the natural world. (26)

Evaluate Savola's argument. You might begin by looking for evidence in the novel that the characters could improve their lives by improving their relationships with the natural world. Does the novel truly suggest this? Analyze, for instance, Jake and Bill's fishing trip at Burguete; does this constitute "a more intimate connection with the natural environment"? Does this trip and the time spent in nature produce any noticeable effects on the two men? You will also want to look for evidence that the novel criticizes "conventional depictions" of nature. In what way does it do this? What exactly are the "conventional depictions" of nature that it criticizes? Write an essay in which you extend, modify, or counter Savola's argument regarding the ecological perspective of *The Sun Also Rises.*

3. **Value(s):** What does *The Sun Also Rises* have to say about values or the relative importance of principles and ideas? What about value in regard to making fair or advantageous exchanges?

Locate and analyze passages that comment on values, such as the following exchange between the Count and Brett:

> "That is the secret. You must get to know the values."
>
> "Doesn't anything ever happen to your values?" Brett asked.
>
> "No. Not any more."
>
> "Never fall in love?"
>
> "Always," said the count. "I am always in love."
>
> "What does that do to your values?"
>
> "That, too, has got a place in my values." (67)

What do you make of this exchange? What does Brett mean when she asks, "Doesn't anything ever happen to your values"? What are the values, generally speaking, of the expatriate group at the center of this novel? What things are important to them? What traditionally important things are not? Are their value systems stable, or do they evolve and adapt?

Look also at the following portion of Jake's narrative in which he discusses the "exchange of values":

> I thought I had paid for everything. Not like the woman pays and pays and pays. No idea of retribution or punishment. Just exchange of values. You gave up something and got something else. Or you worked for something. You paid some way for everything that was any good. I paid my way into enough things that I liked, so that I had a good time. Either you paid by learning about them, or by experience, or by taking chances, or by money. Enjoying life was learning to get your money's worth and knowing when you had it. The world was a good place to buy in. (152)

What is making Jake question his philosophy of life? Does he ultimately abandon it? According to the novel, is life at its foundation a series of exchanges? How might Jake's philosophy of the "exchange of values" be related to the Count's idea of "get[ing] to know the values"?

4. **Masculinity:** Although Brett's sexuality drives much of the novel's plot, ultimately *The Sun Also Rises* seems to be about men. In fact, one of the features that most sets Brett apart from

the other women of the novel is the way she acts like "one of the guys." How does the novel present masculinity? How is it constructed? Who is a good model of masculinity in the novel?

How does the novel define masculinity? Does it present more than one model of masculinity? Compare the ways that various male characters—Bill, Robert Cohn, Mike Campell, and Jake, for instance—establish and maintain masculine identities. Jake makes an especially interesting case, as his impotence prevents him from using sex as a means of anchoring his gender identity. According to Jacob Leland, "Jake Barnes depends upon earning and spending practices to establish an American, male, expatriate identity in Paris. He attributes little value to the things he buys: his ownership of commodities is secondary to his relationship with the money form itself" (37). He goes on to argue that

> Jake's trip to rescue Brett entirely compromises the sexual power of economic practice that he works to establish. He is finally presented with the bill he cannot pay at the Hotel Montana in Madrid. . . . The power that Jake gets from spending money is not only incomplete but conditional, dependent upon maleness being for sale. When the bill has been paid, in the passive voice, Jake is *grammatically* disempowered, surely the worst death a Hemingway writer-hero can die. (45)

Peruse the novel for evidence for and against Leland's argument. You might start by studying the following passage in which Jake provides extensive information about his bank statement:

> One was a bank statement. It showed a balance of $2432.60. I got out my check-book and deducted four checks drawn since the first of the month, and discovered I had a balance of $1832.60. I wrote this on the back of the statement. (38)

Why do you think Hemingway has Jake include this information in the narrative? Of what significance is it? Try to identify other instances in which Jake reveals information about his financial status and spending habits that is apparently unnecessary to the story he is conveying. Are there instances in which Jake comments on the financial behaviors of other males in the novel?

Write an essay in which you describe the models of masculinity presented in the novel, making sure to account for the way that Jake secures his gender identity. Evaluate these models of masculinity. Are they all equally successful in establishing masculinity?

Character

The Sun Also Rises is filled with interesting characters you might choose to analyze as you prepare to write an essay on the novel. You could easily devote the entirety of your essay to a discussion of Robert Cohn, Brett Ashley, Jake Barnes, or any one of several other characters. If you decide to make your essay essentially a character analysis, you will want to record everything you know about the character you have chosen. Pay attention to the character's behavior, speech, and relationships with other characters. You will also want to pay attention to where your information about your character is coming from. For example, if you are writing about Robert Cohn, you will want to take into account Jake's ambivalent feelings for Cohn, since everything we learn is filtered through Jake's perspective.

Sample Topics:

1. **Robert Cohn:** Though *The Sun Also Rises* is presented through a first-person narrator who plays an integral role in the story and who seems to be telling his own story, the novel opens with a long description of Robert Cohn. In fact, the entire first chapter consists of Jake talking about Cohn. Who is Robert Cohn to Jake? Why is he afforded such a central position in the narrative? Does he represent something to Jake? To Hemingway? Look carefully at the description that Jake offers of Cohn in the opening chapters of the novel, the following passage in particular:

> He cared nothing for boxing, in fact he disliked it, but he learned it painfully and thoroughly to counteract the feeling of inferiority and shyness he had felt on being treated as a Jew at Princeton. There was a certain inner comfort in knowing he could knock down anybody who was snooty to him, although,

being very shy and a thoroughly nice boy, he never fought
except in the gym. (11)

What does Cohn's background tell us about him? What do we
know about his relationships with women? How does the publication of his novel change him? Look closely at Cohn's relationship with Brett. What does he find appealing in her? All in all,
what are the main motivational factors in Cohn's life? What are
his goals? How does the narrator, Jake, feel about Cohn? How
might Jake's own feelings color his perception of Cohn and in
turn affect our own interpretation of the character?

2. **Brett Ashley:** When critics condemn Hemingway for making
   all of his independent or powerful women into "bitches," Brett
   Ashley usually figures in the debate. Analyze and evaluate this
   character. Is she an independent woman who uses her sexuality
   as a means to control men and get what she wants? Or, is she
   more complicated than that?

How is Brett like and unlike other women in the society in
which she exists? What other women are there in the text to
compare her to? Why do you think Brett refers to herself as a
"chap"? Why do you think villagers at the fiesta chose Brett as
an image to dance around?

  You will want to take a close look at Brett's relationships,
particularly her relationship with Pedro Romero. What do you
make of the way Brett describes Romero's opinion of her: "They
ragged him about me at the café, I guess. He wanted me to
grow my hair out. Me, with long hair. I'd look so like hell. . . .
He said it would make me more womanly. I'd look a fright"
(246). What does Pedro Romero find lacking in Brett? Why
do you think she ultimately leaves him? When she explains
her decision to Jake, Brett says: "I'm thirty-four, you know.
I'm not going to be one of these bitches that ruins children"
(247). Further, she tells him, "I'm going back to Mike. . . . He's
so damned nice and he's so awful. He's my sort of thing" (247).
Analyze her reasoning here. How might she "ruin" Romero?
What exactly makes Mike her "sort of thing"?

3. **Jake Barnes:** In addition to serving as narrator, Jake also is a central—perhaps, the central—character in the novel. And he is the one about whom we have the most information, because we are made privy to his thought processes. What kind of person is Jake? Does he change, or learn anything, over the course of the novel? Why or why not?

Record what you know about Jake's background. Analyze his personal relationships, especially those with Brett and Robert Cohn. Would you say that Jake is fulfilled? Successful? Why or why not? What motivates Jake to tell the story he does? What seems to be its psychological purpose for him? What do his narrative choices tell us about him and the way he perceives himself and the world?

History and Context

Many readers today think of *The Sun Also Rises* as a novel that accurately depicts the angst and the aimlessness of the so-called lost generation in the wake of World War I. And while it can be fruitful to read contemporary fiction in order to understand better the time period in which it was written, the process works equally well in the opposite direction; using historical research can illuminate many obscured meanings and interpretations of a novel from an earlier time period. In the case of *The Sun Also Rises,* some background reading on World War I, the new woman, the expatriate movement, Prohibition, or a combination of these topics could be particularly useful in helping you develop an interesting interpretation of the text to present in your essay.

Sample Topics:

1. **World War I and the "lost generation":** Malcom Cowley, writing about the importance of the war to the themes of *The Sun Also Rises,* notes that most of the characters have been "physically or morally wounded" and "have lost their original code of values" (72). "Feeling the loss," Cowley writes, "they are now trying to live by a simpler code, essentially that of soldiers on furlough" (72). Do you agree with Cowley? In your analysis, what does the novel have to say about the long-term psychological effects of World War I?

You might wish to begin by considering the evidence for Cowley's conclusions. What support can you locate in the text that the characters are "physically or morally wounded" and that they "have lost their original code of values"? Describe the code that Jake and his cohorts seem to live by. Do you agree with Cowley's assessment that they have adopted the code of "soldiers on furlough"? Cowley also writes that the "war has deadened some of their feelings and has left them capable of enjoying only the simplest and strongest pleasures" and that it has "given them an attitude of resigned acceptance toward all sorts of disasters, including those caused by their own follies" (72). What evidence can you find for or against these conclusions? Write an essay in which you position yourself in relationship to Cowley's argument. You might extend that argument, modify it, or offer an alternative explanation for the behavior that Cowley attributes to the lasting effects of the trauma of World War I.

2. **The "new woman" and new models of romantic love:** What kind of commentary does the novel ultimately make about the new woman and the new models of romantic love that accompany her evolution?

According to scholar Kim Moreland, Hemingway makes his male characters, such as Jake and Robert Cohn, nostalgic for the traditions of chivalry and courtly love. Their attempts to re-create or return to those traditions are thwarted by Brett Ashley, the model of the new woman of the 1920s. Moreland writes:

> [T]he many parallels between the events in this novel and the courtly love tradition are skewed, as though seen through a distorted and distorting lens. These distortions certainly suggest the breakdown of romantic love in the modern world, yet it is important to recognize that each of the male protagonists continues to feel a powerful nostalgia for romantic love, and specifically for the courtly love tradition which is at its base. . . . The distortions of the courtly love tradition that are revealed in *The Sun Also Rises* primarily result from and thus act implicitly to criticize Brett's morals, actions,

and personality, and therefore the morals, actions, and personality of the new modern woman (31).

Begin with some background reading into the traditions of chivalry and courtly love such as Andreas Capellanus's *The Art of Courtly Love* or Denis De Rougoment's *Love in the Western World*. What were the relationships like between men and women in the courtly love tradition? What was required of each gender? Who was in control? Think particularly about the role of the woman in this type of society. Now, do some background reading on the new woman of the 1920s and 1930s, starting with sources such as *Women of the 20s* by George H. Douglas and the pertinent chapters of Sheila Rowbotham's *A Century of Women: The History of Women in Britain and the United States in the Twentieth Century*. How was she different from the women who took part in the courtly love traditions? How would a relationship between a new woman and her partner be similar to and different from a relationship between a lady and gentleman in the courtly tradition? Once you have all of this background information, evaluate Moreland's argument. Do you agree that Hemingway is using a nostalgia for courtly love and chivalry to criticize the new woman? Is this technique effective? Is it misleading in any way?

3. **Expatriatism:** What kind of commentary does *The Sun Also Rises* make about the expatriates who lived abroad in the post–World War I era?

Begin with some background reading on expatriates, for example, Kirk Curnutt's *Ernest Hemingway and the Expatriate Modernist Movement*. Why did so many people choose to leave the United States? What were they rejecting, if anything? What were they searching for? What did they have in common? Identify and analyze any references to their national affiliations in the text. You might examine, for instance, Bill's remarks to Jake:

> Nobody that ever left their own country ever wrote anything worth printing. Not even in the newspapers. . . . You're an

expatriate. You've lost touch with the soil. You get precious. Fake European standards have ruined you. You drink yourself to death. You become obsessed by sex. You spend all your time talking, not working. You are an expatriate, see? You hang around cafés (120).

Is Bill at all serious here? Is there any truth to his remarks? What does the novel as a whole seem to think about the expatriate crowd?

4. **Alcohol and Prohibition:** What does *The Sun Also Rises* have to say about alcohol and Prohibition?

You might wish to begin with some background reading on Prohibition to get a better understanding of the cultural and social context in which Hemingway was writing. *Prohibition: Thirteen Years That Changed America* by Edward Behr or *Deliver Us From Evil: An Interpretation of American Prohibition* by Norma H. Clark are good introductions. How did the majority of Americans feel about Prohibition and alcohol in general in the 1920s? Was this perception shared by Europeans? According to critic Jeffrey Schwartz, "Hemingway viewed drinking and getting drunk as an initiation rite and an adventure." For Schwartz, *The Sun Also Rises* "actualizes Hemingway's own views of drinking, and signifies both communal enjoyment of life and its pleasures and a manner of rebelling against prohibition and its nationalist agendas" (196). You may want to read Schwartz's argument in its entirety. Do you agree with Schwartz's assessment? What evidence can you find for and against it? Ultimately, what message do you think Hemingway is sending regarding alcohol and Prohibition in this novel?

Philosophy and Ideas

When you set out to write about philosophy and ideas, you are in essence evaluating the philosophical underpinnings or ideological positioning of a piece of literature. In the case of *The Sun Also Rises*, you might focus your attention on Catholicism and prayer or on tragedy and pessimism, for example, two ideological frameworks with a clear presence in the novel. In either case, your job is to discern and articulate the novel's particular relationship to the ideological framework you have chosen to investigate. In the case of pessimism, for example, you want to determine whether the novel endorses or challenges this perception of the world and to uncover any nuances in the relationship as well. You might decide, for example, that *The Sun Also Rises* presents an essentially pessimistic view, although it allows that some redemption and meaning might be found through humans' relationship with the natural world. Or you might conclude that the novel considers but ultimately rejects a pessimistic worldview, that it chooses to emphasize the human bonds that can be forged as a result of shared suffering rather than the suffering itself.

Sample Topics:

1. **Catholicism and prayer:** The world of this novel is one thoroughly rooted in secularism and even decadence, and, therefore, Jake's occasional moments of religious observance really stand out as noteworthy. How do these moments figure in the novel? What is it that Jake actually believes in? What does *The Sun Also Rises* have to say about the role and value of Catholicism and prayer?

   Jake seems to have ambivalent feelings regarding his religion and spirituality. Before the bullfights, he

   > knelt and started to pray and prayed for everybody I thought of, Brett and Mike and Bill and Robert Cohn and myself, and all the bullfighters, separately for the ones I liked, and lumping all the rest, then I prayed for myself again. . . . I was a little ashamed, and regretted that I was such a rotten Catholic, but realized there was nothing I could do about it, at least for a while, and maybe never, but that anyway it was a grand religion, and I only wished I felt religious and maybe I would the next time. (102–03)

   Analyze this passage along with others you locate in the novel that comment on Jake's religious feelings. Make sure to look also at the following exchange between Jake and Brett:

   > Brett looked at the yellow wall of the chapel. . . .

"Let's go in. Do you mind? I'd rather like to pray a little for him or something."

We went in through the heavy leather door that moved very lightly. . . . We knelt at one of the long wooden benches. After a little I felt Brett stiffen beside me, and saw she was looking straight ahead.

"Come on," she whispered throatily. "Let's get out of here. Makes me damned nervous."

Outside in the hot brightness of the street Brett looked up at the tree-tops in the wind. The praying had not been much of a success.

"Don't know why I get so nervy in church," Brett sid. "Never does me any good."

We walked along.

"I'm damned bad for a religious atmosphere," Brett said. "I've the wrong type of face. . . . I've never gotten anything I prayed for. Have you?"

"Oh, yes." (212)

Reading these two passages and any others you have located and analyzed, what conclusions can you draw about Jake's relationship to religion and spirituality? How about Brett's? What is the novel as a whole saying about the power (or lack thereof) of religion in this postwar, expatriate society?

2. **Tragedy and pessimism:** According to critic Günther Schmigalle, though some critics describe *The Sun Also Rises* as demonstrating a "sporty superficiality," it actually "carries on the tradition of philosophical pessimism by its emphasis on the transitory, insignificant nature of all human action, and on human will or desire as the source of all suffering" (19). Write an essay that extends, modifies, or counters Schmigalle's claim.

Begin by searching the novel for evidence that human nature is "insignificant" and "transitory." Look also for evidence to the contrary. Are there instances that prove human actions are meaningful and lasting? Peruse the text for evidence of the second part of Schmigalle's argument as well. Does it indicate that "human will or desire" is the "source of all suffering"? Are there other factors that cause suffering? Does human will or desire sometimes result in something other than suffering?

Language, Symbols, and Imagery

Language, symbols, and imagery are foundational elements of literature. Not surprisingly, a sharp analysis of a set of symbols or pattern of language can lead you to interesting discoveries about a text, which can ultimately serve as the basis of your argument. A focus on the discussion of writing and reading, the novel's title and epigraphs, or the descriptions of the bullfights in *The Sun Also Rises* would make good starting points for an essay. Remember that you may or may not use all of your analysis as you draft your actual essay. You may generate a great deal of material if you analyze every mention of reading and writing in the novel, for example, but not all of that material will make it into your essay. You will use your notes to draw a conclusion or interpretation that you would like to present in your essay. At that point, you will be able to select the material that best supports your conclusion and incorporate it into your essay.

Sample Topics:

1. **The power of writing:** What kind of commentary is the novel ultimately making about writing and the power of the written word?

   Think about the many characters that populate this novel. Which of them are writers? What kind of writing do they do? How successful are they? What are their motivations and obstacles? Which characters are not writers? How do these characters feel about literature and their more literary friends? Think about Frances, for example, and her own attempts at writing as well as the sarcastic remarks she makes about Cohn when she believes that he is leaving her in order to have some more varied experiences he could then parlay into literary material: "We all ought to make sacrifices for literature. Look at me. I'm going to England without a protest. All for literature. We must all help young writers" (57). What do these comments say about the general social attitude toward literature and writers? How does Mike Campbell fit into this equation? What does he think of literature and literary types?

In addition to studying the characters' varying relationships with and attitudes toward writing, you will also want to locate passages in the novel that refer directly to writing or reading, such as the following, and analyze them:

> [Cohn] had been reading W. H. Hudson. That sounds like an innocent occupation, but Cohn had read and reread "The Purple Land." "The Purple Land" is a very sinister book if read too late in life. It recounts splendid imaginary amorous adventures of a perfect English gentleman in an intensely romantic land, the scenery of which is very well described. For a man to take it at thirty-four as a guide-book to what life holds is about as safe as it would be for a man of the same age to enter Wall Street direct from a French convent, equipped with a complete set of the more practical Alger books. Cohn, I believe, took every word of "The Purple Land" as literally as though it had been an R. G. Dunreport (17).

What dangers are described in this passage? How can the sentiments in this passage be connected to your analysis of the characters and their relationship to the written word?

2. **Epigraphs and title:** Discuss the significance of the epigraphs and title of *The Sun Also Rises*.

Examine the following epigraphs closely:

> *"You are all a lost generation."*—Gertrude Stein in conversation

> *"One generation passesth away, and another generation cometh; but the earth abideth forever.... The sun also ariseth, and the sun goeth down, and hasteth to the place where he arose.... The wind goeth toward the south, and turneth about unto the north; it whirleth about continually, and the wind returneth again according to his circuits.... All rivers run into the sea; yet*

the sea is not full; unto the place from whence the rivers come, thither they return again."—Ecclesiastes

Why do you think Hemingway chose to include these quotations at the start of the novel? How do they relate to the themes of the book? Why do you think he chose the title he did? How does the title connect with the epigraphs and the themes of the novel?

3. **Bullfighting:** Bullfights operate as extremely rich symbols in *The Sun Also Rises*. The fights themselves are full of pageantry, ritual, and symbol, and clearly Hemingway intends us to see symbolic significance for the characters through the bullfights as well. What symbolic significance do they have in the novel?

Peter L. Hays writes:

> [I]f one believes, as I do, that *The Sun Also Rises* is concerned with spiritual values, a search for what to believe in, then the bullfight scenes should not be looked upon as secular diversions, a plot device necessary to introduce Brett to Romero or as opportunities merely to introduce those virtues Romero possesses as a model for Jake. Rather, bullfighting in the novel should be seen as an attenuated form of religious worship culminating in live sacrifice. . . . Bullfighting, therefore, as Hemingway uses it in the novel, is not in opposition to the Catholic Church, but parallel to it, an altered mirror image. (47)

What do you make of Hays's argument? Do the bullfights provide some type of spiritual fulfillment for any of the characters? What might the bullfights provide that the Catholic Church does not? In what way might it be "an altered mirror image" of the Catholic Church?

Compare and Contrast Essays

Setting two elements side by side can really help you notice features that might otherwise have escaped you and thus is a good way to generate ideas for an essay. In the case of *The Sun Also Rises,* you might compare and contrast Robert Cohn and Jake Barnes, for example. Getting a better sense of their similarities and differences might help to explain Jake's ambivalent feelings for his friend and Brett's attraction to both of them. It is also important to remember that you are not bound by the confines of a particular text when you think about interesting comparisons to make. You might, for example, want to compare Brett to another iconic female character, Daisy Buchanan from F. Scott Fitzgerald's *The Great Gatsby.* Since these two classic works of American literature were published around the same time, you might use a comparison of Daisy and Brett to discuss the evolving role of women in the early 20th century, or you might write an essay that details the differences between Fitzgerald's perception of women and Hemingway's, using Daisy and Brett as your primary examples.

Sample Topics:

1. **Robert Cohn and Jake Barnes:** Jake and Robert operate in the same expatriate society, and they seem to have a lot in common, including an obsession with Brett Ashley. How can comparing and contrasting these two characters help us to understand better the psychological workings of each?

   Begin by listing the similarities between Robert and Jake. What interests do they share? What makes them friends? How are their backgrounds similar? What attracts each of them to Brett? Next, move to their differences, beginning with what you feel is the most significant. You will also want to examine their relationship with each other. Pay particular attention to the way that Jake tells Cohn's story. What can his narrative choices tell us about the way he perceives Cohn? Do the two men ultimately become rivals?

2. **Daisy from *The Great Gatsby* (1925) and Brett from *The Sun Also Rises* (1926):** Daisy and Brett are two of the most memorable female characters in early 20th-century fiction. Are they memorable for the same reasons? Taken together, what might an analysis of Brett and Daisy tell us about the changing role of women in the 1920s?

You will want to reread each of these novels, taking careful note of the similarities and differences between Daisy and Brett. What are their goals? What are their relationships like with the men in their lives? Pay close attention to how each woman is defined or defines herself in the context of her culture. Notice also who tells each woman's story and how that affects our perceptions of her.

Bibliography for *The Sun Also Rises*

Behr, Edward. *Prohibition: Thirteen Years That Changed America.* New York: Arcade, 1996.

Capellanus, Andrews. *The Art of Courtly Love.* Trans. John Jay Parry. New York: Columbia UP, 1960.

Clark, Norma H. *Deliver Us From Evil: An Interpretation of American Prohibition.* New York: Norton, 1976.

Cowley, Malcolm. *A Second Flowering: Works and Days of the Lost Generation.* London: Andre Deutsch, 1956.

Curnutt, Kirk. *Ernest Hemingway and the Expatriate Modernist Movement.* Detroit: Gale, 2000.

de Rougemont, Denis. *Love in the Western World.* Trans. Montgomery Belgion. New York: Pantheon, 1956.

Douglas, George H. *Women of the 20s.* Dallas, TX: Saybrook, 1986.

Frohock, W. M. *The Novel of Violence in America.* Dallas, TX: Southern Methodist UP, 1957.

Hays, Peter L. "Hunting Ritual in *The Sun Also Rises*." *Hemingway Review* 8.2 (1989): 46–48.

Hemingway, Ernest. *The Sun Also Rises.* New York: Scribners, 1995.

Leland, Jacob Michael. "Yes, That Is a Roll of Bills in My Pocket: The Economy of Masculinity in *The Sun Also Rises*." *Hemingway Review* 23.3 (2004): 37–46.

Moreland, Kim. "Hemingway's Medievalist Impulse: Its Effect on the Presentation of Women and War in *The Sun Also Rises*." *Hemingway Review* 6.1 (1986): 30–42.

Rowbotham, Sheila. *A Century of Women: The History of Women in Britain and the United States in the Twentieth Century.* New York: Penguin, 1999.

Rudat, Wolfgang E. H. "Sexual Dilemmas in *The Sun Also Rises*: Hemingway's Count and the Education of Jacob Barnes." *Hemingway Review* 8.2 (1989): 2–13.

Savola, David. "'A Very Sinister Book': *The Sun Also Rises* as Critique of Pastoral." *Hemingway Review* 26.1 (2006): 25–46.

Schmigalle, Günther. "'How People Go to Hell': Pessimism, Tragedy, and Affinity to Schopenhauer in *The Sun Also Rises*." *Hemingway Review* 25.1 (2005): 7–21.

Schwartz, Jeffrey A. "'The Saloon Must Go, and I Will Take It with Me': American Prohibition, Nationalism, and Expatriation in *The Sun Also Rises*." *Studies in the Novel* 33.2 (2001): 180–201.

THE OLD MAN
AND THE SEA

READING TO WRITE

ORIGINALLY PUBLISHED in the September 1, 1952, issue of *Life* magazine, *The Old Man and the Sea* was Hemingway's first attempt at novel-length fiction after the critically condemned *Across the River and into the Trees.* It certainly proved a successful comeback in terms of sales, and the initial critical reception was warm. More than 5 million copies

> were sold in the first forty-eight hours. Scribner's first printing of 50,000 became available the next week and the book soon reached the best-seller list, where it remained for six months. The Book-of-the-Month Club chose it as a main selection with a first printing of 153,000 copies, and it was translated into nine foreign languages within the year. Soon *The Old Man and the Sea* was being taught in middle schools and high schools, and it became a favorite outside the classroom as well (Cain 112).

Since its publication, the poignant simplicity of this work has garnered it both praise and criticism. While some admire Hemingway's ability to sketch out a tale with many possible meanings in sparse prose, many others complain that the characters are not fleshed out sufficiently or that the story is too psychologically or symbolically unsophisticated. Because of this alleged lack of sophistication, *The Old Man and the Sea* is not generally considered by critics to be one of Hemingway's finest works.

There is an argument to be made, however, that the complexity and depth that some find missing is in fact present in the story if one looks hard enough. Take for example Santiago's reflections and memories, this one in particular:

> He remembered the time he had hooked one of a pair of marlin. The male fish always let the female fish feed first and the hooked fish, the female, made a wild, panic-stricken, despairing fight that soon exhausted her, and all the time the male had stayed with her, crossing the line and circling with her on the surface. He had stayed so close that the old man was afraid he would cut the line with his tail which was sharp as a scythe and almost of that size and shape. When the old man had gaffed her and clubbed her . . . and then, with the boy's aid, hoisted her aboard, the male fish had stayed by the side of the boat. Then, while the old man was clearing the lines and preparing the harpoon, the male fish jumped high into the air beside the boat to see where the female was and then went down deep, his lavender wings, that were his pectoral fins, spread wide and all his wide lavender stripes showing. He was beautiful, the old man remembered, and he had stayed.
>
> That was the saddest thing I ever saw with them, the old man thought. The boy was sad too and we begged her pardon and butchered her promptly.
>
> "I wish the boy was here," he said aloud. (49–50)

In this passage, Santiago's struggle with the great marlin he has hooked causes him to reflect on another memorable experience he had with a marlin. It is worth spending some time thinking about why this experience resonates so powerfully for Santiago as well as what we can infer about him based on his attachment to the story of these two marlins. What seems to have made this experience important to him is the bond that the male and female fish shared. Santiago seems to interpret the male marlin's behavior as a show of devotion to his mate, faithfully staying with her through an agonizing death, even at the risk of his own life. Once the marlin sees his mate dead he goes "down deep," in what Santiago likely construes as grieving, since he interprets the scenario as the "saddest" thing he has ever seen fish do. Is Santiago's interpretation of the marlin's behavior an objective, unbiased one, or is he creating a tragic romance out of strictly biologically driven animal behavior? Why exactly is Santiago so touched by the behavior of the male marlin? Could he possibly be associating the fish with himself in some way? What do we know about Santiago's own relationships with women? What do we know or what can we infer about Santiago's feelings for his departed wife?

As he recalls this experience, Santiago remembers that the boy had helped him with this particular fish. They boy (Manolin) too had been saddened by the experience and had joined Santiago in "begging [the fish's] pardon and butchering her promptly" (50). At this point in his recollections, Santiago says out loud, "I wish the boy was here" (50). What conclusions can we draw from the fact that Santiago's memory of this experience results in his voicing this particular sentiment out loud? How might Santiago and Manolin's relationship be reflected in the story of the two marlins? Can we assume that Santiago is not simply thinking of the help the boy could be in terms of catching the fish but is thinking of the companionship he has lost? Are there other passages in the story that suggest Santiago and the boy share a devotion and a dependency on each other as the two marlins did? If Santiago draws a parallel between the marlins and himself and Manolin, which of them does he cast in the role of the caught fish and of its loyal, grieving partner?

In stopping to analyze the above passage and consider its relevance to the rest of the story, we have noted that the memory of the two marlins is likely connected to Santiago's lost wife as well as his (temporary) loss of the boy. How might focusing on Santiago's feelings of loss, love, and loneliness—his relationships with other humans rather than his relationship with the natural world—change our interpretation of him and his journey? If you became interested in pursuing this topic, you might locate and analyze other passages that seem relevant to Santiago's need for human contact. Then, once you have devoted a good deal of time and energy to studying them, you would synthesize your findings, using them to develop a thesis sentence that puts forth an argument having to do with Santiago's need for human relationships. You might argue, for instance, that Santiago's entire struggle is fueled by a desire not to pit himself against nature but to restore his close relationship with Manolin; if he brings in a big enough fish, Manolin's parents will once again allow the boy to fish with the old man. Alternatively, you might argue that while Santiago certainly experiences loneliness, isolation from other humans is absolutely necessary for him to experience the harmony with nature that he ultimately finds.

TOPICS AND STRATEGIES

In the following pages, you will find a wide variety of ideas for essays on *The Old Man and the Sea.* By no means is this list exhaustive. Reading through it may inspire you to come up with a topic of your own, or you might decide to modify an existing topic or combine two or more topics. If you decide to use one of the suggested topics, be careful not simply to answer each of the subquestions in order. Use these questions, and the suggested passages as well, to generate new ideas. Spend some time thinking about the questions and passages, taking careful notes as you proceed. Then comes what is perhaps the most difficult task in crafting an essay; you will want to synthesize your findings into one single argument, or interpretation, that will serve as the foundation of your essay. If you are unable to do this, you will simply need to return to the questions and suggested passages and continue working with them until you are able to do so. Realizing all the work that has to be done before you actually begin to draft your essay will help you to remember to allow sufficient time for the thinking and planning process. The good news here is that if you have done a good, thorough job in your planning, drafting the essay will come fairly easily.

Themes

The Old Man and the Sea engages many interesting and important themes, including the meaning of success, the relationship between man and nature, and the role of the artist in society. You might choose to write about any one of these themes or on another theme you identify in the novel. Once you have selected the theme you wish to study, it is a good idea to reread the novel, looking for passages and scenes relevant to your topic. Once you have identified these elements, you can analyze them carefully, using them to help you come to some conclusion regarding precisely what the novel has to say about the meaning of success, the relationship between man and nature, or the role of the artist in society.

Sample Topics:

1. **Success:** How does *The Old Man and the Sea* define success?

   What are Santiago's goals? What are his priorities? He clearly won his long-fought battle with the marlin, but his attempt to bring the fish in to sell its flesh is ruined when the sharks attack.

Does the novel portray Santiago as victorious or defeated? How do the townspeople view him? How about Manolin? Most important, how does Santiago himself conceptualize his experience, and what does his conceptualization tell us about the message that Hemingway is attempting to convey in this text?

2. **Man versus nature/man's relationship with nature:** What does the novel have to say about man's relationship with nature?

Identify and analyze passages that seem to comment on humans' relationship with nonhuman nature. How does Santiago imagine himself? How does he perceive his relationship with the marlin he has hooked? How does he see himself in relation to the sea? Does Santiago perceive himself as competing with—struggling against—nature or as an integral part of it? Critic G. R. Wilson, Jr., argues that Santiago is unlike the majority of Hemingway's heroes because his connection to nature allows him to overcome nihilism. He writes:

> In place of the code hero, who accepted a nihilistic universe more or less passively and whose only effort was to try to come to terms with that dark vista through some personal accommodation, we have here the hero incarnate, who achieves meaning, not only personally but universally, by a full commitment to his world and through an intimate relationship with the world's creatures. Only because of this unity with nature can Santiago exercise, indeed expand, his strength and endurance as a man to achieve his final symbolic but meaningful triumph in the face of literal disaster, a triumph that carries a redemptive message for all who share the human condition. (373)

Return to the novel with Wilson's claim in mind and assess its validity. Write an essay in which you support and extend his claim or modify it in some way. Alternatively, you might fashion an essay that argues against Wilson, claiming that Santiago, in fact, retains a competitive, rather than harmonious, relationship with nature throughout the course of the novel.

You will want to examine passages that describe Santiago's relationship with the great marlin. At one point, "he began to pity the great fish that he had hooked. He is wonderful and strange and who knows how old he is, he thought. Never have I had such a strong fish nor one who acted so strangely. . . . I wonder if he has any plans or if he is just as desperate as I am" (49). At another, he says to the fish, "I love you and respect you very much. But I will kill you dead before this day ends" (54). After the sharks have begun to destroy the body of the fish, Santiago "did not like to look at [it] anymore"; when "the fish had been hit it was as though he himself were hit" (103). What do Santiago's remarks about the fish reveal about his relationship to the fish? What can his relationship with the fish tell us about his relationship to the larger natural world?

3. **The artist:** What does *The Old Man and the Sea* have to say about art and the artist?

The Old Man and the Sea is read by many as an allegory about writing. The old man can be imagined as the artist and his craft; fishing can be read as writing. If you read the novel in this way, what exactly is Hemingway saying about the artist and his craft? What are the obstacles he faces? What qualities are necessary for him to succeed? How is he different from the rest of his community? If one reads the story in this way, is Santiago's fishing expedition a success? Why or why not?

Character

You could, of course, write an essay that analyzes the main character of *The Old Man and the Sea*, arguing whether Santiago learns some kind of lesson during the course of the novel or whether he is ultimately victorious or defeated. You could also opt to study one of the other characters in the story, including the boy, the sea, or even Joe DiMaggio. When preparing to write an essay about a character, first record everything you know about that character. You will also want to note where the information you receive about a character comes from. Does it come from that character himself? From another character? From the narrator? Is the source of your information reliable? Be alert for changes in your character as the story progresses and for hints as to whether this change is viewed in a positive or negative light. Especially in regard to minor characters, you will want to spend some time thinking about what the work would be like without that particular character. Why did Hemingway choose to add this particular character to the story? What about the character is significant to the story's meaning or message?

Sample Topics:

1. **Santiago:** Analyze the main character of *The Old Man and the Sea*. Would you consider Santiago a tragic hero?

In your opinion, does Santiago's downfall result from his own error or flaw as a tragic hero's must? According to one way of reading the story,

> when the sharks come, it is almost as a thing expected, almost as a punishment which the old man brings upon himself in going far out "beyond all people. Beyond all people in the world" and there hooking and killing the great fish. For the coming of the sharks is not a matter of chance nor a stroke of bad luck: "the shark was not an accident." They are the direct result of the old man's action in killing the fish. (Burhans 449)

Analyze the passages in the novel that speak to this issue. Do you agree that Santiago committed a grave error by going out too far? Why or why not? Do you believe that the sharks' attack on the marlin is punishment, or is it simply chance? Think about how your interpretation of the entire novel would change depending on your answers to these questions. Write an essay in which you argue that Santiago is or is not a tragic hero, and discuss the implications of your answer on the overarching meaning of the text.

2. **Manolin:** Analyze and evaluate the character of Manolin.

Begin by recording everything you know about Manolin. What do you know about his parents? What about his relationship with Santiago? What are his priorities? His goals? What conflicts does he experience? Does he change from the beginning of the story to the end? If so, what sparks this change, and does the novel view it as positive or negative?

3. **The sea:** Analyze the sea as a character, and discuss its role in the novel.

   Hemingway offers two potential ways of characterizing the sea:

   > [Santiago] always thought of the sea as *la mar* which is what people call her in Spanish when they love her. Sometimes those who love her say bad things of her but they are always said as though she were a woman. Some of the younger fishermen, those who used buoys as floats for their lines and had motorboats, bought when the shark livers had brought much money, spoke of her as *el mar* which is masculine. They spoke of her as a contestant or a place or even an enemy. But the old man always thought of her as feminine and as something that gave or withheld great favours, and if she did wild or wicked things it was because she could not help them. (30)

   Locate other passages in the text that describe the sea, and study them carefully. Does the novel create a sea that is more like the one Santiago perceives or closer to the image that the younger fishermen have of it? What are the implications for our interpretation of the novel of the way in which Hemingway portrays the character of the sea?

4. **Narrator:** Analyze the narrator's point of view and discuss how it affects your interpretation of *The Old Man and the Sea.*

   Although the anonymous narrator is not a character in the strictest sense of the word, we can still learn a great deal about the book by analyzing his role in the story. First of all, what information is the narrator privy to? Does he present only events as they occur, or does he seem to have access to the characters' thoughts and emotions? Does he present a completely objective, unbiased account of Santiago's battle with the marlin? Or does the narrator seem to have an opinion or interpretation of his own in regard to Santiago's struggle? How can you tell? After analyzing the narrator's perspective, what kind of argument can you make about how Hemingway intended readers to interpret Santiago's story?

History and Context

Taking the time to familiarize yourself with cultural and historical contexts can really help you arrive at a fuller understanding of a literary work. In the case of Hemingway's *The Old Man and the Sea,* you might research Hemingway's life at the time in which he was writing this novel, the role of baseball in the 1940s and '50s, or Cuban life in this time period. Armed with this knowledge, you are much less likely to make errors by analyzing the novel with ill-fitting 21st-century assumptions that cannot apply to 1940s Cuba. In addition, you will be prepared to pick up on nuances and to ascertain whether Hemingway is reflecting contemporary social norms or whether he is responding to or challenging them in some way. In short, time learning about context is time well spent, as it will certainly enable you to make more informed comments when you discuss the novel in your essay. Further, your research into cultural and historical context might become integral to your argument, especially if you decide to write about a topic such as the setting of the story, the connections between Hemingway's life and his art, or the role of women or of baseball in society.

Sample Topics:

1. **Women:** Analyze what the story has to say about women and their relationship to men.

    According to critic Martin Swan,

    > The only real live woman in the story is set up right from the beginning: through a simple misunderstanding, a female American tourist made to represent the full force of Woman's flippant, uncomprehending, emasculating ridicule of Man's achievement—

> "What's that?" she asked the waiter and pointed to the long backbone of the great fish that was now just garbage waiting to go out with the tide.
>
> "Tiburon," the waiter said, "Eshark." He was meaning to explain what had happened.
>
> I didn't know sharks had such handsome, beautifully formed tails."
>
> "I didn't either," her male companion said.

> What is particularly damaging about the woman's accidental scorn is that the Marlin, stripped of its flesh, is a phallic symbol now flaccid or "spent"—all she sees of it or chooses to see of it is "just garbage waiting to go out with the tide." (155)

Reread the story, keeping Swan's arguments firmly in mind. Analyze for yourself the passage that Swan quotes. What does it say to you about the relationship between men and women? Can you locate any other passages in the story that comment in some fashion on gender roles or relationships? Once you have assessed the validity of Swan's claim, write an essay in which you extend, modify, or argue against his thesis.

You might find it helpful to do some background reading on what women's roles were like in the 1940s and 1950s. Try *The Home Front and Beyond: American Women in the 1940s* by Susan M. Hartmann, which while focusing mostly on how World War II altered gender roles in the United States reveals much about how those gender roles were perceived by both men and women before, during, and after the war. Some background knowledge will help you to place Hemingway's work in context. Was he expressing ideas about gender roles consistent with social norms, or was he reacting to these norms in some way?

2. **Joe DiMaggio and baseball:** Why does Hemingway include Joe DiMaggio, a contemporary baseball player, in this novel? What is the significance of the baseball references, and why is DiMaggio important to the story?

Begin with some background reading. You might try *Joe DiMaggio: An American Icon* by Joseph J. Bannon, Joanna L. Wright, and Susan M. McKinney and *Past Time: Baseball as History* by Jules Tygiel. Once you have a good sense of the role of baseball and an understanding of Joe DiMaggio's role within baseball culture, particularly in the late 1940s, go back to the text, and locate and analyze all references to baseball and particularly to DiMaggio himself. At one point, Santiago says to himself:

> I must have confidence and I must be worthy of the great DiMaggio who does all things perfectly even with the pain of the bone spur in his heel. . . . Do you believe the great DiMaggio would stay with a fish as long as I will stay with this one? he thought. I am sure he would and more since he is young and strong. Also his father was a fisherman. But would the bone spur hurt him too much? (68)

What does DiMaggio represent for Santiago? What do the two men have in common? What does Santiago's fascination with baseball and DiMaggio in particular reveal about him?

3. **Setting:** What is the significance of the setting that Hemingway used for this novel?

   How does Hemingway's decision to set this story in a small fishing village near Havana, Cuba, in the 1940s affect your interpretation of the novel? Do some background reading on this period in Cuban history. You might start with Clifford L. Staten's *The History of Cuba*, particularly chapters 1 and 4. Once you have a solid understanding of the cultural and historical context, what new insights can you derive about the story? Imagine that it was set in the United States or in present-day Cuba. How would the story be different?

4. **Biography:** Interpret *The Old Man and the Sea* as a commentary on Hemingway's own personal struggles at the time in which he was writing this novel.

The Old Man and the Sea can be viewed as a return to serious writing for Hemingway; it was the first novel he penned after the unpopular and ill-received *Across the River and into the Trees.* Do some background reading on Hemingway's life. Start with Carlos Baker's *Ernest Hemingway: A Life Story.* How might *The Old Man and the Sea* be read as a commentary on Hemingway's own struggles with writing?

Philosophy and Ideas

The Old Man and the Sea can be interpreted in terms of many philosophical and ideological approaches. You might investigate what this novel says about the concept of *nada* that Hemingway is famous for developing in his early works or what it has to say about Christianity, since there are many references to Christian symbols in the text. Alternatively, you might investigate what the novel is saying about fate and free will as references to choice and luck recur rather frequently in the work. Finally, you might take a cue from critic Eric Waggoner and discuss *The Old Man and the Sea* from a Taoist perspective.

Sample Topics:

1. **Chance and choice:** What kind of commentary does the novel make about free will and chance?

At one point in the story, Santiago reflects that both he and the fish made choices that resulted in the situation that they found themselves in at present: "His choice had been to stay in the deep dark water far out beyond all snares and traps and treacheries. My choice was to go there to find him beyond all people. Beyond all people in the world. Now we are joined together and have been since noon. And no one to help either one of us" (50). This passage suggests that one's fate is decided by the choices he makes combined with the choices of others. Does the remainder of the novel support this claim, or does the novel indicate elsewhere that one's fate is determined not by choice but by chance?

How does luck play into one's destiny, according to the novel? Analyze Santiago's comments about luck, including what he says to himself before he catches his big fish: "Only

I have no luck anymore. But who knows? Maybe today. Every day is a new day. It is better to be lucky. But I would rather be exact. Then when luck comes you are ready" (32). What does this reveal about how Santiago thinks luck works? How is it connected to free will? After he has caught the marlin and is having difficulty bringing him in, he thinks: "Maybe I'll have the luck to bring the forward half in. I should have some luck. No, he said. You violated your luck when you went too far outside" (117). What does this statement tell us about Santiago's thinking regarding fate, chance, and free will?

2. **Nada:** What does *The Old Man and the Sea* have to say about the concept of *nada*?

According to critic Jogendra Kaushal,

> Darkness in which the human life is engulfed is simply irremovable. One has to live in the midst of it, in spite of it. The darkness will remain, looming as large for ever, and so will the mysterious sea. *The Old Man and the Sea,* viewed as the most optimistic of Hemingway's works, has nada in the beginning and *nada* in the end (116).

You might reread Hemingway's short story "A Clean, Well-Lighted Place" to remind yourself of the way that Hemingway uses the concept of *nada*. Once you have done so, return to *The Old Man and the Sea,* and evaluate Kaushal's remarks. Does the sea seem to be associated with *nada* in your reading? Does Santiago's life seem to be "engulfed in darkness"? Write an essay in which you extend or modify Kaushal's basic argument that *The Old Man and the Sea* presents a vision of human existence as filled with *nada*, or craft an argument that refutes this idea, arguing instead that *The Old Man and the Sea* presents a new kind of world for Hemingway, one in which *nada* gives way to a sense of harmony with the natural world.

3. **Christianity:** What does the novel ultimately have to say about Christianity?

Santiago claims not to be religious, yet he tries to bargain with God, offering prayers in exchange for his request, more than once in the course of the story: "Now that I have him coming so beautifully, God help me endure. I'll say a hundred Our Fathers and a hundred Hail Marys. But I cannot say them now" (87). Additionally, the story makes associations between Santiago and Christ. Wolfgang Wittkowski theorizes that Hemingway uses these ambiguous Christian references for a specific literary reason:

> by bringing the basic form of life and the valid answer to it (namely suffering and acting) to perfect realization in battle and in the demiurgic fighter's ethos, he demonstrates and attains outside of Christianity a perfection which Heming-way, with the pride of Lucifer, places alongside and in opposition to that of Christianity. Furthermore, the fighter's ideal encompasses that which is truly authentic in Christ. It lays claim to the respect and esteem usually rendered to Christianity and its creator. It takes the place of Christ. For this reason Santiago's suffering and fighting are stylized into two models, one of which subsumes the other in antithetical fashion: the fighter-in-the-ring and Christ on the Cross. (17)

Identify and analyze passages in the story that seem to speak about religion, particularly Christianity. In your opinion, is Hemingway writing a story intended to be read as parable? Does he have a message consistent with the foundational tenets of Christianity? Or do you agree with Wittkowski that Hemingway is using ambiguous Christian references to point out that there are other approaches to life just as meaningful or ethical as Christianity?

4. **Taoism:** Interpret *The Old Man and the Sea* from a Taoist perspective.

Eric Waggoner writes that "Tao may be roughly translated as 'the path,' or 'the way,' and refers to the passage of the spiritual initiate who attempts to remain balanced or centered in the world, neither a slave to emotions, nor an automaton resistant to the constant changes of which our lives are comprised" (89). According to Waggoner, if we read the story in terms of this Eastern philosophy, we see that Santiago, far from being defeated, actually learns and grows from his experience with the marlin. He discusses in particular the passage in which Santiago ignores the sharks and sails for home, noting that while "[m]ost criticism sees this passage, especially the section detailing Santiago's refusal to notice the hitting sharks, as indicative of his failure," this is actually an epiphany for Santiago, who is learning to yield to the ways of nature. Waggoner writes: "Santiago, who recognizes the 'rightness' of events, does not cry for loss. Manolin, whose understanding of success or failure is bound up (like the townspeople's) with possession of the marlin, does weep" (102).

Read Waggoner's complete argument in "Inside the Current: A Taoist Reading of *The Old Man and the Sea*," and then reread the novel with these arguments in mind. Write an essay in which you agree with and expand on Waggoner's interpretation or in which you argue against his reading.

Language, Symbols, and Imagery

Hemingway's *The Old Man and the Sea* is rife with symbolism and imagery. Critics and readers have interpreted the symbolism in various ways, and they have used their interpretations to help them develop their own unique readings of the novel. Similarly, you can identify a symbol, image, or group of symbols in the novel, analyze Hemingway's use of the symbols, and then develop a thesis for your essay based on your analysis. What does the symbol you have identified stand for? How do you know? Is Hemingway using the symbol in a traditional way, or is he doing something new and different with his use of the symbol? How can an analysis of this symbol help you to understand the novel in a new way?

Sample Topics:

1. **Lions in Santiago's dreams:** What is the significance of Santiago's repeated dream about lions?

> Hemingway emphasizes that Santiago no longer dreamed of storms, nor of women, nor of great occurrences, nor of great fish, nor fights, nor contests of strength, nor of his wife. He only dreamed of places now and of the lions on the beach. They played like young cats in the dusk and he loved them as he loved the boy. He never dreamed about the boy. (25)

What are lions typically associated with? What do these particular lions stand for? How might they be connected to the boy? Why do you think Santiago never dreams about the boy?

2. **Sharks:** What do the sharks symbolize, and how is this symbolism important to the overall themes of the novel?

Some scholars have claimed that the sharks that plague the old man and rob him of his great treasure actually represent literary critics. If this is so, then who is the writer, and what represents the literary work? What is the relationship between the sharks and the writer and the works? Are there different types of sharks? Some better than others? Write an essay in which you discuss what the sharks are meant to symbolize and how that symbolism fits in the larger scheme of the novel.

3. **Christ imagery:** Analyze and interpret the Christ imagery in the text.

Locate and analyze passages that associate Santiago with Christ, such as the description of him after his return from his battle with the fish, lying "face down on the newspapers with his arms out straight and the palms of his hands up" (122). In what ways is Santiago Christ-like? In what ways is he not? Why do you think Hemingway includes this imagery? How is it connected to the larger themes and meanings of the novel?

Compare and Contrast Essays

If you compare and contrast elements across two or more novels by the same author, you will have more material to work with and a broader perspective as well. If you are interested in Hemingway's portrayal of the relationship between human beings and the natural world, for example, you could certainly write an essay that articulates what *The Old Man and the Sea* has to say about this issue. It might be even more interesting, though, to compare Santiago with Robert Jordan from *For Whom the Bell Tolls* or Francis Macomber from "The Short Happy Life of Francis Macomber" in order to throw into relief the variations that Hemingway offers on this theme. Or you might even compare and contrast all three of these characters. Then, you could use the similarities present to make a more general argument about Hemingway's thoughts regarding the relationship between human beings and nature.

Sample Topics:

1. **Robert Jordan of *For Whom the Bell Tolls* and Santiago:** Compare and contrast these two characters.

   Analyze Robert Jordan and Santiago, paying particular attention to their feelings about the natural world. How does each imagine his relationship with nature? Trace Robert Jordan's and Santiago's evolving feelings about nature and their places in it through these two works. From your analysis of the two of them, draw some conclusions about Hemingway's conception of human beings' relationship with the natural world.

2. **Francis Macomber from "The Short Happy Life of Francis Macomber" and Santiago:** Compare and contrast these two characters.

   Francis Macomber's main goal in "The Short Happy Life of Francis Macomber" is to kill game, particularly a lion. In *The Old Man and the Sea*, the struggle is between Santiago and the great marlin he is trying to bring in. Reread both of these pieces, and think about the ways in which Macomber and Santiago are alike and different. Why is each man pitting himself against the natural world? What are his motivations? His obstacles? How does each man perceive his relationship with nature? How do the story and the novel seem to feel about the way the main character treats the natural world? What can we tell through an analysis of these pieces about Hemingway's perception of the ideal relationship between human beings and nature?

Bibliography for *The Old Man and the Sea*

Baker, Carlos. *Ernest Hemingway: A Life Story.* New York: Scribners, 1969.

Bannon, Joseph J., Joanna L. Wright, and Susan M. McKinney, eds. *Joe DiMaggio: An American Icon.* New York: Sports Publishing, 2000.

Burhans, Clinton S., Jr. "*The Old Man and the Sea*: Hemingway's Tragic Vision of Man." *American Literature* 31.4 (1960): 446–55.

Cain, William E. "Death Sentences: Rereading *The Old Man and the Sea*." *Sewanee Review* 114.1 (2006): 112–25.

Grebstein, Sheldon Norman. *Hemingway's Craft.* Carbondale: Southern Illinois UP, 1973.

Hartmann, Susan M. *The Home Front and Beyond: American Women in the 1940s.* Boston: Twayne, 1982.

Hemingway, Ernest. *The Old Man and the Sea.* New York: Collier, 1987.

Kaushal, Jogendra. *Ernest Hemingway: A Critical Study.* New Delhi, India: Chandi Publishers, 1974.

Staten, Clifford L. *The History of Cuba.* New York: Palgrave Macmillan, 2005.

Swan, Martin. "*The Old Man and the Sea*: Women Taken for Granted." *Visages de la féminité.* Ed. A. J. Bullier and J. M. Racault. Denis, France: Université de Réunion, 1984.

Tygiel, Jules. *Past Time: Baseball as History.* New York: Oxford UP, 2000.

Waggoner, Eric. "Inside the Current: A Taoist Reading of *The Old Man and the Sea*." *Hemingway Review* 17.2 (Spring 1998): 88–104.

Wilson, G. R., Jr. "Incarnation and Redemption in *The Old Man and the Sea*." *Studies in Short Fiction* 14.4 (1977): 369–73.

Wittkowski, Wolfgang. "Crucified in the Ring: Hemingway's *The Old Man and the Sea*." *Hemingway Review* 3.1 (1983): 2–17.

"A CLEAN,
WELL-LIGHTED
PLACE"

READING TO WRITE

ALTHOUGH "A Clean, Well-Lighted Place" is recognized as one of Hemingway's finest short stories, you might initially find yourself at a loss when trying to devise an essay topic because it is so short and does not include much action. In situations like this, close reading important passages can be extremely helpful. For this story in particular, a close reading of the passage in which the older waiter thinks about why a clean, well-lighted place is necessary should help to clarify the story's themes and get you on your way toward developing an essay topic and argument. The older waiter thinks to himself:

> It is the light of course but it is necessary that the place be clean and pleasant. You do not want music. Certainly you do not want music. Nor can you stand before a bar with dignity although that is all that is provided for these hours. What did he fear? It was not fear or dread. It was a nothing that he knew too well. It was all a nothing and a man was nothing too. It was only that and light was all it needed and a certain cleanness and order. Some lived in it and never felt it but he knew it all was *nada y pues nada y nada y pues nada*. Our *nada* who art in *nada, nada* be thy name thy kingdom *nada* thy will be *nada* in *nada* as it is in *nada*. Give us this *nada* our daily *nada* and *nada* us

our *nada* as we *nada* our *nadas* and *nada* us not into *nada* but deliver us from *nada; pues nada*. Hail nothing full of nothing, nothing is with thee. (291)

In this passage, the waiter tries to pinpoint what exactly the clean, well-lighted place is a refuge from and concludes that it is "nothing." The way that Hemingway refers to "a nothing" suggests that the "nothing" to which he refers is not a lack of something but an entity, some sort of tangible absence. He thinks to himself that "[i]t was all a nothing and a man was nothing too," indicating his conclusion that man's life, even his very existence, has at its center some kind of gaping hole where something—meaning or worth, perhaps—should be.

The waiter continues his reverie, thinking that "[s]ome lived in it and never felt it" and then incorporating the words *nada* and *nothing* into the words of the Lord's Prayer and the Hail Mary. This sequence suggests that some people do not feel the "nothing" or despair that the waiter knows because they find a spiritual system that somehow protects them from it. But this is not to say that they are exempt from *nada*. These people "live in" the same condition that the waiter does; they simply do not "feel it" because of their faith. What does this suggest about religion? What is its function? According to the story, is it a positive or negative force?

The waiter himself keeps despair at bay not with religion but with a clean, well-lighted place. In this passage, he explains exactly what the place must be like. It must be clean, pleasant, lighted, and orderly. Why would a place possessing these qualities be a comfort to one facing despair? Is the place a metaphor for a kind of mental or spiritual state? Why does the waiter insist that the clean, well-lighted place not have music? What problematical element would music introduce? The waiter also says that a bar does not serve the same purpose as a café. What are the differences between a café and a bar, and why would a bar be unsuitable for comforting people who are disturbed by *nada*?

With the observations and questions you have generated through an analysis of this passage, you are prepared to reread the story and identify other passages to analyze that will help you further your thinking about *nada* and the various ways that humanity deals with this condition. You might wind up writing an essay on this topic, arguing that, according to this story, while people might try to comfort themselves with various tactics, including religion and alcohol, the fundamental human condition is despair. Alternatively, based on your analysis, you might conclude and argue that "A Clean, Well-Lighted Place" demonstrates the different ways that people find meaning in their lives, some of them through religion, some through their families, and some through being kind to others. Or you might come to a different conclusion altogether. Whatever you decide to argue, remember to back up your conclusion with evidence derived from the text.

TOPICS AND STRATEGIES

The sample essay topics that follow illustrate just how many possible approaches there are to writing an essay on a story, even one as short as "A Clean, Well-Lighted Place." After reading these suggestions, you might be inspired to create a topic of your own. Or you might find one in the following pages that you would like to pursue. If so, use the topic and its questions and guidelines to help you generate ideas and organize your thoughts. Do not feel compelled to address all of the subquestions suggested in the topic or to limit yourself to the questions and passages presented there.

Themes

"A Clean, Well-Lighted Place" deals with several universal human themes, including courage, despair, and age. If you choose to write an essay on one of these themes, your task is to determine what the story has to say about this particular topic. For example, if you choose to write about despair, you might argue that through "A Clean, Well-Lighted Place," Hemingway suggests that as human beings mature they inevitably begin to face despair as they realize the truth of the human condition. Alternatively, you might decide to argue, as some critics have, that the story is ultimately about hope because it celebrates the tendency of human beings to want to comfort one another in the face of the despair that is part and parcel of the human condition. Before you decide what you will argue, what the claim of your essay will be, you need to consider the question carefully, examining the story for evidence. Most likely you will find evidence that supports several different claims, and you will need to decide what evidence is the most compelling to you before settling on an argument to make in your essay.

Sample Topics:

1. **Courage:** According to the story, how is courage defined?

   Many of Hemingway's novels and stories deal with courage in the face of a great challenge, such as wartime violence. There is no such imminent physical danger present in "A Clean, Well-Lighted Place." How, then, does the story define "courage"? Who displays courage? In the face of what? How is the kind of courage in evidence in this story different from and similar to the courage displayed in other Hemingway stories, such as "Indian Camp"? The younger waiter says at one point: "I have confidence. I am all confidence" (90). Is "confidence" in this sense the same as courage? If not, what is the difference?

2. **Hope or despair:** Would you argue that the major theme of "A Clean, Well-Lighted Place" is despair or hope? On what do you base this argument?

   Although to many readers "A Clean, Well-Lighted Place" centers on the old man and his despair, for scholar Annette Benert the story is really an affirmation of the many positive aspects of humanity as manifested in the older waiter. She writes:

   > "A Clean, Well-Lighted Place" is, without cheating, a totally affirmative story, one of the very few in our literature. It assumes a world without meaning, life on the very edge of the abyss, but that is not what it is about. . . . It is . . . a dramatization of the possibility, given the above conditions, of man continuing to act, to feel even for others, to think even about metaphysics, to create (with a smile), to control and thereby to humanize both himself and his environment. (qtd. in Bloom 30)

   Do you agree with Benert's assessment? Why or why not?

3. **Age:** What kind of commentary is the story making about age?

One of the waiters says, "I wouldn't want to be that old. An old man is a nasty thing," to which the other waiter replies, "Not always. This old man is clean. He drinks without spilling. Even now, drunk" (289). What do you make of this exchange? What associations and implications are made here? As you think about this exchange, consider also what the old man and the older waiter have in common. How are they similar to and different from the younger waiter? How does the soldier fit into these patterns?

Character

Especially in a story such as "A Clean, Well-Lighted Place," which does not include very much in the way of action, it is a good idea to examine the piece's characters in order to get at its themes and meanings. When you analyze a literary character, be sure to consider everything told to you about that character but also remember to evaluate the reliability of that information. From whom is it coming? Also consider any dialogue that character is involved in and examine the reactions of other characters to the character under investigation. Does your character change in any way during the course of the story? If so, chart and evaluate that change. Does your character represent a certain viewpoint or idea? How do you know? If you judge by the way the story treats your character, what does the author think about the viewpoint or idea he or she represents?

Sample Topics:

1. **The two waiters:** Analyze and evaluate the two unnamed waiters in the story.

   Record what you know about each waiter. Examine the dialogue for clues. Which waiter has what information? What is the attitude of each toward the old man and the café? One waiter says to the other, "We are of two different kinds" (290). What does he mean by this? Is he correct? What determines what "kind" each of the waiters is?

2. **The old man:** Analyze and evaluate the character of the old man.

What do you know about the old man? Analyze the two waiters' responses to him. What does he represent for them? Would you argue that the old man is the main character of the story, or is the story more concerned with the waiters' response to him? Why do you think that Hemingway made the old man "deaf"? What is the significance of this choice?

3. **The soldier:** What is the function of the soldier character in the story?

Analyze the passage in which the waiters observe the soldier and his companion walking down the street. What do we know about them? What can we infer? What are the waiters' attitudes toward them? Critic Warren Bennett writes: "The soldier needs the sexual intoxication of this girl as the older waiter and the old man need a drink. The soldier is no more concerned about military regulations than the old man is concerned about financial regulations, and 'would leave without paying' if he became too drunk" (77). Do you agree that the soldier and the old man are similar in these ways? In what other ways are they similar? In what ways are they different? In this sparse story, why do you think Hemingway included the soldier and his companion?

Philosophy and Ideas

When you set out to write about the philosophy and ideas involved in a piece of literature, you begin by asking yourself what philosophical and social ideas the text engages with. For "A Clean, Well-Lighted Place," you might observe that the story deals with the philosophical concept of *nada* as well as the concept of time as it relates to value or meaning. Once you have identified an idea you would like to pursue further, locate passages in the text that deal with this idea, and analyze them carefully. You might also identify any characters who are associated with the idea and consider them as well. Once you have analyzed the relevant material in your text related to nada in "A Clean, Well-Lighted Place," for example, use your observations to construct a claim that will illuminate for your readers what Hemingway means by nada and what he has to say about it in this story. Two essays about nada in "A Clean, Well-Lighted Place" might end up arguing different things, depending on the writers' particular interpretations of the text. There is no right or wrong argument or interpretation. You want to devise an interesting, unique stance whenever possible and to make sure that you can support that stance through the presentation of evidence derived from your analysis of the story.

Sample Topics:

1. **Nada:** Exactly what does *nada* signify in "A Clean, Well-Lighted Place," and what commentary is the story making on this concept?

   Carlos Baker writes about the concept of *nada* in "A Clean, Well-Lighted Place":

   > [T]he word nothing (or nada) contains huge actuality. The great skill in the story is the development, through the most carefully controlled understatement, of the young waiter's mere nothing into the old waiter's Something—a Something called Nothing which is so huge, terrible, overbearing, inevitable and omnipresent that once experienced, it can never be forgotten (124).

   According to Steven Hoffman, "critics have generally come to see the piece as a nihilistic low point in Hemingway's career, a moment of profound despair both for the characters and the author" (173). Reread the story with these observations in mind, paying particular attention to the concept of nada. In your opinion, what exactly is nada, and what is Hemingway saying about it?

2. **Time:** What kind of commentary does "A Clean, Well-Lighted Place" make about the relative value of time?

   The younger waiter, resentful of the old man for keeping him out late, has the following exchange with the older waiter:

   > "I want to go home to bed."
   > "What is an hour?"
   > "More to me than it is to him."
   > "An hour is the same." (290)

Analyze this exchange and the remainder of the story to determine which view the story supports. Is an hour an hour? Or is time more meaningful or valuable for some than for others? Another way to frame the question: Are some people's lives more valuable than others'?

Language, Symbols, and Imagery

Careful use of language, symbols, and imagery is an integral part of good literature. Analyzing these aspects of a work can be very valuable as an attempt to generate an interesting claim on which to base your essay. You might address the poetic qualities of "A Clean, Well-Lighted Place," the irony present in the story, or one of the symbols Hemingway employs in the work, such as the café. In any case, be sure to keep in mind that each word, phrase, and image was carefully selected and crafted by the author; thus, you are justified in drawing conclusions based on the author's choice of one word over another or the inclusion of a particular image in a particular place in the text. Analyzing language, symbols, and imagery requires very careful and precise attention to language and the appreciation of subtle differences in meaning, but it can also be one of the most rewarding and enriching ways of approaching a work of literature.

Sample Topics:

1. **Poetic qualities:** What poetic qualities are present in "A Clean, Well-Lighted Place"?

   According to Sean O'Faolain, "this story by an acknowledged 'realist' is as near, in its quality and its effect, to a poem as prose can be without ceasing to be honest prose" (112). What are the qualities and effects of poetry? Which of them can you locate in this story? What is strange about "an acknowledged 'realist'" writing a story in this style? Why do you think Hemingway did so?

2. **Irony:** What role does irony play in "A Clean, Well-Lighted Place"?

   According to Jackson Benson,

The fundamental irony of the story lies in the skillfully balanced and controlled contrast between the attitude of boredom (self-absorption) displayed by the young waiter, who has "everything," and the active concern and essential "aliveness" of the older waiter, who has "nothing." The ironic paradox that results is that only through the awareness of nothing or non-meaning can meaning be created. (117)

Evaluate Benson's claim. How is the irony he points to manifested? Is it essential to the meaning of the story? How exactly? Is it possible to read the story in a straightforward, rather than ironic, manner? Think about how that changes the meaning of the story.

3. **The café:** What does the café represent in this story?

The title of the story, "A Clean, Well-Lighted Place," refers to the café in which the old man sits drinking. What does the café represent? Why must it be clean and well lighted? Why won't a bar function in the same way as a late-night café? Analyze in particular the exchange in which the older waiter admits that he is "reluctant to close up because there may be someone who needs the café" (290). When the younger waiter replies, "*Hombre,* there are *bodegas* open all night long," the older waiter responds, "You do not understand. This is a clean and pleasant café. It is well lighted. The light is very good and also now, there are shadows of the leaves" (290). Why does the waiter feel the need to keep the café open? What is the significance of the "shadows of the leaves"?

4. **Iceberg principle:** Analyze and evaluate the style of "A Clean, Well-Lighted Place" in the context of Hemingway's ideas of the "iceberg principle."

"A Clean, Well-Lighted Place" is regarded by many critics as one of Hemingway's finest short stories, particularly because of its subtlety and understatement. Hemingway himself considered this story to be one of the best examples of his use of the iceberg principle. He explains this theory as follows:

> If it is any use to know it, I always try to write on the principle of the iceberg. There is seven-eighths of it underwater for every part that shows. Anything you know you can eliminate and it only strengthens your iceberg. It is the part that doesn't show. If a writer omits something because he does not know it then there is a hole in the story. (Mangum 1622)

Reread the story with this iceberg principle in mind. How does it operate in this story? What does Hemingway keep beneath the surface? Do you agree that subtlety and understatement are desirable qualities in literature? Why or why not? Do they enhance the meaning and the power of stories such as "A Clean, Well-Lighted Place"? How exactly?

Compare and Contrast Essays

Compare and contrast essays can be some of the most fun to write and some of the most interesting to read. You can compare and contrast elements within a single work or elements across multiple pieces. You might, for example, compare and contrast the two waiters in "A Clean, Well-Lighted Place," or you might compare the story to another work such as T. S. Eliot's "The Waste Land" or Wallace Stevens's "The Snow Man." Additionally, you might compare and contrast two versions of a single work, such as the original and emended versions of "A Clean, Well-Lighted Place," using your analysis to help you come to a greater understanding of the work's themes. Any comparing and contrasting you do will allow you to speak about the work of literature you are studying with a wider perspective and enable you to perceive subtler nuances of meaning. When you write your essay, make sure to do more than simply list the similarities and differences you have discovered between the two elements you have examined; use your findings in support of a claim that will help your readers appreciate the text(s) in a new or deeper way.

Sample Topics:

1. **"A Clean, Well-Lighted Place" and T. S. Eliot's "The Waste Land":** Read Eliot's poem "The Waste Land," and compare it to Hemingway's "A Clean, Well-Lighted Place."

   Consider the way that each of these literary pieces grapples with the concept of spiritual loss. How does humanity cope with this problem in each of these pieces? Which piece ultimately offers a more hopeful message?

2. **Original versus emended text:** How would your interpretation of "A Clean, Well-Lighted Place" differ if you read the original versus the emended text?

   There has been a great deal of critical controversy over the lines in the story in which the two waiters discuss the old man's suicide attempt. In general, Hemingway does not make clear which waiter speaks which lines. According to William E. Colburn, there is one line that definitely belongs to the younger waiter: "He's lonely. I'm not lonely. I have a wife waiting in bed for me." Colburn claims that if we use this line as a marker and trace the conversation backward, we learn that it is the older waiter who has the information about the suicide attempt. However, if we count forward from the same line—"He's lonely. I'm not lonely. I have a wife waiting in bed for me"—as our initial starting point, we come to the conflicting conclusion that it is the younger waiter who has the information about the suicide (Ryan 80). In order to fix this perceived problem, a scholar named John Hagopian persuaded publishers to emend the text. In the original text, the lines read:

   > "His niece looks after him."
   > "I know. You said she cut him down."

   Texts in the "Hagopian tradition" read this way:

"His niece looks after him. You said she cut him down."
"I know." (Flora 21–22)

You may want to read Ken Ryan's "The Contentious Emendation of Hemingway's 'A Clean, Well-Lighted Place'" and
David Kerner's "Hemingway's Attention to 'A Clean, Well-
Lighted Place'" for some additional background on the controversy. Then, reread the story, paying careful attention to the
dialogue. How is the story different if you read it in the original and then the emended version? Write an essay in which
you make a case that one version works better than the other
with the story's overall themes and patterns.

3. **"A Clean, Well-Lighted Place" and Wallace Stevens's "The
Snow Man":** Read Wallace Stevens's poem "The Snow Man,"
and compare it to Hemingway's "A Clean, Well-Lighted Place."

According to Robert Fleming, Stevens's poem, particularly its
concluding notion that the speaker sees the "Nothing that is
not there and the nothing that is," may have been the inspira-
tion for Hemingway's "nada." Examine the concept of nothing,
or nada, in both of these works. In what ways are Stevens's and
Hemingway's ideas similar? In what ways are they different?

Bibliography for "A Clean, Well-Lighted Place"

Baker, Carlos. *Hemingway: The Writer as Artist.* 4th ed. Princeton, NJ: Princeton UP, 1972.

Bennett, Warren. "Character, Irony and Resolution in 'A Clean, Well-Lighted
Place.'" *American Literature* 42.1 (1970): 70–79.

Benson, Jackson J. *Hemingway: The Writer's Art of Self-Defense.* Minneapolis: U
of Minnesota P, 1969.

Bloom, Harold, ed. *Ernest Hemingway: Comprehensive Research and Study Guide.*
Bloom's Major Short Story Writers Ser. New York: Chelsea House, 1999.

Fleming, Robert E. "Wallace Stevens's 'The Snow Man' and Hemingway's 'A
Clean, Well-Lighted Place.'" *ANQ: A Quarterly Journal of Short Articles,
Notes, and Reviews* 2.2 (1989): 61–63.

Flora, Joseph M. *Ernest Hemingway: A Study of the Short Fiction.* Twayne's Studies in Short Fiction Ser. Boston: Twayne, 1989.

Hemingway, Ernest. "A Clean, Well-Lighted Place." *The Complete Short Stories of Ernest Hemingway: The Finca Vigía Edition.* New York: Scribners, 1987. 288–91.

Hoffman, Steven K. " 'Nada' and the Clean, Well-Lighted Place: The Unity of Hemingway's Short Fiction." *New Critical Approaches to the Short Stories of Ernest Hemingway.* Ed. Jackson J. Benson. Durham, NC: Duke UP, 1990. 172–91.

Kerner, David. "Hemingway's Attention to 'A Clean, Well-Lighted Place.'" *Hemingway Review* 13.1 (1993): 48–62.

Mangum, Bryant. "Ernest Hemingway." *Critical Survey of Short Fiction.* Ed. Frank Magill. Pasadena, CA: Salem Press, 1982. 621–28.

O'Faolain, Sean. "A Clean, Well-Lighted Place." *Hemingway: A Collection of Critical Essays.* Ed. Robert P. Weeks. Englewood Cliffs, NJ: Prentice-Hall, 1962. 112–13.

Ryan, Ken. "The Contentious Emendation of Hemingway's 'A Clean, Well-Lighted Place.'" *Hemingway Review* 18.1 (1998): 78–91.

"HILLS LIKE
WHITE ELEPHANTS"

READING TO WRITE

H EMINGWAY's "Hills Like White Elephants" was published in 1927. Set in a train station in Spain, the story seems merely to present a conversation, or disagreement, between an American man and his female partner. Beneath the surface of this deceptively simple story, however, there is an enormous amount of emotional and psychological maneuvering going on. Although everything is coded in irony and subtleties, the two main characters manage to make their differing perspectives on the woman's pregnancy clear. The man sees it as a hindrance to their self-indulgent lifestyle and wants the woman to abort the fetus so that everything can return to the way it was before. The woman, on the other hand, resists the man's advice, displaying a nascent belief that perhaps the pregnancy could lead them both to a life of greater meaning. By the story's end, it is unclear whether the woman has made her decision, but what does seem to be clear is the growing distance between her and the man. The relationship seems doomed. A close look at the story's opening passage helps set up its themes and meanings:

> The hills across the valley of the Ebro were long and white. On this side there was no shade and no trees and the station was between two lines of rails in the sun. Close against the side of the station there was the warm shadow of the building and a curtain, made of strings of bamboo beads, hung across the open door into the bars, to keep out flies. The American and the girl with him sat at a table in the shade, outside the building. It was

> very hot and the express from Barcelona would come in forty minutes. It stopped at this junction for two minutes and went on to Madrid. (211)

If we are analyzing this passage once we have read the story all the way through, then we know that the couple is facing a decision about the woman's pregnancy and that the two disagree about the best course of action. The fact that the story opens with the couple waiting in a stultifying space for a train that will stop for two minutes at their station before going on to Madrid, where, presumably, the woman could have the abortion performed, emphasizes how critical their decision is. They have some time to talk things over and to make each other aware of their positions, but once the train arrives there will be only a two-minute window either to board or turn away. The suggestion here is that the actual decision is not one that can be gradually implemented; once the path is chosen, there is no way to turn back or choose another course. Getting on that train when it makes its two-minute stop is irrevocable, as is having the abortion.

Think for a moment about the setting that Hemingway describes here. Our main characters are located in a place with "no shade" and "no trees," a place where it is "very hot" and where precautions must be taken to keep out the flies. Such a setting suggests barrenness and decay. If we read the setting as a suggestion of the psychological condition of the couple and their relationship, then it appears that their relationship has no chance to grow or flourish; it is in a state of stagnation and decomposition. Considering the remainder of the story, we have a good idea about why this is. Because the man and the woman have different ideas about how they should handle the pregnancy, it is unlikely that the relationship can be saved, no matter what choice they ultimately make. The man wants the relationship to return to the way it was before the woman became pregnant, but the woman knows that this is not possible. Even if she aborts the baby, life will not return to its pre-pregnancy bliss because she would then have cause to question the self-indulgent way that she and the man have been living their lives.

The initial paragraph offers little in the way of clues as to the decision the couple will make. We might consider, though, how the main characters are introduced for some idea as to their relative power in the decision-making process. They are described as the "American and the girl with him." The man is listed first, and the woman is mentioned only in relationship to the man. We do not have the "American and the girl," but the "American and the girl *with him*." Additionally, the girl is in reality an adult female; the fact that she is referred to as a "girl" instead of a woman indicates that she is the less powerful of the couple and probably is guided and supported by the man. From these factors, we must consider whether the man's wishes—to abort the baby—will likely prevail over the woman's. To give further credence to this idea, we might read the barren landscape described in the opening paragraph as a prediction not of the fate of the couple's relationship but of their unborn baby.

Based on this analysis of the initial paragraph of the story, you might consider identifying other passages that describe the setting and investigate its significance. Do other descriptions of the setting seem to correlate with the couple's psychological state? How can an analysis of Hemingway's depiction of the surrounding environment help you better understand the internal motivations and preoccupations of the characters? You might also continue to think about the power dynamics between the couple and what effect this will likely have on their decision about the pregnancy and their continued relationship. Does the woman seem to be submissive or under the control of the man in the remainder of the story? If not, is the opening intentionally misleading in this way or do the couple's roles evolve in the course of the story?

No matter what line of questioning you decide to pursue or what suggested topic you choose to write about, you will want to reread the story several times in order to identify pertinent passages. Analyzing these passages will help you gain a deeper understanding of the story's complexities and will likely lead you to ask questions and pursue lines of thinking you might not have discovered otherwise. Close reading passages will also be an excellent method of identifying evidence to back up your claim once you have decided what you want to argue in your essay.

TOPICS AND STRATEGIES

The topics suggested in the following pages are by no means exhaustive. Feel free to develop your own topic or to modify one of the topics listed here. If you decide to use one of the suggestions, it is best to think of the subquestions and the suggested passages as a rough guide, as arrows pointing you to new thoughts, new questions, and new ideas. Before you begin to draft your essay, you will need to synthesize your findings and your ideas about the topic you have chosen into one single claim, ideally one that helps your reader to develop new insights and a new appreciation for the story.

Themes

"Hills Like White Elephants" is a story about two people faced with some critical decisions about their future; the short, spare story delves into some complicated and sophisticated themes, including (mis)communication, the nature of romantic love, and the best way to live a life. If you elect to write an essay about one of these themes, you will want to analyze the relevant portions of the text, paying careful attention to the dialogue between the characters as well as the subtext. What can you tell about their feelings by their movements, for example? In addition, you will want to think about the narration and how, despite the fact that it seems objective and unbiased, it might influence your perception of the characters and their relationship with each other.

Sample Topics:

1. **Communication:** "Hills Like White Elephants" consists mainly of dialogue, yet the American and his partner, "Jig," seem to have trouble understanding each other. What do you think the story has to say about communication and the capacity of language to bond or to separate people?

   According to Patricia Smiley's "Gender-Linked Miscommunication in 'Hills Like White Elephants,'" the miscommunication between the two characters is caused by "gender-linked language patterns." Smiley writes:

   > In spite of the sparse details of the plot, the subtle and dramatic dialogue in "Hills Like White Elephants" reveals a clear, sensitive portrait of two strong personalities caught in a pattern of miscommunication due to gender-linked language patterns. Jig's language covers a wide range of moods; but whether she is light, sarcastic, emotional, or deferential, her language is traditionally feminine. The American uses few words, speaks in direct sentences, effectively translates the world and achieves his goals, and is therefore traditionally masculine. (10)

You might wish to read Smiley's argument in its entirety to get a complete sense of it. Additionally, you might want to do your own research into gender differences in language use. Try Mary M. Talbot's *Language and Gender: An Introduction* for starters. Once you have done your research, return to the story and analyze the dialogue. Is there evidence that gender-based language patterns are at the root of the miscommunication? If the problem is not connected to gender-based language, what other explanation is there for the couple's failure to communicate successfully?

2. **Romantic love:** The fate of a romantic relationship is at the center of this poignant, spare story. What does it ultimately have to say about the nature of romantic love?

   What do you know about the two people, the American and the woman called "Jig," who are the main characters in the story? What can you tell about their relationship? How do they usually spend their time? What are their goals? What does their behavior tell you about the way that they treat each other and the way they usually make decisions? Do they appear to be equal partners, or does one of them seem to be in control? How can you tell? Would you call this relationship a healthy one? Why or why not? How do you think it will stand the test of time? Are there any indicators in the story? All told, what kind of statement does "Hills Like White Elephants" make about romantic love? Would you consider it a positive, or at least hopeful, one, or does it suggest that attempts at such a connection are futile and ultimately doomed to failure?

3. **The purpose of life:** According to "Hills Like White Elephants," what is the best, most fulfilling way to live a life? Indulging in one's own wishes or taking responsibility for the happiness of another?

   Begin by thinking about what the man and woman at the center of this story have been living for. What have their goals been? What has given their lives meaning? How has the pregnancy affected their perceptions of their own roles in the world? Does either of them develop a different sense of purpose or possibility from the unexpected pregnancy? What, ultimately, is the story saying about the purpose of life? Does it condemn one way of living in favor of another?

Character

There are three important characters in "Hills Like White Elephants," the unnamed American, his female partner, whom he refers to as "Jig," and their unborn baby. You might focus on any of these as a starting point for your essay. You will want to evaluate whether the character you have chosen remains static through the course of the story or has developed or evolved in some fashion. You will also want to think about how your character appears to other characters, including the narrator, and you will want to think about how self-aware your character is. Finally, you will want to try to determine the overall attitude toward your character inherent in the work. If the story had a voice of its own, for example, would it be singing the praises of the American, making excuses for him, or fervently criticizing him?

Sample Topics:

1. **The American:** Analyze and evaluate the character of the American.

   Why do you think Hemingway opts to give this character no name but to refer to him only as "the American"? Why is his nationality important to the story? Does the American change through the course of the story, or does his character remain static? Is he a sympathetic character? Would you consider him or the woman to be the protagonist of the story? For what reasons?

2. **Jig:** Analyze and evaluate the pregnant woman in "Hills Like White Elephants."

   What do you make of the way the woman is referred to in the story? What does the American call her? How about the narrator? Of what significance are these appellations? What do you know about the "girl"? How does she feel about her pregnancy? How does she feel about the American? Would you classify her as a strong, independent woman or one who is dependent on and submissive to men? Does she change through the course of the story? How, and how do you know? Most critics agree that the woman is a more sympathetic and likable character than the man. Do you agree? If so, what do you think makes the woman the character with whom readers tend to side? What effect does this have on our overall interpretation of the story?

3. **The baby:** "Hills Like White Elephants" has two obvious main characters, the American and his partner. But what about their unborn baby? What role does he or she play in the story?

Perhaps the significance of the baby to the story is its surprising lack of significance to its parents. Margaret Bauer notes that its welfare is of

> little concern to the characters. The man, of course, perceives the child only as a white elephant in the most negative sense of the term.... The woman, the more positively characterized of the two and thus the one receiving more of the author's approval, does apparently recognize that she is carrying a potentially valuable life, but her primary concern seems to be her relationship with her lover. (132)

Reread the text of the story with Bauer's argument in mind. Do you agree with her assessment of the American and the woman's perception of their child? What does this signify about them?

History and Context

It can be counterproductive and even highly misleading to read a piece of literature through our current 21st-century perspective without considering its historical and social context. "Hills Like White Elephants" was published in 1927, after World War I and during a period in history in which many former soldiers were still struggling to readjust to civilian life, and in which many Americans, suffering from disillusionment and despair, declined to live in America, becoming expatriates and often relocating to Europe. We must also keep in mind the difference between modern-day medical care and technology and what was available in the 1920s; though antiseptics were introduced in the late 19th century and so helped to reduce the chances that a woman would die as a result of an abortion, it was still far from as simple a procedure as the American makes it out to be. Some background reading on World War I and the history of abortion and medical practices in the early 20th century will give you a much better perspective on the events and attitudes displayed in "Hills Like White Elephants" and may even provide you with the basis of an essay in which you discuss the story as Hemingway's response to contemporary social ideas.

Sample Topics:

1. **Post–World War I operations/abortion:** Although the American keeps trying to convince his partner that an abortion is a routine, safe, and simple operation, the woman harbors doubts. How are her concerns treated in the story? What does "Hills Like White Elephants" ultimately have to say about abortion?

   Begin by reading some background information on abortion and medical technology in the 1920s. You might begin with *When Abortion Was a Crime: Women, Medicine, and Law in the United States, 1867–1973* by Leslie J. Reagan. Was abortion considered safe at this time? Ethical? What was known about its potential long-term psychological effects? Now return to "Hills Like White Elephants." How is abortion presented in the story? Does Hemingway portray what we would think of as a pro-life or pro-choice stance? Is he accurately depicting social attitudes toward abortion in the 1920s? Is he responding to them in some way?

2. **World War I:** Considering the time period in which this piece was written and is set, Margaret Bauer suggests that the American, "like so many of Hemingway's protagonists, is suffering from what we now call post traumatic stress syndrome" due to wartime experiences (132). She notes that he is an American but has not returned to his home country, and suggests that this is perhaps because he is not yet prepared to resume a "normal" life. Noting

the lack of direct references to the war, however, Bauer warns about the dangers of "imposing a World War I experience on just any Hemingway character" (133). What role, if any, do you think World War I plays in "Hills Like White Elephants"?

Begin with some background reading on World War I and the long-term psychological effects of combat on soldiers, such as *Fallen Soldiers: Reshaping the Memory of the World Wars* by George L. Mosse or *A War of Nerves: Soldiers and Psychiatrists in the Twentieth Century* by Ben Shephard. Then, reread the story with this information and Bauer's comments in mind. Can you locate any references to war or any indications of post-traumatic stress in the story? Can you justify bringing World War I and its psychological effects to bear on the American's behavior? If so, does it make him a more sympathetic character? How might it help to explain his behavior?

Form and Genre

Though we often tend immediately to focus on character or symbolism when we are faced with the challenge of crafting an essay on a particular novel or short story, it can be just as illuminating to focus on other foundational elements of literature. In "Hills Like White Elephants," for example, eschewing the more traditional character and symbolism and opting instead to analyze the story's ambiguous ending, the narrative technique that Hemingway employs to tell the story, or the interaction between setting and theme, can set you on the path to an interesting interpretation that you may not have otherwise arrived at.

Sample Topics:

1. **Ambiguous ending:** Analyze and evaluate the ending of "Hills Like White Elephants."

Critics have long disagreed over the ending to "Hills Like White Elephants." Many argue that the woman submits to the man's wishes and will have the abortion, though the relationship will probably not endure for long afterward. Others have a different take. Stanley Renner, for example, writes that a "study of Hemingway's characterization of the pregnant girl as she struggles with the American's wishes and her own feelings points . . . toward the conclusion that she decides not to have an abortion, and her companion, though not without strong misgivings, acquiesces in her decision" (27). Reread the story, paying particular attention to any clues that Hemingway provides about the ending. Can you make an argument that the woman decides to have the abortion or, conversely, not to have it? Can you tell whether the relationship will likely last? If you believe it will not last, who will be the one to end it? Include in your argument a discussion of why you think Hemingway created such an intentionally ambiguous ending. How does the ambiguity shape the overall story?

2. **Narration:** The praise that Hemingway garnered for the technical virtuosity of "Hills Like White Elephants" seems at odds with the straightforward, uncomplicated narration that he employs to tell the story. Analyze and evaluate the narration of "Hills Like White Elephants" to explain this apparent incongruity.

   How would you describe the narrator? As biased or unbiased? Objective? Observant? Why do you think Hemingway chose to employ a narrator of this type? Of what significance is this choice to the story? It might be helpful to think about how the story would change if it were narrated by someone else, one of the two main characters, for example. Would our perception of the events in the story change? How so?

3. **Setting:** The setting of "Hills Like White Elephants" is described with a great deal of care. Of what significance is the setting to the overall themes and meanings of the story?

   According to literary critic Stanley Renner, Hemingway represents the essential conflict in the story through a careful description of the setting, creating a setting with two "sides," each connected with a different set of values. The side that the couple is on as the story begins is described as follows: "On this side there was no shade and no trees and the station was between two lines of rails in the sun." This setting is connected with the couple's decision to have the abortion; it is associated with "sterility, aridity, the taste of licorice, and the pregnancy as a white elephant on the girl's hands" (Renner 32). However, this is only one option. Through the setting, Hemingway indicates the possibility of a different choice: "Across, on the other side, were fields of grain and trees along the banks of the Ebro." In this element of the setting "are the values associated with having a child: fertility, the water of life, fruitfulness—in short, pregnancy as a precious, even sacred, manifestation of the living power of nature" (Renner 32).

Examine and evaluate Renner's claims. Do you agree with his assessment of the symbolic significance of the setting? If his claims are correct, how does an understanding of the symbolic significance of the setting help you to come to a fuller understanding of the story's themes or meanings? Write an essay in which you expand on, modify, or counter Renner's claims.

Language, Symbols, and Imagery

Because "Hills Like White Elephants," like much of Hemingway's work, is profoundly symbolic, an analysis of any of the story's symbols or images will likely prove fruitful. If you are interested in the symbols and imagery of "Hills Like White Elephants," read the story closely, identifying the particular images you find most striking or significant. Then, analyze the passages in which those images appear. Are they associated with certain characters, perspectives, or ideas? Is Hemingway using the image in a traditional way, or does he seem to be inventing new associations for it? Although there are many symbols and images to choose from in "Hills Like White Elephants," two particularly intriguing ones are the image of the white elephant and the possible metaphorical significance of the abortion. Whichever symbol you decide to focus on, when you are drafting your essay, make sure that you do not simply explore the many possibilities of the meaning of a particular symbol or write what amounts to a list of several symbols and their corresponding meanings. Instead, you want to use your analysis of an image or set of images to help you arrive at an interpretation of the story.

Sample Topics:

1. **White elephants:** What is the symbolic significance of the references to "white elephants" in the story?

According to Lewis Weeks, when we hear the term *white elephant*, we initially think of the "ubiquitous white elephant sale" which "raise[s] money for worthwhile causes by providing an opportunity for people to donate unwanted objects, white elephants, which will be sold at low prices to people who can find some use for them or think they can" (76). Weeks also notes that there is another way to think of the term *white elephant*: "the actual white elephant is a rarity in nature, is considered sacred and precious, and is revered and protected" (77). Weeks suggests that this paradoxical meaning of the term is appropriate, as it accurately describes the way that the American and the woman, respectively, each think of their unborn child, the "white elephant" of the story.

What do you think of Weeks's argument? Can *white elephant* have other meanings as well as the ones he refers to? Do you agree that the white elephant references most likely concern the pregnancy? After you have explored the various possibilities, write an essay in which you offer an interpretation of the story based on the symbolic significance of the references to white elephants. You might use Weeks's remarks as a basis from which to expand, or you might come up with an alternative, and entirely different, explanation of the white elephant references.

2. **Abortion as metaphor:** David Wyche argues that the abortion referenced in "Hills Like White Elephants" should be read as metaphorical, just as most of the story's other elements have been. If you read the story in this way, what might the fetus and its impending abortion represent?

You might wish to develop your own independent reading of the meaning of the abortion metaphor in "Hills Like White Elephants," or you can begin by reading Wyche's essay, "Letting the Air into a Relationship: Metaphorical Abortion in 'Hills Like

White Elephants,'" published in the *Hemingway Review,* and evaluate and respond to the claims and reasoning presented there. In this essay, Wyche claims that the fetus is symbolic of the relationship between the American and the woman and concludes that "[l]ike an aborted fetus, the love affair has died before it had time to grow into a complex and meaningful life" (72). Write an essay in which you expand or modify Wyche's argument, or present an alternative interpretation of the abortion as metaphor in "Hills Like White Elephants."

Compare and Contrast Essays

Comparing and contrasting a piece of literature with another that is similar in some fundamental way can often yield surprising insights about both pieces. You might wish to compare "Hills Like White Elephants" to another of Hemingway's stories, such as "Soldier's Home," for example, to discuss the fate of marriage and family in post–World War I society. Or, building on insights by critic Hildy Coleman, you might compare Hemingway's story to a Grimms fairy tale with which it has much in common. Both "Hills Like White Elephants" and "Clever Hans" feature a "relationship between an obtuse and selfish young man and a patient, giving girl" (70). You might use this comparison to discuss whether gender roles or attitudes toward family life have remained relatively static or whether they have changed in fundamental ways between the recording of "Clever Hans" and the penning of "Hills Like White Elephants."

Sample Topics:

1. **"Hills Like White Elephants" and "Soldier's Home":** Margaret Bauer notes similarities between the American of "Hills Like White Elephants" and Krebs of "Soldier's Home." Most significantly, "the man in 'Hills Like White Elephants' and Krebs do have in common a resistance to marriage and fatherhood." But there are significant differences as well. Bauer continues: "Whereas the woman in 'Hills Like White Elephants' may be perceived as the ultimate victim of this attitude, Krebs seems to be the victim of 'Soldier's Home'—of his community not understanding his resistance to a traditional lifestyle, as epitomized by his mother's attitude toward him" (133).

Reread "Hills Like White Elephants" and "Soldier's Home." What are the most striking similarities between the American and Krebs? What is different about them? Do you agree with Bauer's claim that Krebs is more sympathetic than the American? Why is this? What do these stories, taken together, have to tell us about attitudes toward marriage and family in post–World War I society? What might these attitudes have to do with wartime experiences?

2. **"Hills Like White Elephants" and "Clever Hans":** According to Hildy Coleman, the American is much like Hans of the fairy tale "Clever Hans" in that he "disregards and mishandles the gifts of love and family offered to him by the girl" (71). Compare and contrast these two stories and their male characters, and craft a response to Coleman's claim.

Read or reread "Clever Hans"; you can find it in *The Complete Fairy Tales of the Brothers Grimm.* In what ways are Hans and the American similar and different? What are the fates of the characters in each of the stories? How can a reading of these two tales side by side help you arrive at a greater understanding of the themes and meaning of both stories? Do you think Hemingway used "Clever Hans" as a model? If so, what modifications did he make? To what end?

Bibliography for "Hills Like White Elephants"

Bauer, Margaret D. "Forget the Legend and Read the Work: Teaching Two Stories by Ernest Hemingway." *College Literature* 30.3 (2003): 124–37.

Coleman, Hildy. "'Cat' and 'Hills': Two Hemingway Fairy Tales." *Hemingway Review* 12.1 (1992): 67–72.

Grant, David. "Hemingway's 'Hills Like White Elephants' and the Tradition of the American in Europe." *Studies in Short Fiction* 35 (1998): 267–76.

Hemingway, Ernest. "Hills Like White Elephants." *The Complete Short Stories of Ernest Hemingway: The Finca Vigía Edition.* New York: Scribners, 1987. 211–14.

Mosse, George L. *Fallen Soldiers: Reshaping the Memory of the World Wars.* New York: Oxford UP, 1990.

Reagan, Leslie J. *When Abortion Was a Crime: Women, Medicine, and Law in the United States, 1867–1973.* Berkeley: U of California P, 1997.

Renner, Stanley. "Moving to the Girl's Side of 'Hills Like White Elephants.'" *Hemingway Review* 15.1 (1995): 27–41.

Shephard, Ben. *A War of Nerves: Soldiers and Psychiatrists in the Twentieth Century.* Cambridge, MA: Harvard UP, 2001.

Smiley, Patricia. "Gender-Linked Miscommunication in 'Hills Like White Elephants.'" *Hemingway Review* 8.1 (1998): 2–12.

Talbot, Mary M. *Language and Gender: An Introduction.* Maiden, MA: Blackwell, 1998.

Weeks, Lewis E. "Hemingway Hills: Symbolism in 'Hills Like White Elephants.'" *Studies in Short Fiction* 17.1 (1980): 75–77.

Wyche, David. "Letting the Air into a Relationship: Metaphorical Abortion in 'Hills Like White Elephants.'" *Hemingway Review* 22.1 (2002): 58–73.

"THE SHORT
HAPPY LIFE OF
FRANCIS MACOMBER"

READING TO WRITE

PUBLISHED IN 1936, "The Short Happy Life of Francis Macomber" has remained one of Hemingway's most popular stories. Critical debate has long raged over the ambiguous ending of the story. Some scholars argue that the shooting is accidental; others that it is almost certainly murder. Still others praise it for its very ambiguity. Critics have also differed on their estimations of the integrity of each of the three main characters, some championing Wilson, some Francis, and others Margot. They also differ on the way they believe the story portrays femininity, masculinity, and romantic relationships. The good news about all of this disagreement is that there are plenty of places for you to enter the critical conversation, adding your unique contribution in the form of your essay. To begin, you might identify and perform a close reading of a passage that seems to you to offer answers to some of the story's fundamental questions. You might start, for example, with the passage in which Wilson describes American women:

> They are, he thought, the hardest in the world; the hardest, the cruelest, the most predatory and the most attractive and their men have softened or gone to pieces nervously as they have hardened. Or is it that they pick men that they can handle? They can't know that much at the age they marry, he thought. He was grateful that he had gone through

his education on American women before now because this was a very
attractive one. (9)

Wilson says that he is grateful to have "gone through his education
on American women before now." Where has he learned these things
about American women? Presumably, he has had exposure to them as a
hunting guide as they accompany their husbands on big game hunts in
Africa. If this is so, then Wilson has encountered only a certain class of
American women, those who are wealthy and likely enjoy a high social
standing, for these are the type of women who would find themselves
accompanying their husbands on such expensive vacations while most of
America is suffering through the Great Depression. With this in mind,
you might begin to think more closely about how wealth figures into
the story as a whole. What does it say about Francis and Margot that
they are willing to spend their money on this African hunt in which they
place themselves in danger to kill animals that they do not need for food?
What has value for them? What does the story seem to think about their
use of resources?

You might spend some time thinking about whether Wilson's description of American women would have described most American women
in this period or whether it might have been accurate for the rich, white
American women that Wilson met on his safaris. Bear in mind that Wilson says that he is glad he has had his education in American women in
anticipation of dealing with "this one." While you would need to go outside the story to demonstrate the general accuracy of Wilson's comments,
you can search the text for evidence of whether Wilson's estimation of
American women is correct when it comes to Margot. Is she hard, cruel,
and predatory? If she is predatory, who is her prey? You might decide to
craft an essay in which you evaluate Margot's character, comparing her
to the stereotypical femme fatale that Wilson has in mind.

Wilson also suggests in his comments that the gender roles of American couples have begun to reverse, that women are becoming "hard"
while "their men have softened or gone to pieces nervously." You might
use your essay to investigate the gender roles in the relationship between
Francis and Margot. Is it true that Margot is "hard" while Francis is
"soft"? If it is true that Margot is "hard" and "predatory," then that suggests that she holds the upper hand and possesses the power in the relationship. Is this so? What evidence can you find for this in the text?

Finally, you might think about what Wilson's comments tell us about him and the way that he perceives relationships. He is thinking of Margot not as an individual full of idiosyncrasies but rather as an attractive specimen of a dangerous group. We get the sense that Wilson does not approve of what he sees as the American tendency for women to be hard, cruel, and predatory while the men are soft. How do you think couples ought to operate according to Wilson? Think about the way that his affair with Margot plays out. Is he trying to replace Francis, or is he trying to establish a different sort of dynamic with Margot? How can you tell? What does the narration seem to think of the various sorts of relationship dynamics portrayed in the story? Does it seem to suggest that Margot and Francis had a relatively healthy relationship? Would the sort of relationship that Margot and Wilson would strike up be better?

A careful look at just one paragraph in this compelling story is enough to give you many ideas to pursue as you think about writing your essay. You can perform an analysis like this on almost any paragraph in the story. Once you have identified your topic or at least have a general sense of the kinds of questions you are interested in, you can locate and close read several relevant passages. More than likely, this technique will lead you to new questions and new passages. Ultimately, you will arrive at a conclusion, an answer to some of your most interesting questions, and this will be the thesis, or claim, of your essay.

TOPICS AND STRATEGIES

In the pages that follow you will find many sample topics that you could use to write an essay on "The Short Happy Life of Francis Macomber." The samples will provide you with questions to think about and passages to analyze. Use these to help you generate ideas, but do not feel that you have to restrict yourself to the subquestions provided in the topic you have selected or that you have to answer all of them. Your essay should not be a series of answers to the questions in your topic. Remember that once you have answered the questions and analyzed the passages provided in your topic and followed up on any leads generated in that process, you will need to stop and synthesize your findings before you begin to draft your essay. Using all of your notes, you will want to construct a single, strong claim or argument upon which your essay will rest. Then, you will mine your notes for the strongest and most compelling evidence to support your thesis and incorporate this evidence into the body of your paper.

Themes

When you set out to write about a theme of a literary work, first consider all of the themes the work addresses. Ask yourself, "What is this story about?" Some of a work's concerns may be obvious, like courage or gender roles in "The Short Happy Life of Francis Macomber," and you can certainly select one of these themes to write about. However, spending just a bit more time thinking about the various issues that the story concerns itself with—asking yourself what different topics the story is "about"—will open up additional options. In the case of "The Short Happy Life of Francis Macomber," for instance, you might discover that while the story is certainly about courage and gender roles, it is also about the consequences of wealth and the relationship between the human world and the natural world. And you might find that one of these themes that lies just a little under the surface is more interesting to you than the ones you identified right away. When you select such a theme, you will have to work a little harder to identify passages to analyze and spend a little longer unearthing clues that will help you figure out what the story is saying about your theme. The good news is that this task can be interesting and exciting, and you can wind up with a fresh interpretation of the story and a very successful essay.

Sample Topics:

1. **Courage and fear:** According to "The Short Happy Life of Francis Macomber," what does it mean to have courage? Which character exhibits the most courage?

   Francis Macomber is revealed as a "coward" when he runs from the lion. His actions stem from the deep fear he feels, which Hemingway describes as follows:

   > [H]e was miserably ashamed at it. But more than shame he felt cold, hollow fear in him. The fear was still there like a cold slimy hollow in all the emptiness where once his confidence had been and it made him feel sick. It was there with him now. It had started the night before when he had wakened and heard

the lion roaring somewhere up along the river.... He could hear his wife breathing quietly, asleep. There was no one to tell he was afraid, nor to be afraid with him.... (11)

What can an analysis of this passage tell us about the nature of fear? How is it related to courage? We know that it would require courage to face the lion, but when Wilson offers to go in after the lion without Macomber, Hemingway describes Macomber as "wanting to find courage to tell Wilson to go and finish off the lion without him" (16). What is Macomber most frightened of? What does this tell us about him? Which character performs the most courageous act? Do you think that Macomber discovers courage in the moments before his death? Why or why not?

2. **Gender:** According to "The Short Happy Life of Francis Macomber," how are masculinity and femininity defined?

What can we tell about gender roles in the story based on an analysis of the Macomber marriage? The narrator writes that Margot and Francis "had a sound basis of union. Margot was too beautiful for Macomber to divorce her and Macomber had too much money for Margot to ever leave him" (18). What does this tell us about their roles in the marriage and in society? Identify and analyze passages that speak to this issue, such as the following, in which Wilson remarks to himself about Margot's harsh treatment of Francis once he has proven himself a "coward": "How should a woman act when she discovers her husband is a bloody coward? She's damn cruel but they're all cruel. They govern, of course, and to govern one has to be cruel sometimes. Still, I've seen enough of their damn terrorism" (10). How do Wilson's ideas about what constitutes appropriate femininity compare to or contrast with Francis's? Are you able to get a sense of Margot's own ideas about femininity? What does it suggest about gender roles that the narrator most often refers to Margot as "Macomber's wife"? Ask the same sorts of questions to explore the construction and expectations of masculinity in the story.

3. **Nature:** What kind of commentary does the story make about human beings' relationship with the natural world?

Reread the story, paying careful attention to how human beings are described and how elements of nature, including the lion, are described. How are they similar and different? What is the relationship between humanity and the natural world? Are human beings shown as a cooperative part of the natural world or antagonists of it? Is the relationship between humanity and nature depicted in the story presented as positive or negative? Is Hemingway criticizing or praising it? How can you tell?

As you think about this question, consider how hunting is portrayed in the story. Is it viewed as a necessity for human survival? A sport? Is it viewed in the same manner by each of the characters? Do they consider it ethical? Consider especially Margot's comments as she insists on accompanying the men on the next hunt: "And I want so to see you perform again. You were lovely this morning. That is if blowing things' heads off is lovely" (9). How is hunting a "performance"? Is Margot's the prevailing view of hunting in the story? If not, what is? Consider also the impact of presenting the lion's point of view in the narrative. Why did Hemingway include those passages?

4. **Wealth:** What kind of commentary is the story making about wealth?

The story is presumably set in the time period in which it was written, the 1930s, a period in which most Americans were struggling financially in the throes of the Great Depression. If Francis and Margot can go on a safari in times like these, then they must be wealthy indeed. What can you tell from the story about their wealth and status and the manner in which they use their wealth and status? Critic Virgil Hutton writes that "The bond between Macomber and his wife epitomizes the American values of money and physical beauty, and the destruction of Macomber implies the collapse of any society that places its values on external things" (248). Do you agree that the story is an indictment of the American valorization of the physical and material? Is there a connection between Francis's wealth and his death?

Character

Character analysis is an excellent way to approach this particular story. Interpretations of "The Short Happy Life of Francis Macomber" vary greatly based on the writers' perception of the three principal players, Robert Wilson, Margaret Macomber, and Francis Macomber. You might perform a character analysis of any of the three main characters, for example, to help you to come to your own ideas about the meaning of the story. Looking at Margot, you would want to note everything you know about her. Note how she behaves and how other characters respond to her. Consider her motives for behaving the way she does. Finally, you would want to consider the time period in which the story is set and think about how Margot compares to other women of her generation. Once you have analyzed and evaluated Margot's character, you will be able to construct your interpretation of the story. You might, for example, argue that Margot's cruelty forced her husband into putting himself into risky situations and that therefore, whether or not she meant to shoot him, she is still completely responsible for his death. Alternatively, you might argue that Margot, as the aging wife of a wealthy American in the 1930s, lashes out the way she does because she feels that her husband is, in truth, in control of her life and her destiny. You might perform a similar analysis of Wilson or Francis, or you might compare and contrast these two characters.

Sample Topics:

1. **Margot:** Analyze and evaluate the character of Margot.

Many critics have referred to Margot as one of Hemingway's "bitches" or femme fatales because of her behavior toward her husband. Feminist critic Nina Baym, however, presents a more sympathetic view of Margot. In a piece entitled "Actually, I Felt Sorry for the Lion," Baym writes:

Margot does not recognize, it seems safe to say, that she too, in relation to these men, is in the situation of the lion—imagined as

> dangerous, but in fact helpless. . . . She has an illusion of power which she exercises in occasional infidelities to her husband, but such exercises rather than freeing her deliver her from the power of one man to the power of another. (119)

Reread the story with Baym's claims in mind. Do you agree or disagree with her argument? Does this change your view of Margot, and more important, does it change Margot's role in the story?

2. **Wilson:** Analyze and evaluate the character of the "white hunter."

Some critics have identified Wilson as the "moral center" of "The Short Happy Life of Francis Macomber," noting that his code of courage is similar to one Hemingway himself often espoused and arguing that Wilson makes it possible for Francis to enjoy a brief period of happiness before he is killed. Other critics, however, such as Hal Blythe and Charlie Sweet, see Wilson not as the hero but the villain of the piece. Blythe and Sweet write:

> Wilson indeed lured Macomber to his death, and the act is calculated. . . . It is also important to note here that Wilson knows Margot will shoot in these circumstances. He has seen the rift develop between husband and wife, he understands what has kept them together, he has seen Margot's control over her husband diminish with Macomber's sudden maturation, and he has verbally widened the gap between them. Knowing Margot has a motive, Wilson, then, has simply provided her with the means (the light Mannlicher) and the opportunity. (307–08)

What evidence does the story provide to guide your reading of Wilson's character?

3. **Francis:** Analyze and evaluate the character of Francis Macomber.

Do you think that Francis begins the story as a deplorable coward and then develops courage and poise shortly before he is shot? Do you read this as a "coming-of-age" story? Or do you agree with critic Virgil Hutton, who writes in regard to Francis, he "illustrates no dramatic change from boyish cowardice to heroic manhood. He is a man betrayed by his own society, which failed to give him the wisdom he needed to stave off disaster when he was transplanted into the deadly world of big-game hunting" (248). Not only does Hutton feel that Francis's courage is judged too harshly, he goes even further, arguing that "Macomber is a good fellow whose instinctive shock at Wilson's treatment of the native boys serves as a foil for Wilson's own inhuman attitude" (248).

4. **Africans:** Analyze and evaluate the African characters in "The Short Happy Life of Francis Macomber."

How does Hemingway portray the African characters in this story? What do we know about them? Why does he include them? Critic Joseph Harkey writes: "To an extent the Africans function as a chorus in the story." He explains that the "blank expression on the servant's face" in the lion scene "serves as a type of commentary of Macomber's action and helps us grasp its moral significance for Hemingway" (345). What do you make of Harkey's argument? Do you agree that the African characters function as a kind of "chorus" in the story? If so, what do their responses to the action tell us about the meaning of the story? What is the "moral significance" of the lion scene, and the story in general, for Hemingway, and how do these characters help create and convey that significance?

Philosophy and Ideas

It can be productive to consider what philosophies, ideas, and social issues a particular work is concerned with and to devote your essay to articulating and then evaluating what the piece has to say about one of those philosophies or ideas. What philosophies or ideas are at play in "The Short, Happy Life of Francis Macomber"? The biggest question in this story, the one readers and critics return to again and again, is whether the shooting at the end is accidental. This question introduces the ideas of fate and chance, which you might choose to examine in an essay. Alternatively, you might choose to examine and evaluate Wilson's philosophy of life, which he expresses in the form of a Shakespeare quotation.

Sample Topics:

1. **Fate and chance:** What does "The Short Happy Life of Francis Macomber" have to say about fate and chance?

    Reread the story, particularly the ending, with an eye toward its messages about fate and chance. What role does fate or chance play in the outcome of this story? Do you think that Macomber's death was an accident? If so, why does Hemingway have this accident occur right after Macomber believes he has had an epiphany? Do you believe that Macomber was somehow fated or destined to die as he did? What evidence in the story supports this interpretation? How does this perspective affect your view of the story as a whole?

2. **Wilson's philosophy:** Analyze and evaluate Wilson's philosophy.

    Some literary scholars have claimed that the moral code espoused by Wilson is similar to Hemingway's own. Analyze the following passage in which Wilson lays his code bare:

    > Worst one can do is kill you. How does it go? Shakespeare. Damned good. See if I can remember. Oh, damned good. Used to quote it to myself at one time. Let's see. "By my troth, I care not; a man can die but once; we owe God a death and let it go which way it will, he that dies this year is quit for the next." Damned fine, eh? (25)

    What does this quotation from Shakespeare mean? How does Wilson interpret it into a philosophy of life, and how is it reflected in his actions? Does the story portray this philosophy as positive or negative? How can you tell?

Form and Genre

A close look at the manner in which a story is crafted can often result in interesting insights and new interpretations of the literary work. In the case of "The Short Happy Life of Francis Macomber," think about the authorial decisions that Hemingway made as he constructed this story. He chose, for instance, to begin the story in medias res, beginning not with the shooting of the lion, which is the earliest event eventually described in the story, but to start it after Francis "had just shown himself, very publicly, to be a coward" (6). Without doubt, this was a deliberate choice on the part of the author, so delving into the chronology of the story and investigating its significance would be a good way to start thinking about an essay. Additionally, many critics agree that Hemingway crafted an intentionally ambiguous ending for "The Short Happy Life of Francis Macomber." Certainly this was deliberate as well; Hemingway could easily have tipped the scales one way or the other, letting readers know whether Margot truly intended to murder or to rescue her husband. You might devote your essay to an analysis of this ambiguity and an evaluation of its success. Does it make for a more meaningful story? How so?

Sample Topics:

1. **Chronology:** Analyze the order in which the story is presented and discuss the significance of this sequence on your interpretation of the story.

   Reread the story paying careful attention to the order in which events unfold. Why do you think Hemingway opted to present the events in this way? Imagine how the story would be different if it began with the shooting of the lion and proceeded in strict chronological order. How would your interpretation of the story be different?

2. **Ambiguous ending:** Analyze and evaluate Hemingway's use of the ambiguous ending in this story.

   Study the ending of "The Short Happy Life of Francis Macomber." In your opinion, is there a way to tell definitively whether the shooting of Francis Macomber by his wife is intentional or accidental? If not, why do you think Hemingway chose to make the ending so ambiguous? How does this ambiguity affect your interpretation of the story? Are there other instances of ambiguity in the story? How do they contribute the effect evoked by the ending?

Language, Symbols, and Imagery

It is helpful to keep in mind the extraordinary number of decisions that an author must make as he or she creates a story. Not only the plot and characters but each symbol, image, and word of a literary work is carefully selected by its author. Thus, it can be quite illuminating to fix your attention on a particular image, symbol, or language pattern. Consider what the work would be like without a certain image or with a different image in its place, for example. Think about why a particular symbol is used in a certain place in the text. Think also about whether the author is drawing on traditional meanings or associations or whether he or she is modifying traditional associations or inventing completely new ones when incorporating a particular symbol or image, such as the lions or red faces in "The Short Happy Life of Francis Macomber." Finally, ask yourself why the author presents information with the precise words that he does when there are so many different ways to convey information in the English language. What other, similar words or phrases might Hemingway have used to title this story, for example? Often, imagining other possibilities can help us to realize the nuances that are latent in the author's choices.

Sample Topics:

1. **Lion:** What does the lion represent in "The Short Happy Life of Francis Macomber"?

The narrator describes the lion's perceptions as he sees the vehicle approaching:

> Then watching the object, not afraid, but hesitating before going down the bank to drink with such a thing opposite him, he saw a man figure detach itself from it and he turned his heavy head and swung away toward the cover of the trees as he

heard a cracking crash and felt the slam of a .30-06 220 grain
solid bullet that bit his flank and ripped in sudden hot scalding
nausea through his stomach. (13)

Analyze this passage and others that give you insight into the
lion's point of view. How is the lion portrayed? Does it represent another character—Margot, perhaps, as some critics have
suggested—or idea in the story? Why do you think Hemingway devotes so much attention to describing the hunt and the
kill from the lion's vantage point?

2. **Red faces:** What are the significance of red faces in the story?

When Wilson is described, the narrator takes pains to mention his red face, and later, Margot comments on it:

> "You know you have a very red face, Mr. Wilson," she told him
> and smiled again.
> "Drink," said Wilson.
> "I don't think so," she said. "Francis drinks a great deal, but
> his face is never red."
> "It's red today," Macomber tried a joke.
> "No," said Margot. "It's mine that's red today, but Mr. Wil-
> son's is always red."
> "Must be racial," said Wilson. (6)

What are the various reasons for a red face mentioned in this
exchange? Locate other instances in the story in which the
colors of characters' skin, particularly their faces, are mentioned. What does Wilson's red face signify? What does it tell
us about him?

3. **Title:** Analyze and evaluate the title of the story.

Think carefully about the title of this story. As you consider its meaning and significance, it will help you imagine
other possible titles that Hemingway might have given the

story, including ones that he tried out and rejected, such as "Dangerous Game." When you read the title of the story only, what are your expectations? How does the story meet and frustrate these expectations? Write an essay in which you demonstrate how the title of the story affects your interpretation of its meaning.

Compare and Contrast Essays

A good way to achieve fresh and interesting insights about a piece of literature is to compare and contrast it with another literary work. In the case of "The Short Happy Life of Francis Macomber," you might choose to compare it to another of Hemingway's short stories set in Africa, "The Snows of Kilimanjaro," and use your essay to discuss the significance of the setting in each of the pieces. Or you might compare and contrast similar characters across Hemingway's pieces—Margot and Brett Ashley, for example—or across works by Hemingway and one of his contemporaries—Francis Macomber and F. Scott Fitzgerald's Jay Gatsby, for instance.

Sample Topics:

1. **"The Short Happy Life of Francis Macomber" and "The Snows of Kilimanjaro":** Compare and contrast these two short stories.

   Hemingway biographer and literary critic Carlos Baker finds significant similarities between these two stories, noting that both concern "the achievement and loss of moral manhood. Both look further in to the . . . men-without women theme. The focal point in each is the corrupting power of women and money" ("The Two" 45). Reread "The Short Happy Life of Francis Macomber" and "The Snows of Kilimanjaro" with Baker's argument in mind. Do you agree with his assessment? What fresh insights about these stories can you obtain by comparing and contrasting them?

2. **Margot and Brett Ashley from *The Sun Also Rises*:** Compare and contrast these two female characters.

Reread these two works of literature, focusing on the female characters, particularly Margot and Brett. Many critics have identified these two women as typical of Hemingway's female characters who step beyond the traditional submissive female role. What kind of portrait does Hemingway create of "nontraditional" women? Are they individual, idiosyncratic characters, or does Hemingway employ stereotypes, such as the femme fatale, in his creation of these women? What does his portrayal of these two female characters tell us about Hemingway's perception of women?

3. **Francis Macomber and F. Scott Fitzgerald's Jay Gatsby from** *The Great Gatsby*: Compare and contrast these two characters. How similar or different are Hemingway's and Fitzgerald's portrayals of rich Americans?

Read each of these pieces focusing on Francis and Jay Gatsby. What do we know about their goals, their relationships with women, the way they spend their money and their free time? What has the apparent achievement of the American Dream gained each man? What has it cost him? As portrayed by these two characters, how are Hemingway's and Fitzgerald's perception of wealth and status similar and different?

Bibliography for "The Short Happy Life of Francis Macomber"

Baker, Carlos. *Ernest Hemingway: A Life Story.* New York: Scribners, 1969.

———. "The Two African Stories." *The Short Stories of Ernest Hemingway: Critical Essays.* Ed. Jackson J. Benson. Durham, NC: Duke UP, 1990. 45–53.

Baym, Nina. "Actually, I Felt Sorry for the Lion." *New Critical Approaches to the Short Stories of Ernest Hemingway.* Ed. Jackson J. Benson. Durham, NC: Duke UP, 1990. 118–19.

Bloom, Harold, ed. *Ernest Hemingway.* Bloom's Major Short Story Writers Ser. New York: Chelsea, 1999. 50–67.

Blythe, Hal, and Charlie Sweet. "Wilson: Architect of the Macomber Conspiracy." *Studies in Short Fiction* 28.3 (1991): 305–10.

Harkey, Joseph H. "The Africans and Francis Macomber." *Studies in Short Fiction* 17.3 (1980): 345–48.

Hemingway, Ernest. "The Short Happy Life of Francis Macomber." *The Complete Short Stories of Ernest Hemingway: The Finca Vigía Edition.* New York: Scribners, 1987. 5–28.

Hutton, Virgil. "The Short Happy Life of Francis Macomber." *The Short Stories of Ernest Hemingway: Critical Essays.* Ed. Jackson J. Benson. Durham, NC: Duke UP, 1990. 239–50.

Kravitz, Bennett. "'She Loves Me, She Loves Me Not': The Short Happy Symbiotic Marriage of Margot and Francis Macomber." *Journal of American Culture* 21.3 (1998): 83–87.

McKenna, John J., and Marvin V. Peterson. "More Muddy Water: Wilson's Shakespeare in 'the Short Happy Life of Francis Macomber.'" *Studies in Short Fiction* 18.1 (1981): 82–85.

Meyers, Jeffrey. "Wallace Stevens and 'The Short Happy Life of Francis Macomber.'" *AN&Q* 21.3–4 (1982): 47–49.

Morgan, Kathleen, and Luis A. Losada. "Tracking the Wounded Buffalo: Authorial Knowledge and the Shooting of Francis Macomber." *Hemingway Review* 11.1 (1991): 25–29.

Seydow, John J. "Francis Macomber's Spurious Masculinity." *Hemingway Review* 1.1 (1981): 33–41.

Sugiyama, Michelle Scalis. "What's Love Got to Do with It? An Evolutionary Analysis of 'The Short Happy Life of Francis Macomber.'" *Hemingway Review* 15.2 (1996): 15–32.

"THE SNOWS OF KILIMANJARO"

READING TO WRITE

HEMINGWAY SCHOLAR Kenneth G. Johnston notes that before "The Snows of Kilimanjaro," which was published in 1936, Hemingway "had not published a novel since *A Farewell to Arms* in 1929" and that his "production of short fiction had been slight since the publication of *Winner Take Nothing* in 1933" ("The Snows" 223). Based on these lapses, Johnston concludes that Hemingway likely wrote this story "to exorcise his guilt feelings for having neglected his serious writing, and to re-dedicate himself to his craft." "The Snows of Kilimanjaro" certainly has much to say about writers and the passion and the guilt that can plague them. But what exactly? And how does the story's message about writing connect to its other themes? To investigate these questions, we might start with a close reading of a singe paragraph:

> We must all be cut out for what we do, [Harry] thought. However you make your living is where your talent lies. He had sold vitality, in one form or another, all his life and when your affections are not too involved you give much better value for the money. He had found that out but he would never write that, now, either. No, he would not write that, although it was well worth writing. (45)

When Harry mentions in this paragraph that he has been selling vitality all of his life, we can assume he believes that being a soldier, a writer, and the husband of a rich wife—the roles we know he has occupied—all involve the selling of vitality. It is worth spending some time considering how these three roles are alike and what each requires. What can it tell us about the way that Harry perceives writing, for instance, that he compares it in this way with soldiering and marrying a rich woman? It is also worth thinking about how these roles are different. Harry indicates that he has been selling his vitality "in one form or another, all his life." In precisely what form does he sell it as a soldier? A writer? A husband?

We must also consider what exactly "selling one's vitality" means. Does Harry actually lose some of his "life force"? Does he become smaller or less alive by fulfilling the roles of soldier, writer, and husband? You might comb the story for evidence of Harry's life in each of these roles to find out. How exactly does each affect him? What does he lose or forfeit in each role? Also, you might think about why it might be—if being Helen's husband is costing him vitality just as writing would—that Harry finds it easier to be husband than writer. What challenges are posed by writing that are not present in his relationship with Helen? How do you think both of these roles compare to the role we learn about through the flashbacks, Harry's life as a soldier? Of course, when doing a close reading, it is crucial to be very attentive to the language of the passage, and this passage does not say exactly that Harry sold *his* vitality, just that he "had sold vitality" all his life. Does this mean that he somehow contributes to the vitality of those around him, perhaps without losing anything of his own in the process?

From the way that Harry introduces his remarks about selling his vitality—he mentions being cut out for what one does and making a living—we can assume that he imagines this selling of vitality as a job. In the way that another person might rely on his knowledge and work as a teacher, or use his leadership skills to run a business, Harry trades in vitality. What does this say about him? Is this his talent? His remarks that "you make your living where your talent lies" and that "[w]e must all be cut out for what we do" seem to suggest as much. Is Harry to be pitied because he does not have anything else to sell except his very life force, or does this somehow translate into a greater degree of nobility or importance for him? Does this suggest that Harry operates as some sort of Christ figure in the story? What about Harry's conclusion that "when your affections are not too involved you give much better value for the money"? This remark seems to indicate that selling one's vitality entails living an inauthentic life. If Harry is selling himself without involving his emotions, does he gain anything meaningful from his experiences? You probably also want to think about whether Harry is offering an unbiased assessment when he says that he gives "better value for the money" when his "affections are not too involved," or whether this attitude is a way for him to protect himself from painful situations.

Once you have thought about all these questions raised by the above passage, you might decide to write an essay that discusses and evaluates Harry's perception of writing, including what it requires of a person and what it provides for the world. Or if you find yourself interested in Harry's genuineness, or lack thereof, especially when it concerns giving others—Helen in particular—a better "value" by keeping his affections out of the way, you might write an essay that evaluates Harry's integrity as a human being. Does the story suggest that Harry's ideas about "value" and emotions are plausible? Still another option would be to use your essay to attempt to trace Harry's psychological development, considering his life as a soldier, a writer, and a husband, and attempting to discover what factors shaped him into the person he is at the time of his death.

Whatever direction you decide to take with your essay, you will want to locate and close read several passages from the story that deal with your topic before you begin to write. This technique will help you narrow your focus, and ultimately, it will prove indispensable to you as you develop the thesis, or main claim, of your essay. Finally, bits of your analysis will find their way into the body of your essay, serving as the evidence with which you will support your thesis.

TOPICS AND STRATEGIES

The topics and ideas that follow are designed to set you on the path to writing a successful essay on Hemingway's "The Snows of Kilimanjaro." Begin by reading through the topics, identifying those you find most interesting or significant. Once you see how diverse these suggestions are, you may be inspired to come up with a topic of your own that is not listed here, or you may wish to combine two or more of the suggestions in a unique way. Remember to use the suggested questions and passages to spark your thinking. Allow them to inspire you to develop your own questions and to identify other passages to analyze for answers. Once you have done what you feel is a sufficient amount of thinking about your topic, you will need to use your notes to come up with a claim, or thesis, on which your essay will rest. The body of your essay will consist of an orderly presentation of the analysis and evidence that you have gathered to support your claim.

Themes

"The Snows of Kilimanjaro" touches on several universal human themes, including artistic expression, romantic love, death, and war. If you decide to perform a thematic analysis of the story, you will want to select just one theme to work with, and then, depending on how broad your theme is, you may need to narrow it down further, working on a particular aspect of the theme you have selected. If you select love, for instance, you might want to focus on the effects of money on love or the effects of wartime trauma on Harry's ability to love. In any case, you will want to identify and analyze passages that you find pertinent to your topic in an attempt to answer the question what exactly is "The Snows of Kiliman-jaro" saying about romantic love, or artistic expression, or the long-term psychological effects of war?

Sample Topics:

1. **Artistic expression:** What kind of commentary is the story making about artists or artistic expression, particularly writing?

   Reread the story, paying careful attention to Harry's remarks about writing. You will certainly want to analyze passages such as the following one in which Harry reflects on his death: "Now he would never write the things that he had saved to write until he knew enough to write them well. Well, he would not have to fail at trying to write them either. Maybe you could never write them, and that was why you put them off and delayed the starting" (41). What does this passage tell us about Harry's hopes and fears about writing?

   Look also at Harry's reflections on his relationship with the rich:

   > [Y]ou said that you would write about these people; about the very rich; that you were really not of them but a spy in their country; that you would leave it and write of it and for once it

would be written by some one who knew what he was writing of. But he would never do it, because each day of not writing, of comfort, of being that which he despised, dulled his ability and softened his will to work so that finally, he did no work at all. The people he knew now were all much more comfortable when he did not work. (44)

What can this passage tell us about the way in which Harry's writing is affected by luxury and comfort? What conditions would be more conducive to a writer's goals? What connections are being made here between wealth and self-expression? With all of Harry's comments regarding writing in mind, think about his motivation. What did he hope to accomplish through writing? What were his obstacles, real and imagined? Based on your observations and analysis, write an essay that articulates the message that "The Snows of Kilimanjaro" contains about artists or artistic expression.

2. **Love:** What does "The Snows of Kilimanjaro" have to say about love?

Examine Harry and Helen's relationship. What is it based on? Look in particular at Harry's comments about love, such as his comment to Helen: "Love is a dunghill. . . . And I'm the cock that gets on it to crow" (43). What do you think Harry means by this? What is he saying about himself here? Look carefully also at the dialogue between Harry and Helen as they discuss their relationship. Harry insults Helen, insisting that it is her money that has ruined him. "Your damned money was my armour," he accuses (43). Shortly after his outburst, however, Harry begins to feel remorse, and says to her: "I didn't mean to start this, and now I'm crazy as a coot and being as cruel to you as I can be. Don't pay any attention, darling, to what I say. I love you, really. You know I love you. I've never loved any one else the way I love you" (43). Although Harry attempts to placate Helen, it appears that he can no longer sustain the deception. In the following lines he reveals that his love for Helen has always been a lie:

> He slipped into the familiar lie he made his bread and butter by.
>
> "You're sweet to me."
>
> "You bitch," he said. "You rich bitch. That's poetry. I'm full of poetry now. Rot and poetry. Rotten poetry." (43)

Why do you think Harry is revealing these things to Helen now? Why does he abandon his attempts to soothe her? Why does he begin to talk about poetry when he accuses her of being a "rich bitch"? What connection is there in Harry's mind between Helen's money and his writing? From your analysis of these passages as well as other relevant portions of the text, why do you think Harry is with Helen? What does he gain from the relationship? Also, you will want to think about the relationship from Helen's point of view. As far as you can tell, what are her feelings for Harry? Are they genuine? Considering both of their points of view, what is this story saying about the nature of romantic relationships?

3. **Death:** What does "The Snows of Kilimanjaro" have to say about death and dying?

At one point, Harry reveals that "For years [death] had obsessed him; but now it meant nothing in itself. It was strange how easy being tired enough made it" (41). Why do you think Harry spent years of life obsessed with death? Does the narrative provide us with any clues? What do you think he means when he says of death that "now it meant nothing in itself"? Does he mean that death is causing other things to take on unusual significance? What things might these be?

What do you make of the way that death stalks Harry? Trace it as it approaches him, paying particular attention to passages such as the following:

> "[D]eath had come and rested its head on the foot of the cot and he could smell its breath.

> "Never believe any of that about a scythe and a skull," he
> told [Helen]. "It can be two bicycle policemen as easily, or a
> bird. Or it can have a wide snout like a hyena."
>
> It had moved up on him now, but it had no shape any more.
> It simply occupied space. (54)

Of what significance is it that death does not in fact appear
as "a scythe and a skull" but can be any shape at all? What
is the significance of Harry's suggestions—that death can be
"two bicycle policemen" or a "bird" or that it can "have a wide
snout like a hyena"? Finally, you will want to look at Harry's
final vision of Mount Kilimanjaro. What does this vision tell
us about death and dying?

4. **War:** What kind of message does "The Snows of Kilimanjaro"
   offer about wartime experiences and their long-term effects?

As a writer suffering from disillusionment and despair in the
aftermath of World War I, Harry can be considered a member
of the "lost generation." You might want to begin your thinking
about this topic with some background reading, such as *Modern
Lives: A Cultural Re-reading of "The Lost Generation"* by Marc
Dolan or *Sylvia Beach and the Lost Generation: A History of Literary Paris in the Twenties and Thirties* by Noel Riley Fitch. Once
you have a grasp of the characteristics of the lost generation,
think about what it means for Harry to be a part of this group.

You will next want to analyze Harry's flashbacks, paying
particular attention to what they have to tell us about his
wartime experiences and the consequences of those experiences. You will certainly want to examine passages like this,
for example:

> *The Turks had come steadily and lumpily and he had seen the
> skirted men running and the officers shooting into them and
> running then themselves and he and the British officer had run
> too until his lungs ached and his mouth was full of the taste of*

*pennies and they stopped behind some rocks and there were the
Turks coming as lumpily as ever. Later he had seen the things
that he could never think of and later still he had seen much
worse. So when he got back to Paris that time he could not talk
about it or stand to have it mentioned.* (49)

What does this passage tell us about Harry and his experiences in the war? Why do so many of his flashbacks as he is dying have to do with the war? Is there any evidence in the story of a connection between Harry's traumatic experiences in war and his failure at romantic relationships or his failure to write?

Character

Because so much of the text of "The Snows of Kilimanjaro" is devoted to Harry's interior monologues and flashbacks, this story is particularly suited to character analysis. In fact, if you make Harry the focus of your essay, you will have so much material to work with that you will have to narrow your topic further. You could certainly write an essay that focuses on the whole of Harry's character, either deciding whether he has redeemed himself by story's end or attempting to trace the factors that have shaped him into the character we see in the opening passages. Alternatively, you could narrow your focus and devote your essay to a discussion of the effect of the war on Harry, to his relationship with Helen, or to his struggles with writing. Another interesting approach to this story would be to analyze Helen, attempting to describe the true nature of her character based on details provided by the story and then comparing and contrasting this image of Helen with the one that Harry offers us. Finally, you might pick an extremely minor character such as Tristan Tzara and use your essay to explain that character's significance to the story's themes and meanings.

Sample Topics:

1. **Harry:** Analyze and evaluate the character of Harry.

   Look in particular at the passages in which Harry reveals his true state of mind as it has been since he met Helen:

> It was not her fault that when he went to her he was already
> over. How could a woman know that you meant nothing that
> you said; that you spoke only from habit and to be comfortable?
> After he no longer meant what he said, his lies were more suc-
> cessful with women than when he had told them the truth.
>
> It was not so much that he lied as that there was no truth
> to tell. He had had his life and it was over and then he went on
> living it again with different people and more money, with the
> best of the same places, and some new ones.
>
> You kept from thinking and it was all marvellous. (44)

What do these passages tell us about Harry? What is the state
of his soul when he enters into a relationship with Helen?
Does the story give us clues as to why Harry has ended up this
way?

You will also want to look carefully at the following passage in which Harry expresses his desire to make some positive changes:

> Africa was where he had been happiest in the good time of his
> life, so he had come out here to start again. They had made this
> safari with the minimum of comfort. There was no hardship;
> but here was no luxury and he had thought that he could get
> back into training that way. That in some way he could work
> the fat off his soul the way a fighter went into the mountains to
> work and train in order to burn it out of his body. (44)

What exactly is Harry trying to accomplish on the safari? Is
he ultimately successful? Has Harry redeemed himself in a
meaningful way before he dies? How can you tell?

2. **Helen:** Analyze and evaluate the character of Helen.

First, take a look at what Harry has to say about his wife. He
describes her as a woman "who had all the money there was,
who had had a husband and children, who had taken lovers
and been dissatisfied with them, and who loved him dearly as

a writer, as a man, as a companion and as a proud possession"
(45). He also notes that Helen

> had a great talent and appreciation for the bed, she was not
> pretty, but he liked her face, she read enormously, liked to ride
> and shoot and, certainly, she drank too much. Her husband had
> died when she was still a comparatively young woman and for
> a while she had devoted herself to her two just-grown children,
> who did not need her and were embarrassed at having her about,
> to her stable of horses, to books, and to bottles. (45)

Does this information make Helen a more sympathetic character? What are her motivations for being in a relationship with
Harry? Is there evidence in the story of her treating Harry as
"a proud possession"?

Pay particular attention to the conflicting information Harry
gives us about Helen. At one point he thinks to himself: "She
shot very well this good, this rich bitch, this kindly caretaker
and destroyer of his talent," although he quickly backtracks on
this accusation, adding, "Nonsense. He had destroyed his talent
himself. Why should he blame this woman because she kept
him well?" (45). Why do you think Harry harbors such con-
flicted feelings about Helen? When you take these ambivalent
feelings into account, how realistic and reliable do you think
Harry's portrayal of Helen is? All things considered, how does
Helen come off in this story? Is she a victim of Harry's deception to be pitied? Or is she a spoiled rich woman who always get
what she wants?

3. **Tristan Tzara:** What is the significance of this character, who
   is based on a real historical figure, to the overall themes and
   meaning of "The Snows of Kilimanjaro"?

   Tristan Tzara was a major figure in the Dada movement, which
   Kenneth Johnston defines as

   > an avant-garde artistic and literary movement that flourished
   > in Western Europe, and to some extent in New York City,

between 1916–1923. Its aim was to discredit all previous art and literature, and to discover reality by a technique of comic derision in which irrationality, chance, and intuition were the guiding principles. ("The Silly Wasters" 53)

Johnston notes that "Hemingway and Tzara were light-years apart concerning the literary tradition, the role of the artist, and the creative process. Hemingway did not reject tradition; instead, he saw himself in competition with the great writers of the past" ("The Silly Wasters" 54). To get a fuller sense of the movement and its objects, do some background reading; you might start with *Dada* by Rudolf Kuenzli. Once you have a strong grasp of Dadaism, you can turn your thoughts to the reasons Hemingway includes a character like Tzara in "The Snows of Kilimanjaro." Why would he invoke the Dada movement, which he despised, as Harry reflects on his traumatic war experiences? How is this reference connected to Harry's difficulty pursuing his goals as a writer?

Philosophy and Ideas

No work of art is created in a vacuum. This is as true of Shakespeare's plays or Cézanne's paintings as it of Hemingway's short stories and novels. Many of the ideas prevalent after World War I—such as the distrust of technology and progress, the loss of faith in a benevolent God, the anxiety of living in an indifferent universe, the meaninglessness of existing in a world dominated by war and arbitrary violence, and the struggle to maintain belief in individual autonomy and freedom—were organized and eventually given systematic expression during this era by Jean-Paul Sartre in the philosophical movement of existentialism. Hemingway, however, responded to and expressed his understanding of these ideas in a very individual and often startlingly original fashion. His was a unique voice that readers recognized as an authentic expression of the difficulties inherent in the struggle to exist. "The Snows of Kilimanjaro" explores and extends some of these ideas. An essay that takes this approach to interpreting the story will be similar in some respects to a thematic essay, but it will be more concerned with the appropriateness and general coherence of the chosen idea as expressed in the story. For instance, such an essay may examine Hemingway's heroic code of "grace under pressure" as a comprehensive response to the problem of how to live with dignity in a violent, indifferent world where the life of the individual lacks any intrinsic meaning. It might begin by asking whether there is evidence in the story that Harry lives by such a code, and if so, what Harry's most important values are.

Sample Topics:

1. **Hemingway's heroic code of "grace under pressure":** Heroism is an essential aspect of Hemingway's work. He consistently defined his heroes through a set of characteristics that form an individualistic moral code. These characteristics include the ability to impose order upon a chaotic world through adherence to a strong set of personal values and the ability to endure pain with dignity. In this fashion, the Hemingway hero adds meaning to his existence.

   An essay about this topic would first establish the values usually demonstrated by other Hemingway heroes, such as Jake Barnes in *The Sun Also Rises*, Robert Jordan in *For Whom the Bell Tolls*, or perhaps Krebs in "A Soldier's Home" and Nick Adams in "A Way You'll Never Be" and "Big Two-Hearted River." Determine the personal values that constitute Harry's code and compare these values to those of the other Hemingway heroes mentioned. In what ways does Harry exemplify the Hemingway hero, and in what ways does he fall short? How does he act or fail to act upon his values? In addition, one might consider why Hemingway consistently creates such heroes. What is he saying about the world and about the place of individuals in that world?

2. **Existentialism:** Existentialism is a mid-20th-century philosophical movement that defines human existence through such themes as freedom and responsibility, the anxiety created by our awareness of existing, and the dread experienced due to our awareness of the inevitability of death. In light of these themes, existentialism considers the struggle to discover or create meaning in life as the most important of all human activities. These basic concerns of existentialism are of great importance

to Hemingway as well. How does he present these concerns in "The Snows of Kilimanjaro"?

An essay on this topic would be similar to the essay on Hemingway's heroic code (as the two are very closely related) but would be more concerned about the philosophical basis of that code as a response to an indifferent, absurd world in which nothing has meaning. Such an essay might look for examples of when Harry remembers being most happy and attempt to answer the simple question "Why?" Alternatively, an essay on this topic might locate those events in Harry's examination of his past that best demonstrate the indifference of the world and the meaningless of life. Such an essay would also seek to determine which events best demonstrate his awareness of the different ways in which people attempt either to avoid recognizing this indifference or to create some sense of order and meaning? How has Harry given into this indifference? How does he struggle against it? In what way is Harry's code a response to this meaninglessness? What role does his obsession with death play in his value system?

Form and Genre

Thinking about a story like "The Snows of Kilimanjaro" as a crafted piece of literature can help you develop your own unique insights about the story. If you examine the most obvious element of craftsmanship in "The Snow of Kilimanjaro," Hemingway's use of italics, for example, you might wind up writing an essay that shines new light on what the story has to say about Harry's state of mind or reality versus imagination. Or you might focus on the story's somewhat controversial ending, which has been faulted for being "unearned." Your essay could put forth your own viewpoint on whether the ending to "The Snows of Kilimanjaro" seems tacked on and inauthentic or whether you see it as emerging naturally and harmoniously from the story that leads up to it.

Sample Topics:
1. **Flashbacks and the use of italics:** Examine and interpret Hemingway's use of italics in the story.

Reread the story, paying careful attention to Hemingway's decisions regarding which portions of the text are italicized and which are set in roman type. What is the significance of the type change? In the main, the pattern seems to be that Harry's flashbacks or memories—events that are occurring only in Harry's mind—are set in italics, while the main part of the story is set in roman. If this is so, why do you think Harry's dream or vision of Mount Kilimanjaro is set in roman type and not italics? What effect does this have on your interpretation of the story? Imagine how the story would be different if, instead of italics, Hemingway had demarcated Harry's flashbacks by use of narrative indicators—such as "Harry remembered . . ."—or by chapter breaks.

2. **"Wow" ending:** Analyze and evaluate the story's ending. Does it provide an appropriate conclusion to the rest of the story?

According to Kenneth G. Johnston, Hemingway added a "wow" ending to "The Snows of Kilimanjaro" by which he means the story has an "ending that cannot be supported by the narrative." Johnston explains: "Harry's few bitter regrets and remarks in his dying moments concerning his betrayal of craft and self do not atone for a wasted artistic life. Clearly he has not earned the flight to Mt. Kilimanjaro" ("The Snows" 225). Return to the story with this argument in mind. Do you agree that the ending is unearned, or do you think that Harry has sufficiently redeemed himself by the time of his death to warrant the vision of Kilimanjaro? Write an essay in which you assess the story's ending, either supporting and extending Johnston's claims or arguing against them.

Language, Symbols, and Imagery

Like other authors of his caliber, Hemingway makes frequent and carefully considered use of images and symbols to express ideas and convey meaning. To identify a literary symbol, you should look for objects or creatures that seem to take on a great significance in the narrative or that recur periodically throughout the text. Once you have settled on a particular symbol or image to analyze, your job is to figure out and then convey to the reader of your essay precisely what Hemingway is trying to communicate with the use of that symbol.

1. **Hyena and vultures:** What do the hyena and the vultures symbolize? What does Hemingway use these symbols to convey?

   Reread the story with careful attention to references to vultures and hyenas. When and where do they appear? How does each of the characters react to them? What do these animals typically stand for? Is Hemingway using them in a familiar way or is he modifying the traditional meaning of these symbols?

2. **Mount Kilimanjaro and the leopard at its peak:** What do the mountain and the leopard symbolize in the story, and how do these symbols help us interpret the story's meaning?

   Begin with a close look at the epigraph:

   > Kilimanjaro is a snow-covered mountain 19,710 feet high, and is said to be the highest mountain in Africa. Its western summit is called the Masai "Ngàje Ngài," the House of God. Close to the western summit there is the dried and frozen carcass of a leopard. No one has explained what the leopard was seeking at that altitude. (38)

   Think about how the story would be different if this epigraph were not included. How does it set up readers' expectations? What about the symbols introduced here? Is the leopard supposed to represent Harry? Helen? Some ideal held by one of them? In what ways? What is represented by Kilimanjaro? Look closely at the end of the story, in which Harry dreams of the mountain. What is its significance for him at this point? What does the scene tell us as readers of the story about Harry's state of mind as he dies?

3. **Harry's wound:** What is the symbolic significance of Harry's wound? In what ways is his external injury reflective of his internal problem?

Kenneth G. Johnston writes: "Harry's death . . . is caused by gangrene: the local death of soft tissues due to the loss of blood supply; the death of one part of the body while the rest is still alive. The word 'gangrene' derives from the Greek *gangraina*, meaning 'eating sore,' from *gran*, 'to gnaw'" ("The Snows" 224). Johnston claims that the wound represents Harry's literary self, which "has been 'dying' for a long time" (224) and that the trip to Africa, which was to help return his focus to his artistic goals, was not enough or not in time to save him from the effects of the wound. Return to the story with Johnston's remarks in mind, paying careful attention to the descriptions of Harry's injury. Do you agree with Johnston's interpretation? Write an essay in which you support and extend Johnston's arguments, or develop an alternative theory about the symbolic significance of Harry's wound. Is it not his artistic self but his capacity to love, for instance, that might be symbolized by his wound?

Compare and Contrast Essays

Another good way to derive a topic and thesis is to compare and contrast two works or elements of two works that seem similar in some significant way. For example, you can compare and contrast the two female characters in Hemingway's short stories set in Africa. Or you might decide to compare Harry to a similar character created by one of Hemingway's contemporaries, such as F. Scott Fitzgerald. Both Harry and Dick from *Tender Is the Night* are troubled by their wives' money, finding that comfort and luxury, far from making it easier to devote oneself to one's intellectual pursuits, actually makes it more difficult. Setting these two characters side by side, you might craft an essay that discusses the perception of wealth in the 1930s. When you plan and write a compare and contrast essay, remember that you are not simply pointing out similarities and differences to demonstrate your ability to identify them; you will use your observations to make a point about the two texts you are studying. A paper that compares and contrasts Margot from "The Short Happy Life of Francis Macomber" and Helen, for example, would not be a simple list of their similarities and differences but would use that information in the service of a larger, more interpretive argument.

You might argue, for instance, that these two characters demonstrate that Hemingway's women are essentially submissive, even though they may seem to be aggressive and powerful. Or you might argue that these stories demonstrate that money more than gender decides which person in a couple has more control in a relationship.

Sample Topics:

1. **Helen and Margot from "The Short Happy Life of Francis Macomber":** Compare and contrast these strikingly parallel female characters.

   Reread these stories, focusing on Helen and Margot. Record what you know about each of them. How are they similar? What are their significant differences? Note how similar these two women are in circumstances: Both of them are richer than their respective husbands; they both accompany their husbands on safari in Africa, where the male characters seem desperate to prove something about themselves; and both women lose their husbands while in Africa. Keeping these close parallels in mind, look at the relationship that each woman shares with her husband. How much control does she possess? What is her relationship with her husband based on? How does her husband seem to feel about her and their relationship? Can you draw any conclusions about Hemingway's portrayal of women based on your analysis of these two characters?

2. **Harry and F. Scott Fitzgerald's Dick Diver from *Tender Is the Night*:** Compare and contrast these two characters.

   Return to these texts with a particular focus on Harry and Dick and their relationships with wealth. How are their desires to work—to write and to practice psychology—affected by their wives' money? How does this, in turn, affect their relationships with their wives? Taken together, what do these two literary works have to say about the effect of luxury and wealth on the will to work? What implications does this have for those who are seeking the American Dream?

Bibliography for "The Snows of Kilimanjaro"

Davidson, Richard Allan. "Hemingway's 'Homage to Switzerland' and F. Scott Fitzgerald." *Hemingway Review* 12.2 (1993): 72–77.

Dolan, Marc. *Modern Lives: A Cultural Re-reading of "the Lost Generation."* West Lafayette, IN: Purdue UP, 1996.

Fitch, Noel Riley. *Sylvia Beach and the Lost Generation: A History of Literary Paris in the Twenties and Thirties.* New York: Norton, 1983.

Gajdusek, Robert E. "Purgation/Debridement as Therapy/Aesthetics." *Hemingway Review* 4.2 (1985): 12–17.

Hemingway, Ernest. "The Snows of Kilimanjaro." *The Complete Short Stories of Ernest Hemingway: The Finca Vigía Edition.* New York: Scribners, 1987. 39–56.

Johnston, Kenneth G. "The Silly Wasters: Tzara and the Poet in 'The Snows of Kilimanjaro.'" *Hemingway Review* 8.1 (1988): 50–57.

———. "'The Snows of Kilimanjaro': An African Purge." *Studies in Short Fiction* 21.3 (1984): 223–27.

Kuenzli, Rudolf. *Dada.* New York: Phaidon, 2006.

Stephens, Robert O. "Hemingway's Riddle of Kilimanjaro: Idea and Image." *American Literature* 32.1 (1960): 84–88.

Stoltzfus, Ben. "Sartre, Nada, and Hemingway's African Stories." *Comparative Literature Studies* 42.3 (2005): 205–28.

Wagner-Martin, Linda. "A Note on Henri Rousseau and Hemingway's 'The Snows of Kilimanjaro.'" *Hemingway Review* 11.1 (1991): 58–60.

"THE KILLERS"

READING TO WRITE

ERNEST HEMINGWAY's short story "The Killers" was first published in *Scribner's* in 1927 and later included in the short story collections *Men Without Women, Snows of Kilimanjaro,* and *The Nick Adams Stories* and has been one of Hemingway's most popular and most anthologized short stories. Literary critics Cleanth Brooks and Robert Penn Warren collaboratively produced one of the more nuanced and well-received interpretations of this piece. They point out that Hemingway's heroes tend to live by a strict ethical code no matter what their fidelity to this code ultimately costs them. Ole's code is the gangster's. Though it is "brutal and dehumanizing," Ole adheres to it in order to make sense of and create meaning in his world. His determination not to run away from his would-be assassins but ultimately to face his fate is his way of remaining devoted to that code. The story, however, is not only about Ole; it is also fundamentally concerned with Nick. Brooks and Warren explain that Hemingway often treats his basic theme on more than one level:

> There is the story of the person who is already initiated, who already has adopted his appropriate code, or discipline, in the world which otherwise he cannot cope with. . . . There is also the story of the process of the initiation, the discovery of evil and disorder, and the first step toward the mastery of the discipline. This is Nick's story. (193)

As you think about the story's themes and meanings and begin to evaluate Brooks and Warren's interpretation, you may want to turn your attention to a close reading of the interaction between Nick and Ole, the two characters at the heart of their analysis:

Nick looked at the big bag lying on the bed.

"Don't you want me to go and see the police?"

"No," Ole Andreson said. "That wouldn't do any good."

"Isn't there something I could do?"

"No. There ain't anything to do."

"Maybe it was just a bluff."

"No. It ain't just a bluff."

Ole Andreson rolled over toward the wall.

"The only thing is," he said, talking toward the wall, "I just can't make up my mind to go out. I been in here all day."

"Couldn't you get out of town?"

"No," Ole Andreson said. "I'm through with all that running around."

He looked at the wall.

"There ain't anything to do now."

"Couldn't you fix it up some way?"

"No. I got in wrong." He talked in the same flat voice. "There ain't anything to do. After a while I'll make up my mind to go out." (221)

In this exchange, Nick seems to be desperately trying to save Ole. In the world in which he lives, men do not get assassinated as a matter of course. He offers to get the police and asks if there is anything he can do to help Ole. When this fails, he tries to envision other solutions, such as having Ole run away or "fix it up" somehow with the people who are after him. Ole's responses indicate how the world of organized crime he belongs to—the world he says he "got in wrong"—operates according to its own particular set of rules. First of all and perhaps most significantly, Ole's world exists apart from the law that governs most people's lives and is designed to provide us with safety and protection. Secondly, there is no way to "fix" whatever the problem is between Ole and the people who have ordered him killed. Nick is imagining settling the issue with communication or perhaps financial arrangements, but in Ole's universe, the settling is done with violence, and Ole seems reconciled to this.

Ole's determination to embrace his fate but to do so on his own terms—whenever he "make[s] up [his] mind to go out," he knows he will be killed—makes him, as noted by Brooks and Warren, one of Hemingway's heroes whose ability to live and even die by a code enables him to cope with and make meaning in what might be perceived as a chaotic and disordered universe. For Brooks and Warren, Nick's exposure to this situation is an initiation for him into knowledge of the evils of the world as well as into the codes and discipline that some use to exist in that world. On the surface, at least, Nick rejects Ole's code; unable to accept its terms, he determines to get out of town.

Nick's response to Ole's stoic resignation to his fate brings up additional questions. If Ole is our hero, does Nick's reaction and desire to escape make him an antihero? Is his idea that he can escape crime and corruption by leaving town realistic? Do you think he ultimately will leave town, or is he simply saying this as he adjusts to a new worldview that incorporates the evil and violence he has been exposed to? Alternatively, you might consider whether Nick's resistance to Ole's inaction is designed not to highlight Nick's initiation into the world of corruption at all but rather to call into question Ole's commitment to the gangster code. After all, Nick's reactions to Ole's situation, including his advice to Ole and his offer to help, seem appropriate and reasonable rather than cowardly.

A look at a seminal critical interpretation of "The Killers" combined with a close reading of a passage from the story has yielded some significant questions to pursue. After additional thinking and analysis, you might decide to extend and modify Brooks and Warren's argument, arguing, for instance, that in resisting initiation into Ole's world with its strict, unyielding code, Nick is forfeiting the chance to be heroic in the Hemingway sense. Alternatively, you might dispute Brooks and Warren, claiming that Nick's logical and appropriate reactions to Ole's predicament demonstrate that "The Killers" does not, in fact, celebrate Ole as a hero but instead reveals the futility of remaining devoted to a brutal, unforgiving code of ethics even in the face of death.

TOPICS AND STRATEGIES

The topics that follow are designed to demonstrate the incredibly wide range of essay subjects you might choose to write on, even when your assigned literary piece is as short as Hemingway's "The Killers." You should feel free to invent your own topic or to modify or combine any of the suggested topics that appeal to you. In any case, remember that much of the work that goes into a successful essay happens before you even begin drafting. Set aside some time for settling on a topic and for investigating that topic by rereading the story, taking notes, and analyzing passages. Only after you have done this preliminary work are you ready to synthesize your findings into a thesis, or claim. This is the point at which you decide what your essay will "say"; you will articulate your particular interpretation of the story based on what you have discovered about the topic you have chosen. Then, you will select the most compelling evidence for your claim from your notes to present as evidence in the body of your essay.

Themes

When writing about theme in "The Killers," you have several options. First, the story definitely concerns the move from innocence to experience for Nick Adams. You might elect to focus your essay on what the story has to say about the discovery of evil. Or if you find that the story is more fundamentally concerned with Ole Andreson than with Nick Adams, you might want to examine Ole's role very closely and use your essay to explore what the story says about "heroic fatalism." Is Ole's attitude one to be admired? Why or why not? Finally, you might devote your essay to an examination of the models of masculinity presented in "The Killers," articulating for your readers what, according to "The Killers," it means to act like a man.

Sample Topics:

1. **Discovery of evil:** What does "The Killers" have to say about the discovery of evil?

   According to critics Cleanth Brooks and Robert Penn Warren, "The Killers" is fundamentally concerned with Nick's progression from innocence to experience. They cite the following passage from the story:

   > "I'm going to get out of this town," Nick said.
   >   "Yes," said George. "That's a good thing to do."
   >   "I can't stand to think about him waiting in the room and knowing he's going to get it. It's too damned awful."
   >   "Well," said George, "you'd better not think about it." (222)

For Brooks and Warren, this passage makes it clear that it is "Nick on whom the impression has been made. George has managed to come to terms with the situation. By this line of reasoning, it is Nick's story. And the story is about the discovery of evil" (188–89). Do you agree that this is in fact the central theme of the story? If so, what point is Hemingway trying to make about it?

2. **Heroic fatalism:** What kind of commentary does the story make about "heroic fatalism"?

According to Philip Booth, "Heroic fatalism, or fatalistic heroism, a dignified, graceful acceptance of one's circumstances in the face of personal disaster up to and including one's death, is a theme that surfaces in Ernest Hemingway's short story 'the Killers' and elsewhere in his short fiction and novels" (410). Who exhibits heroic fatalism in this story? How do the other characters feel about this attitude? What perspective does the story seem to take on heroic fatalism?

3. **Masculinity:** What kind of commentary does "The Killers" make about masculinity?

What models of masculinity are offered in "The Killers"? How do they compare to the modes of masculinity presented in other Hemingway texts? You will want to look in particular at the following comments made by Al and Max. At one point, Al says to Max that he has Sam and Nick "tied up like a couple of girl friends in the convent" (218). After George cooks a sandwich for a customer, Max says, "Bright boy can do everything. . . . He can cook and everything. You'd make some girl a nice wife, bright boy" (219). What is the significance of Al and Max referring to these men as "girl friends" and a potential "wife"? What is it that makes them "feminized"? What does this tell us about the way that Al and Max perceive masculinity? Does the story as a whole seem to endorse Al and Max's idea of masculinity? How can you tell? Does it offer an alternative?

Character

Analyzing one or more characters in a literary work is a good way to figure out what the piece is fundamentally concerned with and what messages it ultimately conveys. In the case of "The Killers," you might focus on Nick Adams, Ole Andreson, George, Sam, or even Max and Al. No matter which character you choose, you will need to analyze closely any dialogue that the character engages in as well as his behavior. In addition, you will need to study the way that other characters react to him and consider carefully any information the narration supplies regarding his personality and his internal motivations. You will want to ascertain whether your character evolves in any way and whether any change he undergoes is construed by the narrative as positive or negative. If your character remains essentially static through the course of the work, then you will want to look carefully at his role in the story. Why did the author include that particular character? Does he represent some idea or philosophy, or is he intended to serve as a foil for another character?

Sample Topics:

1. **Ole Andreson:** Analyze and evaluate the character of Ole Andreson.

   Record everything you know about Ole Andreson. What kind of a person is he? How is he described and perceived by other characters? Look closely at Ole's reaction to Nick's warning. Why do you think he had been hiding in his room all day? What do you think he means when he tells Nick: "No. I got in wrong. . . . There ain't anything to do. After a while I'll make up my mind to go out" (221)? Why do you think Ole seems to accept his fate? How does Nick react to Ole's behavior? Are you sympathetic to Ole and his predicament? What point is Hemingway attempting to convey by having Ole behave in the way he does?

2. **Nick Adams:** Analyze and evaluate Nick's character in "The Killers."

   What do you know about Nick? How is he similar to and different from the other characters? Would you consider Nick the protagonist of this story or simply a minor character? On what do you base this decision? How does Nick change from the beginning of the story to the end? Is there a lesson he learns?

3. **George:** Analyze and evaluate George's character.

What do you know about George? What can you tell about him from his reaction to Max and Al? Why do you think George tells Nick "you better go see Ole Andreson," but then, when the cook tells Nick to stay out of the situation, adds, "Don't go if you don't want to" (220)? Where exactly does he stand? What do you make of his advice to Nick at the story's end? Do you think Hemingway designed George's character to represent a certain ideology or perspective in this story?

4. **Max and Al:** Analyze and evaluate the characters Max and Al.

Record everything you know about Max and Al. Why does Hemingway have them look and act as they do? Are they two distinct individuals or are they interchangeable? Why might this be important? What kind of code do they live by? What are their values and priorities? Do they change in the course of the story or remain static? Does the reader feel any sympathy or connection with these characters, or are they the clear villains of the piece? What do you think Hemingway is using these characters to demonstrate?

History and Context

When we read works of literature written and set in a time period greatly different from our own, there is a strong tendency to interpret and evaluate the story based on our own perspective. Because of the vast social and historical difference in context, this can create misinterpretations and unfounded conclusions. It is definitely worth your time to do some background reading to familiarize yourself with the context of a literary piece before you begin to write about it. Not only will any argument you make be better informed, but you might even find the entire basis of your essay in the consideration of historical and contextual kinds of questions. For example, you might devote your essay to determining precisely what the story has to say about Prohibition and organized crime. Or you might research the historical basis for the story of Ole Andreson and use your essay to discuss the significance of that historical connection, focusing on how understanding this connection can help readers more fully understand the story. Finally, you might study the history and philosophy associated with vaudeville and examine what the story ultimately has to say about this early 20th-century form of popular entertainment.

Sample Topics:

1. **Prohibition and organized crime:** What kind of commentary is the story making about Prohibition and organized crime?

Hemingway wrote this story in 1926, at the height of the Prohibition era, a time in U.S. history in which organized crime flourished. Do some background reading on Prohibition and organized crime to get a fuller understanding of the context for "The Killers." You might start with Thomas Reppetto's *American Mafia: A History of Its Rise to Power* or Edward Behr's *Prohibition: Thirteen Years That Changed America.* Then, return to the story with an eye toward what it has to say about organized crime. Look closely at Max and Al and their attitude toward killing a person they have never seen before "to oblige a friend" (218). How is their behavior connected to the values of organized crime? Also, you will want to examine the following exchange in particular: George tells Nick of Ole, "He must have got mixed up in something in Chicago," and when Nick wonders what he could have gotten mixed up in exactly, George responds, "Double-cross somebody. That's what they kill them for" (222). According to this story, what is the world of organized crime like? What are its values and codes? What happens when this world infringes on the ordinary world outside its boundaries?

2. **Historical basis for Ole Andreson:** Discuss the significance of the historical model for Ole Andreson's character.

Critic Philip Booth writes:

> The Hemingway character most willing, and perhaps even most eager, to accept his own terrible destiny is Ole Andreson,

a former boxer also referred to as the Swede, in "The Killers." The character, according to "The Art of the Short Story," an essay Hemingway wrote while in Spain during May and June 1959, was inspired by "Agile" Andre Anderson, born in Denmark. Anderson, on one occasion, beat his opponent after agreeing to throw a fight, as Hemingway told Gene Tunney, a heavyweight boxing champion of the late '20s: "All afternoon he had rehearsed taking a dive, but during the fight he had instinctively thrown a punch he didn't mean to" (Young 35). The boxer had knocked down Jack Dempsey in a 1916 bout that ended in no decision, and was shot to death a decade later in a Chicago cabaret. (404)

How can this additional knowledge of the historical figure upon which Ole's character is based help you better understand the story? Are there insights into the story's meaning that become clearer to you once you have this information? How closely did Hemingway adhere to the historical facts? What did he change, and why?

3. **Vaudeville:** Hemingway writes that Max and Al, "[i]n their tight overcoats and derby hats . . . looked like a vaudeville team" (219), and critics have noted that they act like one as well. What is it about Max and Al's actions that allows us to make this connection between the killers and a vaudeville act? What is the significance of such a connection?

Vaudeville refers to a type of entertainment popular in late 19th- and early 20th-century America. A vaudeville show consisted of multiple unrelated acts with singers, acrobats, magicians, dancers, comedians, and various other sorts of entertainers. Critic Ron Berman probes the intellectual underpinnings of the vaudeville phenomenon, postulating a connection between vaudeville and both the literary modernist movement and the artistic Dada movement. He writes that like these other movements, "the art of vaudeville was above all an accurate response to the postwar world and 'the bewildering confusion of the modern city'" (82). To get a fuller understanding of vaudeville, its philosophical basis, and its connection to other artistic movements, you might begin by reading Ron Berman's article, entitled "Vaudeville Philosophers: 'The Killers.'"

Do you think that Hemingway invokes vaudeville in this story because of its underlying philosophy? What is the connection between vaudeville and the themes and meanings of "The Killers"?

Philosophy and Ideas

In order to write about the philosophy and ideas of a literary work, you should begin by rereading the piece with your focus on identifying what ideas and philosophies are openly discussed in the work and which might be underneath its surface. Once you have identified ideas that the piece is concerned with—you will usually be able to identify several—choose one central idea or philosophy on which to focus in your essay. In the case of the "The Killers," you might focus on how the story is connected to recent discoveries in the world of physics. Familiarizing yourself with Albert Einstein's theory of relativity and Werner Heisenberg's principle of indeterminacy would be your first step. Then, take some time to imagine what it would be like to live in a world in which these discoveries are brand new. How might these discoveries affect how ordinary citizens view and interpret their world? Then, return to the story and attempt to decode Hemingway's response to these new ideas. Alternatively, you might consider the story and its relationship to "nada." After careful consideration, you might argue that Hemingway employs the concept of nada in "The Killers" in much the same way as he does in many of his other works—only this time without referring to it by name. Or if you decide that "The Killers" offers an entirely different conception of the human condition from Hemingway's other works, you might use your essay to describe and evaluate this alternative worldview.

Sample Topics:

1. **New discoveries in physics:** Discuss the relationship between "The Killers" and Albert Einstein's theory of relativity and Werner Heisenberg's principle of indeterminacy.

According to Quentin Martin,

> "The Killers" can be seen as a concise and dramatic represen-
> tation of certain aspects of Albert Einstein's theory of relativ-
> ity and Werner Heisenberg's principle of indeterminacy (or
> uncertainty). In general and simplified terms, relativity argues
> that time and mass are relative, not absolute, measurements,
> and that therefore seemingly fixed things, such as the motion
> of clocks and the shape of tables, are in fact dependent on their
> actual motion (as through space) and the perspective of the
> viewer. (53–54)

Martin concludes that the "story's powerful confusion, then,
is emblematic of a post-Newtonian scientist who has to dis-
card seemingly solid, commonsensical principle and find his
or her way in a mirage-world" (56). Further, he argues that the
story demonstrates that just "as time, mass, motion, and other
concepts are discovered to be unfixed, relative, and indeter-
minate, so too are moral precepts: the ability to judge whether
something is evil is part of the positivistic, determinable,
Newtonian universe" (56–57).

With these arguments in mind, return to the story and
assess whether it does in fact reflect or comment upon these
newly posited scientific theories. If it does, what kind of commentary is it making? Is the story actually suggesting that
relativity and indeterminacy have rendered "good" and "evil"
meaningless?

2. *Nada:* What does "The Killers" have to say about *nada*?

"The Killers" has been called one of Hemingway's bleak-
est works. Think about the philosophical underpinnings of
this story. Does it refer in any way to the concept of nada as
described in Hemingway's other work, such as "A Clean, Well-
Lighted Place"? Reread "A Clean, Well-Lighted Place," or try
Ben Stoltzfus's article "Sartre, *Nada,* and Hemingway's African

Stories," published in *Comparative Literature Studies*, to familiarize yourself with Hemingway's concept of *nada*. Would you argue that this concept is a fundamental element of "The Killers," or would you argue instead that this story presents a different, perhaps even a more life-affirming, worldview than some of Hemingway's other work?

Language, Symbols, and Imagery

Symbols, images, and creative use of language are what make literature possible. The study of them can help you develop unique insights and interpretations that you can put forth in an essay. In "The Killers," you might choose to focus on the misleading and intentionally confusing images and languages that abound in the story. Remember that each of these misunderstandings is an intentional element of a very spare story. Why did Hemingway include them? Alternatively, you might look for and interpret any symbolic reference to bullfighting in the story. In either case, you will want to identify and close read passages that reference your selected topic and try to determine how Hemingway is using the particular images or symbols you have selected. Why has he included them? What would be missing in the story if they had been omitted? What major theme(s) does the image contribute to or comment on?

Sample Topics:

1. **Misunderstandings:** What is the significance of the misunderstandings and false impressions in this story?

   According to Robert E. Fleming, misunderstandings and false impressions abound in this short, spare story. He cites the mix-up of the killer's orders, the broken clock, and the killers' appearance as a "vaudeville team" (219), among other things. Return to the story and keep your eye out for more of these misunderstandings and false impressions. Why do you think Hemingway weaves them into this story? For Fleming, they emphasize what Nick learns in the story, "that a great disparity exists between the normal signposts in life and the features of the real world to which those guides refer," or, to put it more simply, that "life refuses to play fair" (42). What do you make of Fleming's interpretation? Write an essay in which you support and extend, modify, or counter Fleming's argument.

2. **Bullfight:** How might the events in "The Killers" be analogous to a bullfight? What insights might such a comparison offer?

Hemingway initially titled "The Killers" "The Matadors," and critic George Monteiro finds several "analogies between bullfighting and the events in Summit. The bullring has become Henry's lunchroom, the matador(s), 'the killers,' Max and Al. Replacing the bull is 'the Swede'—the prizefighter Andreson, whose first name is suggestively, Ole" (40). Monteiro believes that these analogies are important because they stress the ritualized nature of the killing that is supposed to take place in the story, as well as the fact that the "killing does not take place only because the human being marked for death does not play his part that day" (40). What do you make of these parallels between bullfighting and the planned assassination in "The Killers"? How do they affect your interpretation of the story? Is it surprising that Ole does not play his part in this ritual? What can we make of his refusal if we compare him to a bull in a bullfight?

Compare and Contrast Essays

Comparing and contrasting is a good way to notice details or nuances that you might otherwise miss. Comparing and contrasting can also allow you to speak more broadly or assertively about your topic, as you have more material from which to draw and, therefore, more evidence to cite. In the case of "The Killers," you might compare and contrast the Nick Adams who appears in this story with the same character in any one or several of Hemingway's other stories that feature Nick as protagonist. You might also compare and contrast Hemingway's story with one or more of the movie adaptations that have been made of it. Finally, you might want to make a more adventurous comparison, setting Al and Max against Shakespeare's Rosencrantz and Guildenstern, for example. Though the literary works that contain them were written in different centuries and in different countries, these pairs share enough in common to warrant your pitting them against each other, and comparing and contrasting them can probably tell you something significant about the themes and meanings of each of these literary works.

Sample Topics:

1. **Nick Adams and Nick Adams:** Compare and contrast the Nick Adams of "The Killers" with the Nick Adams of *In Our Time*.

   To compare and contrast the Nick Adams of "The Killers" with the Nick Adams of Hemingway's short story collection *In Our Time*, you might pick out a couple of stories from *In Our Time* to focus on. Can you create a time line of Nick's life based on the stories you have selected? How old does he seem to be in each of your selections? How is Nick different and the same in each of the stories you examine? Based on your analysis, does Hemingway's character learn some lessons and grow in maturity, or is he a static character who possesses the same flaws in each of his appearances?

2. **"The Killers" and movie adaptations of the story:** Compare and contrast Hemingway's story to one or more of the movie adaptations of "The Killers."

   Three films were based on Hemingway's "The Killers": "Robert Siodmak's feature, a black-and-white film noir starring Burt Lancaster, Ava Gardner, and Edmond O'Brien, was released in 1946, followed a decade later by Andrei Tarkovsky's black-and-white short." And finally, "Don Siegel's color made-for-television adaptation with Lee Marvin, Clue Galager, John Cassavetes, Angie Dickinson, and Ronald Reagan, played theaters in 1964" (Booth 404). Select one or more of these films and compare it to the story. Make a list of the similarities and differences you discover. What new insights can you gain about the story by comparing it to the movie adaptation(s)? What modifications did the movie director(s) make? What effect did these changes have on the story? Which version did you find the most powerful? Why?

3. **Al and Max and Rosencrantz and Guildenstern:** Compare and contrast Al and Max of "The Killers" with *Hamlet*'s Rosencrantz and Guildenstern.

Steven Carter identifies the following similarities between Al and Max and Shakespeare's Rosencrantz and Guildenstern:

> Both pairs act as instruments of another's will to dispose of victims who are well aware of their terrible situations. Like Rosencrantz and Guildenstern, moreover, Al and Max willingly play the role of what Rosencrantz calls 'the indifferent children of the earth' (II.ii.222). All four are oblivious to the grim consequences of revenge, a vicious cycle which they enthusiastically (and literally) buy into. And both pairs are pleased to find a grisly humor in their calling. (68)

Reread *Hamlet* and "The Killers" paying special attention to Al and Max and Rosencrantz and Guildenstern. Assess Carter's observations. Do you agree with the similarities he cites in the two pairs? Why do you think Hemingway would echo these characters in *Hamlet* in this particular story? Do the two works share a larger theme or message?

Bibliography and Online Resources for "The Killers"

Behr, Edward. *Prohibition: Thirteen Years That Changed America.* New York: Arcade, 1996.

Berman, Ron. "Vaudeville Philosophers: 'The Killers.'" *Twentieth Century Literature* 45.1 (1999): 79–93.

Booth, Philip. "Hemingway's 'The Killers' and Heroic Fatalism: From Page to Screen (Thrice)." *Literature and Film Quarterly* 35.1 (2007): 404–11.

Brooks, Cleanth, and Robert Penn Warren. "The Killers." *The Short Stories of Ernest Hemingway: Critical Essays.* Ed. Jackson J. Benson. Durhan, NC: Duke UP, 1975. 187–96.

Carter, Steven. "Rosencrantz and Guildenstern Are Alive: A Note on Al and Max in Hemingway's 'The Killers.'" *Hemingway Review* 17.1 (1997): 68–71.

Davis, William V. "'the Fell of Dark': The Loss of Time in Hemingway's 'The Killers.'" *Studies in Short Fiction* 15.3 (1978): 319–21.

Desnoyers, Megan Floyd. "Ernest Hemingway: A Storyteller's Legacy." Available online. URL: http://www.jfklibrary.org/Historical+Resources/Hemingway +Archive/Online+Resources/eh_sto ryteller.htm. Retrieved August 7, 2007.

Fleming, Robert E. "Hemingway's 'The Killers': The Map and the Territory." *Hemingway Review* 3.2 (1984): 40–43.

Hemingway, Ernest. "The Killers." *The Complete Short Stories of Ernest Hemingway: The Finca Vigía Edition.* New York: Scribners, 1987. 215–22.

Johnston, Kenneth G. "'The Killers': The Background and the Manuscripts." *Studies in Short Fiction* 19.3 (1982): 247–51.

Martin, Quentin E. "Hemingway's 'The Killers.'" *Explicator* 52.1 (1993): 53–57.

Monteiro, George. "The Hit in the Summit: Ernest Hemingway's 'The Killers.'" *Hemingway Review* 8.2 (1989): 40–42.

Reppetto, Thomas. *American Mafia: A History of Its Rise to Power.* New York: Holt, 2004.

Stoltzfus, Ben. "Sartre, *Nada,* and Hemingway's African Stories." *Comparative Literature Studies* 42.3 (2005): 205–28.

"INDIAN CAMP"

READING TO WRITE

Hemingway considered "Indian Camp," which "dramatizes what is apparently the young Nick Adams's first confrontation with profound personal suffering," one of the best stories in his 1925 collection, *In Our Time* (Tyler 38). In this short but powerful story, we meet Nick Adams—who is featured in many other Hemingway works, such as "Big Two-Hearted River"—as a young boy. The young Nick accompanies his father and his Uncle George to an Indian camp in order to assist a Native American woman who is having trouble giving birth to her baby. Once there, Dr. Adams concludes that a cesarean section is necessary. He proceeds to operate, without proper equipment or anesthesia, and is very proud of himself when the operation results in saving the mother and successfully delivering the baby. The elation quickly dissipates, however, when Dr. Adams discovers that the woman's husband, who has been lying in an upper bunk, has committed suicide. While much of the action centers on the doctor and the Indian woman, many readers interpret this as a coming-of-age story for Nick as he is exposed to both birth and death on this momentous occasion, and he peppers his father with questions about both.

You might notice right away that aside from Nick's questions, there is relatively little dialogue in "Indian Camp." To fully experience a story such as this one, it is often helpful to reread the story, visualizing the events as they unfold, paying special attention to the sights, sounds, and smells that the narrator describes for you. Take the following scene, for instance:

> Later when he started to operate Uncle George and three Indian men
> held the woman still. She bit Uncle George on the arm and Uncle George

said, "Damn squaw bitch!" and the young Indian who had rowed Uncle George over laughed at him. Nick held the basin for his father. It all took a long time. (17)

In this scene, Dr. Adams performs a medically necessary procedure, but imagine how it looks. There are four men holding down a woman who has not been anesthetized, while a doctor cuts her open with a jackknife and a young boy observes and minimally participates by holding the basin of water for his father. The woman, obviously in intense pain, is surrounded and literally controlled by men; the other women, who would usually assist at childbirth, are relegated to the background. For the most part, there is no sound, and the narrator notes that the procedure "took a long time." So, add to the visual image of Dr. Adams cutting open the prone woman who is surrounded and held down by a group of men a seemingly interminable silence broken only by the words "Damn squaw bitch!" and the laughter of one of the Indians. The scene becomes one, not of a simple medical procedure, but of a group of males conspiring to violate a female body.

Consider also the racial and ethnic identities of the players in this scene. The person in the most control would certainly be the doctor, who is white. Uncle George and Nick, who are assisting the doctor, are also white. The woman who is being held down and operated on is Native American, as are three of the men holding her still. The only exchange in this scene beyond the actual operation occurs when the woman bites Uncle George, and he responds by saying "Damn squaw bitch!" The fact that the woman selects Uncle George instead of one of the Indian men to bite suggests that she is lashing out at not only the men who are controlling her but, in particular, the white men, which makes sense as it is Dr. Adams who is calling the shots here. It is also worth noting that the woman bites Uncle George; in a way she violates the integrity of his body just as hers is being violated by Dr. Adams. Do not forget to consider also the only response to the exchange between the woman and Uncle George: the laughter of one of the Indian men. Although the man is helping to hold down the woman so that the white man can operate, his laughter at the woman's retaliation indicates that while there is an alliance among the men, there is also an alliance of some sort along racial lines. One cannot help but interpret the laughter as the Indian's way of saying that Uncle George is getting what he deserves.

An examination of this short passage makes clear that "Indian Camp" is fundamentally concerned with questions of power, and it should prompt us to investigate the remainder of the story with these kinds of questions in mind. You might want to ask yourself, for instance, whether gender or race is the most significant factor in determining how much power an individual possesses in this fictional world. You might consider as well what these control and authority issues might have to do with the husband's decision to commit suicide. If you decide to focus on these kinds of issues in your essay, you will want to analyze closely several other key passages for evidence before drawing any conclusions.

TOPICS AND STRATEGIES

Hemingway's "Indian Camp" is a thought-provoking story that can be approached from many different angles. The topics listed below represent only a fraction of the approaches you might take. Once you have read through them and have gained a better sense of the possibilities, you might develop a topic of your own. Or you might decide to combine or modify some of the existing topics. If you do decide to use one of the topics presented here, remember that while the topic you choose should help you to begin thinking deeply about a specific issue, the topics are not designed to serve as road maps to the perfect essay. Said another way, you would not want your essay to turn into a catalog of your answers to the series of questions provided in a topic. Instead, your answers to the questions should lead you to new questions and new ideas. It remains your responsibility to synthesize your thoughts into a coherent argument to present in your essay.

Themes

Hemingway's "Indian Camp" is a very short story that manages to engage multiple complex themes. The story certainly asks important questions about power dynamics, empathy, and identity construction. You might use your essay to investigate the relationship between empathy and power that Hemingway sets up in this story and then relate your findings to Nick's search for identity. How do the choices he makes regarding empathy and power help to shape his personality? Alternatively, you might decide to consider Nick's search for identity from a different angle, examining "Indian

Camp" as a coming-of-age story, analyzing and evaluating Nick's move from innocence to experience. Finally, you might focus on the question of race in the text. What can the story reveal about the way Hemingway conceived of race as a concept or the light in which he viewed Native Americans? You should feel free to develop additional thematic topics as well, as there is much to be mined in this deep and sophisticated short story.

Sample Topics:

1. **Empathy and power:** What does "Indian Camp" have to say about power dynamics between individuals? Between genders and racial groups? In this story, how is power connected to one's capacity for empathy?

   According to Lisa Tyler, in much of Hemingway's work, "men's characters are determined, in part, by their responses to human and animal suffering, and (in 'Indian Camp') especially women's suffering" (37–38). In the case of "Indian Camp," Nick can either "empathize with the woman . . . as the Indian's husband chooses to" or he can "identify with his father and deem her screams unimportant" (39). "Those seem to be Nick's choices: obliterate the Indian woman by declaring her screams, her pain, 'not important,' or become so attuned to her suffering that, like her husband, he surrenders his identity to hers and (figuratively or literally) ceases to exist" (39). What choice does Nick ultimately make? What is the significance of that choice? Could Hemingway have presented Nick with any other options? What can you infer from the two options the author provided for Nick about the way in which he views relationships and the power dynamics on which they are based?

2. **Rites of initiation:** At first glance, "Indian Camp" seems to be a rite-of-passage story in which Nick moves from innocence to experience and knowledge. What does Nick learn in this story? Is Hemingway portraying the experience as a positive and successful rite of passage for Nick?

   Think about Nick at various points throughout the story. How does he change? What new things is he exposed to? Is Nick enlightened in some way after his "initiation"? Was this experience a necessary step in Nick's development? What typically happens in a rite-of-passage or initiation story? How is "Indian Camp" similar to and different from other stories of this type?

3. **Race:** The title of this story, "Indian Camp," tips us off right away that it will likely have race as one of its central themes. But is the story primarily about the Indian camp and the people who live there, or is it about the whites who transgress its boundaries in an attempt to help the pregnant Indian woman? Or would you say that the story is about the apparently tense relationship between the two racial groups? What does "Indian Camp" ultimately have to say about race and racial relationships?

Think about the way that the whites and the Native Americans are described and referred to in "Indian Camp." What is the relationship between the two groups like? Jeffrey Meyers notes that in Hemingway's Indian characters,

> there is no evidence of humanity, love, or solidarity. The Indians are strikingly affectless and isolated. The men moved out of the range of the screams, the husband rolled over against the wall, and the only direct contact with the squaw is made by the three Indians who, with Uncle George, held her down. (213)

Reread the story with this in mind; what do you make of Meyers's observations? Can you locate evidence of "humanity, love, or solidarity" in the Native American characters of "Indian Camp?" Write an essay in which you describe and evaluate Hemingway's portrayal of race and racial relationships in "Indian Camp."

Character

When you decide to write an essay on a particular character, you will want to examine closely that character's behavior, dialogue, and, if you are privy to them, the character's thoughts and feelings. You will want to consider the way that other characters react to your character as well as the way the narrator presents him or her. You will want to assess whether your character develops in the course of the work or remains static. If he or she changes, you will want to determine what prompts the change and whether the narrative construes it as positive or negative. Character analysis of this sort is often one of the most direct ways of getting at the heart of a literary work. By examining Nick in "Indian Camp," for instance, and evaluating precisely how he is affected by witnessing his father perform a cesarean and the discovery that the woman's husband has committed suicide, you can also begin to put your finger on the story's most significant themes and meanings. In fact, while sometimes a character analysis might be only that—an analysis and evaluation of a particular character in a literary work—the best character analyses go beyond that and use the analysis to arrive at a more holistic, comprehensive interpretation of the work. To get to this next level, you will want to ask yourself why the author creates a character such as the one you have examined. Is this particular character serving as a mouthpiece for the author, expressing or embodying what seem to be the author's values? Is the character there to serve as a foil for another character? Which one and to what end? Answering these kinds of questions about your character will help you to construct a more sophisticated and interesting argument.

Sample Topics:

1. **Nick Adams:** Analyze and evaluate the character of Nick Adams, either as he appears in "Indian Camp" only or in multiple stories.

   Because Nick is a character in many of Hemingway's short stories, you will need to decide first on the boundaries of your analysis. Will you be looking at Nick only as he appears in "Indian Camp," or will you be considering other stories that feature Nick as well? Which ones? When you are thinking about Nick's role in "Indian Camp," you will want to decide whether you think Nick changes at all in the course of the story. You will also want to compare him with his father, Dr. Adams. Is Nick like his father? Is he going to grow up to be like his father? How do you know?

2. **Uncle George:** Why do you think Hemingway included Uncle George in this story? What is the significance of his role?

Some critics have suggested that Uncle George is actually the father of the American Indian woman's baby. Reread the story with this theory in mind. List any evidence you can find for and against this theory. If you think there is enough evidence that George may in fact be the baby's father, then how does this affect your interpretation of the story? Does the story take on a different meaning when we consider that George, rather than the Indian husband, might be the father of the child? Where do you think Uncle George goes after the Indian husband is found dead?

3. **Dr. Adams:** Is Nick's father a likable character? Do you find him sympathetic? Would you say he is a good father to Nick? Use your essay to analyze and evaluate the character of Dr. Adams.

Record everything you can discern about Nick's father from "Indian Camp." What kind of man is he? What is his attitude toward the Native Americans? How does he envision his role as doctor? Why do you think he brings Nick along on this trip? Do you think Dr. Adams learns anything in the course of this story? Does he change or evolve at all? In what way? How can you tell?

History and Context

Investing some time and effort into learning about the context of the work of literature you are studying will always pay off. Even if you do not use the information you glean directly in your essay, your understanding of the material will be much greater, and your argument will be that much sounder for your efforts. In some cases, your investigation into context will wind up being absolutely integral to your argument. For example, if you wanted to study the issue of race in "Indian Camp," particularly the relationship between the whites and the Native Americans, and you used today's norms to judge the story, your conclusions would be skewed by a perspective incongruent with the prevailing social ideas of Hemingway's world. To avoid making such a blunder, you would first want to do some research into what the prevalent social ideas were at the time in which Hemingway was writing this story. How much did whites know about Native American culture? What was the relationship between whites and Native Americans like in this era? Was race perceived as a biological fact or as a cultural construction? Once you learn about the context in which Hemingway was writing, you can better ascertain whether his views were in line with prevailing cultural and social values or whether he was responding to or challenging these values in some way. It is perfectly possible, for instance, to decide that while Hemingway's story might seem racist and insensitive judged by today's standards, his work actually represented a significant step forward in tolerance and sensitivity when compared with the racial ideas of his contemporaries.

Sample Topics:

1. **Beliefs about race and Native American culture:** Understanding and appreciation of Native American culture has evolved a great deal since Hemingway wrote "Indian Camp." After you conduct some research, write an essay in which you evaluate Hemingway's understanding of and treatment of Native American peoples, taking into account the context in which he was writing.

Take some time to research prevailing views of Native American culture at the time that Hemingway was writing. You might begin with *Reimagining Indians: Native Americans through Anglo Eyes, 1880–1940* by Sherry L. Smith, *Native Americans in the Twentieth Century* by James S. Olson and Raymond Wilson, or *Going Native: Indians in the American Cultural Imagination* by Shari M. Huhndorf.

Once you have a better grasp of the evolving perception of Native Americans by European Americans, return to the story and ask yourself how Hemingway's portrayal of Native Americans compares to the prevailing conception of Native Americans in early 20th-century America. Is Hemingway simply mirroring his society's notions of what Native American culture and people were like, or is he attempting to change those notions in some way? How can you tell?

2. **Autobiographical connections:** Nick Adams is thought to be based largely on Hemingway himself. What is the significance of any connection between the Nick Adams of "Indian Camp" and Hemingway?

Do some background reading on Hemingway's life, particularly his childhood and his relationship with his father. Start with Carlos Baker's *Ernest Hemingway: A Life Story*, then reread "Indian Camp" with this information in mind. What similarities can you find between Nick and Hemingway? Between Nick's father and Hemingway's father? How can an understanding of these connections help you better understand "Indian Camp"? How can it help you better understand Hemingway?

Philosophy and Ideas

Thinking about the philosophical and ideological stances that are adopted or questioned in the work you are studying can help lead you to an interesting topic and thesis for your essay. For example, in the case of "Indian Camp," you might use your essay to explore what the piece has to say about consumption versus conservation. Does it associate each of these ideologies with a particular racial or ethnic group? Does it endorse or condemn either of them? Alternatively, you might discuss what "Indian Camp" has to say about the various ways that human beings communicate. How many types of communication can you identify in "Indian Camp"? Does communication always make interactions smoother? What are the reasons for and results of the misunderstandings or miscommunications that happen in "Indian Camp"? Finally, you might investigate the concept of "couvade," in which the partner of a pregnant woman experiences her symptoms and pain in order to draw the attention of any bad spirits to him and away from his partner and their baby. You will want to find out what cultures embrace couvade and ask yourself what the presence of couvade in a certain group signifies about that culture. Then, you will want to explore how Hemingway is using couvade in "Indian Camp," using your knowledge to help you construct a new and insightful reading of the story.

Sample Topics:

1. **Consumption versus conservation:** What does the story have to say about consumption and/or conservation? What racial group is associated with consumption? With conservation? Does Hemingway suggest that one of these philosophies is superior to the other?

   Begin with a look at the following passage, which describes the journey from the boat to the Indian camp:

   > They walked up from the beach through a meadow that was soaking wet with dew, following the young Indian who carried a lantern. Then they went into the woods and followed a trail that led to the logging road that ran back into the hills. It was much lighter on the logging road as the timber was cut away on both sides. The young Indian stopped and blew out his lantern and they all walked on along the road. (15)

   Who do you think has been doing the logging that is evident on this road? Indians or white people? How do you know? What kinds of associations do clear-cut forests conjure up? Does it surprise you that the young Indian takes the time to stop and blow out his lantern when it gets light enough to see? What kind of ethic is displayed here?

2. **Communication:** There is not much dialogue in Hemingway's story "Indian Camp," yet there are many attempts, both unsuccessful and successful, at communication. What does the story have to say about the possibilities and pitfalls of human communication?

   What kinds of communication occur in this story? How do people make themselves understood? Think about body language as well as spoken language. Compare the communication of the whites to the communication of the Indians. Is there a difference in their communication styles? Thinking in terms of communication, what do you make of Nick's father's statement "her screams are not important. I don't hear them because they are not important" (16)? Do you agree that the screams are unimportant? What message(s) might they convey?

3. **Couvade:** After learning about couvade among Native American cultures, write an essay in which you explain how it applies to Hemingway's "Indian Camp."

According to Jeffrey Meyers, the Indian husband is engaging in "couvade—in which a man ritualistically imitates the symptoms of pregnancy and the moans during delivery." This practice is supposed to "affirm his fatherhood, protect the child, and deflect potential evil from his wife" (217). Meyers explains that the husband is distressed that the white men have violated taboos; he cannot "bear this defilement of his wife's purity, which is far worse than her screams. In an act of elemental nobility, he focuses the evil spirits on himself, associates his wife's blood with his own death-wound, and punishes himself for violation of taboo" (219).

Do some background reading on the concept of couvade, beginning with Meyers's article, "Hemingway's Primitivism and 'Indian Camp,'" or Mary Douglas's *Purity and Danger: An Analysis of the Concepts of Pollution and Taboo.* Once you have a good understanding of couvade, reexamine "Indian Camp." Do you agree with Meyers's interpretation of the Indian's actions? Write an essay in which you respond to Meyers; you might support and elaborate on his argument, modify it, or offer an alternative interpretation of the evidence he cites.

Form and Genre

You might think of form and genre as the "nuts and bolts" of literary writing as they concern some of the most basic, fundamental decisions that an author makes as he or she creates a work of literature. Once the author, Hemingway, for example, has a story, or plot, in mind and has the characters developed, there are still important decisions to be made. What form will the story take? Will it be a novel? A short story? How short? Where will it be published? In a magazine? A collection of other stories? How will the story be told to the reader—who will be the narrator? What will the narrator know? Will he or she be reliable? Will the work be typical of a certain genre—will it be a mystery or romance, for example? The author must grapple with all of these elements as he or she constructs a piece of literature. By paying attention to the choices an author has made, you can learn some important information about the underlying meaning of the story. When writing about "Indian Camp," for example, you might decide to focus on the narration, analyzing and evaluating not the story but the way that the story is presented to the reader. Or you might analyze the context in which the story appears, as it is the second story of 16 in the collection called *In Our Time.* An examination of the relationship of "Indian Camp" relative to the remainder of the collection would certainly make for an interesting essay.

Sample Topics:

1. **Narration:** The narrator in "Indian Camp" is so unobtrusive that you might be tempted to forget that there is, in fact, a voice telling us the story of "Indian Camp." Take some time to focus on this voice, and use your essay to explore the significance of the narration to the overall themes and meanings of "Indian Camp."

   Reread the story paying particular attention to the narration. Why do you think the narrator refers to Dr. Adams as the "doctor" in some instances and as "Nick's father" in others? Are there any other such shifts that you can identify? With whom does the narrator seem to sympathize? Does the narrator seem to be objective? Dependable? Reliable? All told, how does the narration affect the way the reader ultimately interprets the story?

2. **Relationship of "Indian Camp" to other stories in *In Our Time*:** "Indian Camp" was published in a collection called *In Our Time.* The collection contains 16 stories, of which "Indian Camp" is the second; between the stories are "interchapters," short scenes printed in italic type that usually describe some kind of violence, such as warfare or bullfighting. Use your essay to analyze and evaluate the relationship of "Indian Camp" to *In Our Time* as a whole.

Read *In Our Time* in its entirety. What connections can you find among the various stories? What role do the interchapters play in the text? Why do you think Hemingway chose the particular stories he did for this volume? Why do you think he arranged them in the order he did? Describe what you see as the overarching structure of the collection and note what gives it integrity as a whole. Now think about "Indian Camp" in particular. How would you describe its relationship to the other parts of *In Our Time*?

Language, Symbols, and Imagery

Authors rely on a vast storehouse of literary and mythological symbols and a rich language in which words carry associations well beyond their literal meanings. With this arsenal, they create works of literature with nuances and complexities that delight and sometimes baffle readers. The good news about this is that you can work backward, selecting images and words that seem to you to be important or even those that just seem a little strange. With careful analysis, these images and language patterns can reveal a great deal about the work you are studying. For example, in the case of "Indian Camp," you might focus on Hemingway's choice to have Dr. Adams perform a cesarean (rendered *caesarian* in the text). After investigating all of the connotations of the term *cesarean* and its alternate spellings, you are better prepared to pick up on themes of power and imperialism than you might otherwise have been. Indeed, you might construct an entire argument about the distribution of knowledge and power along racial lines, all prompted by your investigation into the term *cesarean/caesarian*.

Sample Topics:

1. **Cesarean:** Hemingway could have centered "Indian Camp" on a difficult vaginal birth instead of a cesarean section, or he might have had Dr. Adams assist with a different type of surgical procedure. What is the significance of his decision to have Dr. Adams perform a cesarean?

   Jürgen Wolter writes that "in addition to being a technical term in surgery, [cesarean] connotes authority, imperialism, assumption of power, and even tyrannical dictatorship" (92). Why do you think Hemingway chose to center this story on a cesarean section rather than some other event or some other type of medical intervention? Is the story fundamentally concerned with "authority, imperialism, assumption of power," or "tyrannical dictatorship"? Who wields power over whom? What kind of authority is exerted in the story? What does the story seem to be saying about the exertion of power and authority? Be sure to consider how the medical procedure being performed plays into these ideas of power and authority.

2. **Boat crossing the water:** Analyze and evaluate the symbolism of the boat trip in "Indian Camp."

The opening passage of "Indian Camp" describes a nighttime boat trip across a misty lake. What similar mythological scenes might Hemingway be drawing on? What kinds of connections can you draw between these myths and Hemingway's story? Is "Indian Camp" mythological in other ways as well?

3. **Light and dark:** Authors often use light and dark as symbols in literary work; use your essay to discuss Hemingway's unique use of these traditional symbols in "Indian Camp."

Reread "Indian Camp" paying particular attention to any and all references to light, dark, and shadow. What places are dark? Which are lighter? What are the sources of light? Who is in control of the light? Now think about what light and dark traditionally represent and the associations they evoke. Is Hemingway relying on traditional associations in this story or forging new ones? What is he using light and dark to convey?

Compare and Contrast Essays

Comparing and contrasting can be one of the quickest ways to identify significant and meaningful elements in the piece(s) you are studying. You can compare and contrast elements within a single piece of literature, across pieces by the same author, and even across pieces by different authors. It is always a good idea to make sure you have a basis for making your comparison. You do not want to select two random pieces to compare, for example; instead, you might pick two works written in the same time period or two works written by white authors that feature Native American characters. Additionally, while comparing and contrasting might allow you to identify points of interest more quickly, this is not to say that writing this kind of essay is "easier" than writing an essay of a different type. Identifying interesting points of comparison is only half the battle. You must then analyze and interpret your findings, using your observations to help you construct an argument that, ideally, sheds some light on each of the works you are discussing.

Sample Topics:

1. **Race in "Indian Camp" and "The Doctor and the Doctor's Wife":** How does Hemingway present race in these two works? Can you trace the development of Hemingway's views on race from "Indian Camp" to "The Doctor and the Doctor's Wife"? How would you characterize this development?

   Read or reread "Indian Camp" and "The Doctor and the Doctor's Wife," paying careful attention to the presentation of race in each story. Think about how members of each race are characterized. Members of which race are generally in control in each story?

   Once you have made some initial observations, consider the following argument by Amy Strong; Strong writes that in "Indian Camp" Hemingway "present[s] a biologically based view of racial difference and implies almost unwavering success for power relations that rely on white male dominance" (27). However, in "The Doctor and the Doctor's Wife," he "revises this model to create a complex, shifting depiction of race," one that "highlights the social constructedness of racial differences, undoing the hierarchy of power in 'Indian Camp'" (28). What evidence can you find that supports or contradicts Strong's arguments? Do you agree that Hemingway's conception of race evolved from the writing of "Indian Camp" to the writing of "The Doctor and the Doctor's Wife"?

2. **Nick Adams of "Indian Camp" and Nick Adams of other Hemingway stories:** Select two or more of Hemingway's stories

that feature Nick. Can you trace his development from a young boy to a mature adult?

You might begin by reading *The Nick Adams Stories,* a volume that includes all of the stories that Hemingway wrote about Nick Adams arranged in chronological order of Nick's life. Select two or three of the stories to compare and contrast. You might wish to select the ones that seem to you to be the most developmentally significant. What remains consistent about Nick's character? In what ways does Nick change? What prompts his changes, and are they for the most part positive or negative?

Bibliography and Online Resources for "Indian Camp"

Baker, Carlos. *Ernest Hemingway: A Life Story.* New York: Scribners, 1969.

Douglas, Mary. *Purity and Danger: An Analysis of the Concepts of Pollution and Taboo.* New York: Routledge, 2002.

Hemingway, Ernest. "Indian Camp." *In Our Time.* New York: Scribners, 1986. 13–19.

Huhndorf, Shari M. *Going Native: Indians in the American Cultural Imagination.* Ithaca, NY: Cornell UP, 2001.

Lamb, Robert Paul. "Hemingway and the Creation of Twentieth-Century Dialogue." *Twentieth Century Literature* (1996). Available online. URL: http://findarticles.com/p/articles/mi_m0403/is_n4_v42/ai_20119140/pg_3. Retrieved October 20, 2007.

Meyers, Jeffrey. "Hemingway's Primitivism and 'Indian Camp.'" *Twentieth Century Literature* 34.2 (1988): 211–22.

Olson, James S., and Raymond Wilson. *Native Americans in the Twentieth Century.* Provo, UT: Brigham Young UP, 1984.

Strong, Amy. "Screaming Through Silence: The Violence of Race in 'Indian Camp' and 'The Doctor and the Doctor's Wife.'" *Hemingway Review* 16.1 (1996): 18–32.

Tyler, Lisa. "'Dangerous Families' and 'Intimate Harm' in Hemingway's 'Indian Camp.'" *Texas Studies in Literature and Language* 48.1 (2006): 37–53.

Wolter, Jürgen C. "Caesareans in an Indian Camp." *Hemingway Review* 13.1 (1993): 92–94.

Smith, Sherry L. *Reimagining Indians: Native Americans Through Anglo Eyes, 1880–1940.* New York: Oxford UP, 2000.

"BIG TWO-HEARTED RIVER"

READING TO WRITE

FIRST PUBLISHED in 1925 as part of the larger work *In Our Time,* "Big Two-Hearted River" tells the story of a young man by the name of Nick Adams as he goes on a fishing and camping trip. The plot of the story is quite simple; in typical Hemingway fashion, the story's complexity lies in its symbolism and subtle psychological depth. In the words of critic Alex Vernon,

> Ernest Hemingway's 'Big Two-Hearted River' remains perhaps the most famous piece of fiction about war with no mention of the war in it. The absence of war is exactly the point of the story, as Nick Adams, a recently returned veteran of the Great War, attempts to forget the war, to recover his prewar adolescent self by engaging in his favorite prewar adolescent activity, fishing. (36)

A close reading of some of the story's opening lines will help to explain and expand on Vernon's claim:

> Nick looked at the burned-over stretch of hillside, where he had expected to find the scattered houses of the town and then walked down the railroad track to the bridge over the river. The river was there. It swirled against the log piles of the bridge. Nick looked down into the clear, brown water, colored from the pebbly bottom, and watched the trout keeping themselves steady in the current with wavering fins. As he watched them they changed their positions by quick angles, only to hold steady in the fast water again. Nick watched them a long time.

He watched them holding themselves with their noses into the current, many trout in deep, fast moving water, slightly distorted as he watched far down through the glassy convex surface of the pool. . . .

Nick looked down into the pool from the bridge. It was a hot day. A kingfisher flew up the stream. It was a long time since Nick had looked into a stream and seen trout. They were very satisfactory. As the shadow of the kingfisher moved up the stream, a big trout shot upstream in a long angle, only his shadow marking the angle, then lost his shadow as he came through the surface of the water, caught the sun, and then, as he went back into the stream under the surface, his shadow seemed to float down the stream with the current, unresisting, to his post under the bridge where he tightened facing up into the current.

Nick's heart tightened as the trout moved. He felt all the old feeling. (133–34)

The first thing you might notice about the above passage is that although the houses are not where they have been before, where Nick expects them to be, the "river was there." Right away we get the sense that although human-constructed landmarks may not last, natural elements are more enduring. Second, we notice that Nick is heading for a river; the natural element he searches out is one that traditionally represents rebirth and renewal. The fact that the town has been destroyed, coupled with the fact that the symbolic river remains, suggests that the rebirth that Nick needs may not be possible in civilization but only in nature, and perhaps only in isolation.

The fact that Nick looks into the "glassy convex surface of the pool" suggests that he is looking into a mirror. In this light, perhaps the trout should be viewed not merely as Nick's prey, though certainly he plans to catch them, but as a symbolic representation of his spiritual state. Indeed, the narrator's description of the "trout keeping themselves steady in the current with wavering fins" and "chang[ing] their positions by quick angles, only to hold steady in the fast water again" is reminiscent of Nick's actions throughout the story. Nick's deliberate, ritualistic motions and his attention to minute details are perhaps his ways of holding himself "steady in the current." If Nick is in fact dealing with some psychological wounds, perhaps from the war, as Vernon suggests, then holding "steady in the current" may represent a refusal to deal openly with what is bothering him.

The portents are not all foreboding, however. The appearance of the "kingfisher," which connotes abundance and peace, suggests that there is real possibility for healing for Nick. Along this same line, after the kingfisher flies upstream, one of the trout unanchors himself from the streambed and begins to move as well. If we continue to read the trout as symbolic of Nick, then this image suggests that Nick, at some point, will begin to grapple with whatever trauma he has suffered; in this way, he will take advantage of the river's ability to renew instead of fighting the current by occupying his mind entirely with his surroundings and avoiding introspection.

The opening passages, then, suggest that Nick, consciously or unconsciously, has gone to nature, to the river in particular, for some kind of spiritual healing or rebirth. The passages also suggest that Nick will need to deal with the psychic damage he is facing by engaging in some internal reflection in order to take advantage of any healing potential nature provides. It would be interesting at this point to examine the remainder of the story for evidence of Nick's success at achieving a kind of recovery. Is the image of the trout allowing himself to move in the stream a foreshadowing of Nick's ability to face his demons or does it simply show a goal that Nick does not, at least in this particular story, reach? If the latter is so, how much progress does Nick make? How close is he by story's end to that internal inspection necessary to his recovery? Close readings of other passages throughout the story can help you arrive at answers to these questions and, potentially, to a fresh and interesting thesis for your essay.

TOPICS AND STRATEGIES

If you are experiencing some trouble deciding what to discuss in an essay on "Big Two-Hearted River," the topics suggested below will give you a good start. Read through them to get a sense of the wide variety of options you might pursue. Feel free to use them to jump-start your own thinking and to develop a topic of your own. However, if you decide to use one of the suggested topics, you will want to answer the subquestions and analyze the suggested passages well before you begin to draft your essay. Use the notes you generate to lead you to deeper, more complicated questions. Keep brainstorming and analyzing until you feel that you are ready to synthesize your findings and develop a thesis, or claim, to present as the foundational element of your essay.

Themes

When you begin thinking about writing an essay on theme in a particular literary work, you might begin with the broad question "What is this story about?" In the case of "Big Two-Hearted River," you might say that the story is about Nick's recovery from some psychological damage, that it is about the artistic process, or perhaps that it is about the importance of the natural world to human beings. In fact, you might say that the story is about all of these topics, and perhaps additional ones as well, and you would be right. However, as the writer of an essay about theme in "Big Two-Hearted River," it is your job to select one theme about which to write; you might pick what you feel is the most significant theme, the most interesting to you personally, or the one you feel gets the least critical attention. Once you have selected your theme, your next task is to select relevant passages from the text to analyze in an attempt to figure out precisely what the story has to say about your topic. In the case of the recovery process as presented in "Big Two-Hearted River," for instance, you might argue that being isolated in nature and having to focus on his own survival and well-being keeps Nick's mind off the problems he has been facing and thus allows him a necessary respite or retreat from his psychological problems. Or you might argue that Nick's trip promotes his recovery by allowing him to reintegrate himself into the harmonious cycles of nature. Whatever you decide to argue, you will present this claim to your readers and then back it up with a logical and persuasive presentation of the evidence that led you to this conclusion.

Sample Topics:

1. **Recovery:** Many critics have read "Big Two-Hearted River" as a story about Nick Adams's quest for healing after presumably suffering some type of trauma in the war. What does the story have to say about the psychology of recovery?

   Can you find evidence of what is wrong with Nick in the story? Does anything strike you as strange about his behavior? Why do you think Nick chooses a fishing trip to this particular spot to make himself feel better? Is it the contact with nature that somehow helps Nick either to forget or to deal with his troubles? Is it the ritualistic nature of his preparations that comforts him? Or does the story work in a more symbolic way—is

Nick's desire for the river suggestive of his need for a spiritual or psychological rebirth? Once you have figured out exactly what kind of recovery, or healing, is supposed to be taking place here, then you can begin to evaluate its success. Does Nick change as a result of his fishing trip? How exactly? Does it seem as though the trip has done what he expects it to do?

2. **Art and the artist:** Critic B. J. Smith suggests that on one level "Big Two-Hearted River" is about the artistic process; he writes that "Nick's fishing trip is an attempt by Hemingway to write, perhaps for the first time, about the artist and the process of his art" (130). If we read this story as a commentary on the artistic process, what new insights can we reach about Hemingway's perception of that process?

   Think about the story as a metaphor for the artistic process. Who is the artist? What does the river represent? The swamp? The trout? The grasshoppers? What are the obstacles that an artist faces? What are his motivations? His goals? Is the artistic process represented in the story successful? Why or why not? Once you have considered these questions, draft an essay in which you explain for your readers exactly what Hemingway is saying about the process or art or the role of the artist in "Big Two-Hearted River."

3. **Humanity's relationship with nature:** What does "Big Two-Hearted River" ultimately have to say about the relationship between nature and humanity?

   According to critic Glen A. Love, Hemingway's "Big Two-Hearted River," which "most readers . . . regard as a restorative pastoral experience—camping beside, and fishing, a lovingly remembered river," in actuality "illustrates not only the carefully prescribed code of streamside behavior, but also the peculiar drive toward conflict and deathful adventure" in humans' interactions with the natural world (118). In essence, Love argues that Hemingway is not portraying an idyllic, harmonious relationship with nature in "Big Two-Hearted River" but instead revealing that humans engage nature in combat in order to prove themselves and master their individual psychological demons.

Reread the story with Love's remarks in mind. How do you think Hemingway presents the relationship between human beings and nature in this story? Is the relationship an antagonistic one or a cooperative one? Think about the way that Nick treats the fish he has caught as you are answering this question. When you have reached your own conclusions regarding the portrayal of the relationship between humanity and nature in "Big Two-Hearted River," write an essay in which you support and extend, modify, or counter Love's claims.

Character

"Big Two-Hearted River" has one character at its center, who, of course, is Nick Adams. You might write an essay that analyzes Nick's character in this particular story, or you might investigate Hemingway's other stories that feature Nick. You might decide to limit yourself to those included in *In Our Time,* or you might be more adventurous and choose to look at other stories that feature Nick, including those published in different venues and collections. Remember to take into account the desired length of your finished essay as you make these kinds of decisions. If you elect to focus on Nick solely as he is presented in "Big Two-Hearted River," then you will have a piece considerably shorter than one in which you attempt to evaluate Nick as he is presented in multiple works. Alternatively, you might focus on a character who exists only in Nick's memory: Hopkins. Such an essay would likely focus more on the role that Hopkins plays in Nick's psyche or on what Hopkins has come to represent for Nick than on Hopkins himself, as we are given very little information about him. So, in a sense, even if you choose to focus on the only other human character present in the story, you will still be, on some level, discussing Nick.

Sample Topics:

1. **Nick Adams:** Nick Adams is one of Hemingway's best-known fictional creations, and he has often been compared to Hemingway himself. Use your essay to analyze and evaluate this intriguing character.

As he is a character who appears in multiple works, if you choose to write an essay about Nick as a character, you will need to decide on and articulate your boundaries. Are you analyzing the Nick Adams who appears in "Big Two-Hearted River" only, or will you also be analyzing this character as he appears in other works as well? Which other works will you consider? Only those in *In Our Time* or stories that appear elsewhere? Which stories will you exclude? Why?

As you prepare to write your essay, you will want to note what information you have about Nick and where that information comes from. You will want to analyze his behavior as well as his psychological state. Does Nick change in the course of the work(s) you are studying? For better or worse? Is Nick a sympathetic character? Can an analysis of Nick's character tell you something important about Hemingway's perception of coming of age, of masculinity, of the wartime experience, or of coming to terms with the past?

2. **Hopkins:** Analyze and evaluate Hopkins. What is the significance of this character who appears only in Nick's thoughts and memories?

Locate and analyze the few references to Hopkins in "Big Two-Hearted River." What does Nick remember about Hopkins? Why does Nick think about Hopkins on this particular occasion? What does the story suggest happens to Hopkins? To his girlfriend? Why do you think Nick never saw Hopkins again? What does Hopkins represent to him?

History and Context

Doing some background reading on the early 20th century, World War I, and Ernest Hemingway's life, as well as reading some other works by Hemingway that feature Nick Adams, will help you put "Big Two-Hearted River" in its proper context. As a result, you will be much better prepared to pick up on cues within the story that may refer to events outside of it and to develop a fresh insight into the story that you can present to your readers. For example, though the story does not mention World War I, if you know some background—such as the fact that the story was published in 1925, a few years after the end of the war, and that in other stories Hemingway reveals that the character Nick Adams is, indeed, a war veteran—you might consider that Nick of "Big Two-Hearted River" is potentially suffering from some psychological trauma sustained in his wartime experiences. Such a realization may greatly influence your reading of the story; it might, in fact, become the cornerstone of your interpretation.

Sample Topics:

1. **World War I:** Many critics have pointed out that at the start of "Big Two-Hearted River," Nick has likely just returned from service in World War I, basing this conclusion on the time frame of the story, information about Nick that we glean from other stories, and comments that Hemingway himself made about the story years after he wrote it. Many argue that Nick's fishing trip is designed to help him deal with the trauma he suffered in the war and to help him reconnect with his previous hobbies and his life before the war. Do you agree with the critical consensus that the story depicts Nick's attempts to recover from trauma he suffered in war? Why or why not?

   You will want to begin with some background reading on the war and the psychological effects suffered by soldiers who fought in it. You might begin with *A War of Nerves: Soldiers and Psychiatrists in the Twentieth Century* by Ben Shephard. Can you locate evidence in "Big Two-Hearted River" that Nick is suffering from post-traumatic stress disorder or some other psychological problem? Are you convinced that Nick's problems were caused by wartime experience? You might devote your entire essay to making a case for whether it is justifiable to assume that Nick has war-related injuries when the war is not actually mentioned in the story. Or you might begin your essay by arguing the case that Nick has very likely suffered psychological injuries in the war and then use the remainder of your essay to explore what Hemingway has to say about the manifestation of these kinds of psychological wounds and the potential for healing or at the very least assuaging them.

2. **Autobiographical connection:** Critic Howard L. Hannum notes that "autobiographical assumption is virtually automatic among those who write about Nick" (92). What insights can you gain into Nick's character and the themes and meaning of "Big Two-Hearted River" through a study of Hemingway's life?

Begin by doing some background reading on Hemingway; you might start with Carlos Baker's biography, *Ernest Hemingway: A Life Story.* Then, reread "Big Two-Hearted River," and think about the ways in which Nick and Hemingway are similar. You might begin by making a simple list of ways in which this character and his creator are alike and ways in which they differ. Which seem to be the most significant points of comparison? Why are these points important? From your observations, what new insights can you draw about Nick's motivations or psychological state in the story or about Hemingway himself?

Form and Genre

Hemingway's creation of Nick Adams has sparked a great deal of discussion about form and genre. Nick appears in many stories and in multiple venues, and his story is not told in chronological order. Critics have long debated how to treat the Nick Adams stories, whether to consider them all together or whether to group only those that were published in the same collections, for example. Philip Young has published a collection, *The Nick Adams Stories,* in which he presents all of the Nick stories in chronological order so that we see the youngest Nick first and then see him mature as the stories progress. As Hemingway himself never assembled the material this way, a collection like this is somewhat controversial. You might decide to write your essay about the literary creation Nick Adams and how the character should be regarded by critics. Or you might pursue another question that Hemingway's unorthodox publishing forms have prompted, and that is the nature of the relationship between the story "Big Two-Hearted River" and the other stories published in the same collection, *In Our Time.* Alternatively, if you are interested in form and genre but would like to confine your essay to a discussion of "Big Two-Hearted River" only, you might focus on Hemingway's prose style and its relevance to the story's theme.

Sample Topics:

1. **Relationship to other Nick Adams stories:** Scholar Howard L. Hannum notes that "short stories centering on Nick have often been seen as the loose configuration of a novel: creative writers from D. H. Lawrence to Joyce Carol Oates have so viewed them" (92). Another scholar, Philip Young, did more than argue that these stories should be read in tandem by creating a new book, called *The Nick Adams Stories,* in which he gathered the material that Hemingway had written about Nick Adams, both published and unpublished, and arranged it in the chronological order of Nick's life.

   Young explains that as the Nick Adams stories were published over a wide range of time and in various short story collections, most readers did not experience them as a cohesive whole and therefore a great deal of their impact was lost. Read Young's collection, including his preface, in which he provides his justification for creating such a book. Then think about whether Young has done Hemingway readers a great service by assembling material that is truly novel-like in spirit and should be considered in the same context or whether he has created a new literary work entirely, one that should be regarded as distinct from Hemingway's oeuvre.

2. **Relationship of "Big Two-Hearted River" to the other stories that make up *In Our Time*:** Write an essay in which you discuss how the story "Big-Two Hearted River" is connected to the other parts of *In Our Time.* How can we better understand the story by studying the entire volume in which it was published?

   "Big Two-Hearted River" was first published in 1925 in the collection of short stories called *In Our Time.* This collection includes several other stories about Nick Adams, including "Indian Camp," "The Doctor and the Doctor's Wife," "The Three Day Blow," and "The Battler," as well as other stories that do not involve Nick at all. Read the entire collection, paying particular attention to the Nick Adams stories. What is the relationship between "Big Two-Hearted River" and the other stories of *In Our Time*? Do they share some thematic concern? What about the stories that feature Nick? Are these connected to "Big Two-Hearted River" in an especially significant way? What do you make of the "interchapters" that are included between each story, especially chapter 15, which is located between parts 1 and 2 of "Big Two-Hearted River"? If you had to classify *In Our Time*, would you call it a novella or a short story collection? Why?

3. **Short, simple sentences:** Discuss the significance of the prose style of "Big Two-Hearted River." How does it enhance or detract from the story's themes.

To get a sense of the distinctiveness of the style, compare the story to fragments of writing from other writers such as F. Scott Fitzgerald or William Faulkner. What makes Hemingway's prose in "Big Two-Hearted River" different? Why do you think Hemingway uses the style he does in this particular story? Critics have argued that the style of "Big Two-Hearted River" is designed to convey a sense of barely contained panic in Nick. How would this work exactly? Reread the story, and try to locate evidence for and against this theory. Can you propose an alternative explanation for the thematic meaning of the style that Hemingway employs here?

Language, Symbols, and Imagery

Although "Big Two-Hearted River" is a story in which not much happens when one considers only the plot—in essence, it simply amounts to Nick walking to his fishing spot, making camp for the night, catching fish the next morning, and deciding not to fish in the swamp—there is a tremendous amount going on when we consider the symbols and images that Hemingway employs in this deceptively simple tale. Almost everything in this story—from the burned town of Seney to the black grasshoppers, the river, and the swamp—can be read symbolically, and the way that we interpret these symbols helps to determine our overall understanding of the story in its entirety. For example, we might interpret the grasshoppers to be reflections of Nick and the damage he suffered in the war. Just as the grasshoppers changed to accommodate their new, desolate surroundings, so, perhaps, did Nick. We might easily construct an entire reading of the story based on this symbolic interpretation, arguing that Nick has undergone fundamental changes due to his wartime experiences and that only enough time in a healthier environment can possibly help him return to his former condition of, if not innocence, at least peace.

1. **Burned and deserted town:** At the beginning of the story, the narrator takes pains to describe the town at which Nick disembarks from the train. What is the significance of this town to the themes of "Big Two-Hearted River"?

   Begin by analyzing the narrator's description of Seney:

   > There was no town, nothing but the rails and the burned-over country. The thirteen saloons that had lined the one street of Seney had not left a trace. The foundations of the Mansion House hotel stuck up above the ground. The stone was chipped and split by the fire. It was all that was left of the town of Seney. Even the surface had been burned off the ground.
   >   Nick looked at the burned-over stretch of hillside, where he had expected to find the scattered houses of the town and then walked down the railroad track to the bridge over the river. (133)

   Why does Hemingway include this description? How is this setting significant to the themes of the story? Might the deserted town somehow reflect Nick's spiritual or psychological condition? Write an essay in which you discuss the thematic significance of the burned town.

2. **The river and the swamp:** Discuss the thematic significance of the river in which Nick fishes and the swamp into which he declines to go.

   Explore the significance of the river and the swamp. What do rivers traditionally represent? What does the river seem to represent here? What might the swamp be symbolic of? Locate and analyze relevant passages describing the river and swamp, such as the following, to help you sort out the symbolism:

> The swamp looked solid with cedar trees, their trunks close together, their branches solid. It would not be possible to walk through a swamp like that. The branches grew so low. You would have to keep almost level with the ground to move at all. You could not crash through the branches. . . . Nick did not want to go in there now. He felt a reaction against deep wading with the water deepening up under his armpits, to hook big trout in places impossible to land them. In the swamp the banks were bare, the big cedars came together overhead, the sun did not come through, except in patches; in the fast deep water, in the half light, the fishing would be tragic. In the swamp fishing was a tragic adventure. Nick did not want it. He did not want to go down the stream any further today. (155)

Why do you think Nick uses the word *tragic* to describe fishing in the swamp? Do you think that Nick really does not want to fish the swamp or that he secretly wants to? How can you tell? When you have decided on the symbolic meaning of the river and the swamp, use them and Nick's reaction to them to help you develop an interpretation of the story. From your analysis, what does it mean that Nick decides not to go into the swamp? Would you consider this a positive or negative step in his psychological development?

3. **Grasshoppers:** Discuss the significance of the grasshoppers to the themes and meanings of "Big Two-Hearted River."

Begin by analyzing the following description of the grasshoppers:

> As [Nick] smoked, his legs stretched out in front of him, he noticed a grasshopper walk along the ground and up onto his woolen sock. The grasshopper was black. As he had walked along the road, climbing, he had startled many grasshoppers from the dust. They were all black. They were not the big

grasshoppers with yellow and black or red and black wings whirring out from their black wing sheathing as they fly up. These were just ordinary hoppers, but all a sooty black in color. Nick had wondered about them as he had walked, without really thinking about them. Now, as he watched the black hopper that was nibbling at the wool of his sock with its fourway lip, he realized that they had all turned black from living in the burned-over land. He realized that the fire must have come the year before, but the grasshoppers were all black now. He wondered how long they would stay that way. Carefully he reached his hand down and took hold of the hopper by the wings. He turned him up, all his legs walking in the air, and looked at his jointed belly. Yes, it was black too, iridescent where the back and head were dusty. (135–36)

Why do the grasshoppers that Nick sees look different from normal grasshoppers? What has happened to them? Why do you think Nick finds them so interesting? What might these grasshoppers represent? Does Nick identify with them in some way?

Compare and Contrast Essays

It is helpful to remember that when you are writing an essay that compares and contrasts two or more literary elements, you are essentially placing these elements next to each other in order to discern details and nuances more closely that you might otherwise have missed. But the analysis does not stop there. You will use your observations to make some larger point about both of the pieces you are studying and, with hope, enrich your readers' understanding and appreciation of both pieces. Keeping this firmly in mind will help prevent you from turning your essay into a mere catalog of similarities and differences and ensure that you base your essay on a strong and interesting thesis.

Sample Topics:

1. **"Big Two-Hearted River," "Now I Lay Me," and "A Way You'll Never Be"**: Compare and contrast these three fundamental Nick Adams stories.

Hemingway wrote many stories about Nick Adams, but according to Margot Sempreora, "Big Two-Hearted River," "Now I Lay Me," and "A Way You'll Never Be" are perhaps the three that are most closely linked. Sempreora notes that these stories follow Nick during and after the war. She writes that "A Way You'll Never Be" "looks at the youngest Nick, a soldier recovering from a head wound who returns too early to the Italian front," while "Big Two-Hearted River" "gives us the soldier back home, fishing a Michigan river," and in "Now I Lay Me," "a postwar Nick remembers a summer night behind the front lines when he held off sleep to keep his soul from leaving his body" (21).

Read these three stories with careful attention, and compare and contrast the Nick Adams who appears in each of them. Does looking at these three stories together help you better understand Nick's character? What do you know about Nick now that you wouldn't know if you had read only "Big Two-Hearted River"? Can you trace Nick's psychological development through the course of the three stories?

2. **Nick of "Big Two-Hearted River" and Jake Barnes of _The Sun Also Rises_**: Each of these characters suffered some sort of injury in the war. Taken together, what can their stories tell us about Hemingway's perception of the psychological effects of combat?

Read or reread _The Sun Also Rises_ and "Big Two-Hearted River," focusing on Nick and Jake, particularly the time they spend fishing. What are the similarities between these two characters? What do you know about their backgrounds? Does fishing serve the same purpose for both of them? How can you tell? What does each character seem to gain from the fishing experience? You will want to think also about what makes Nick and Jake different from each other. How are these differences significant? What can you learn through a study of these two characters about Hemingway's view of the psychological effects of war and the potential healing power of nature?

Bibliography for "Big Two-Hearted River"

Baker, Carlos. *Ernest Hemingway: A Life Story.* New York: Scribners, 1969.

Carabine, Keith. "'Big Two-Hearted River': A Re-interpretation." *Hemingway Review* 1.2 (1982): 39–44.

Hannum, Howard L. "'Scared sick of looking at it': A Reading of Nick Adams in the Published Stories." *Twentieth-Century Literature* 47.1 (2001): 92–113.

Hemingway, Ernest. "Big Two-Hearted River." *In Our Time.* New York: Scribners, 1986. 133–56.

———. *The Nick Adams Stories.* Preface by Philip Young. New York: Scribners, 1972.

Love, Glen A. "Hemingway Among the Animals." *Practical Ecocriticism: Literature, Biology, and the Environment.* Charlottesville: U of Virginia P, 2003. 117–34.

Sempreora, Margot. "Nick at Night: Nocturnal Metafictions in Three Hemingway Short Stories." *Hemingway Review* 22.1 (2002): 21–35.

Shephard, Ben. *A War of Nerves: Soldiers and Psychiatrists in the Twentieth Century.* Cambridge, MA: Harvard UP, 2001.

Smith, B. J. "'Big Two-Hearted River': The Artist and the Art." *Studies in Short Fiction* 20.2 (1983): 129–32.

Vernon, Alex. "War, Gender, and Ernest Hemingway." *Hemingway Review* 22.2 (2002): 36–57.

"SOLDIER'S HOME"

READING TO WRITE

"SOLDIER'S HOME," published in the collection *In Our Time* (1925), centers on Harold Krebs, a young man just back from service in World War I. By the time Krebs returns, "the greeting of heroes was over," and many of the other hometown boys have settled back into their ordinary lives. Krebs, however, has a great deal of trouble readjusting to civilian life. He does not have a job, and he is not very interested in dating or romance. He seems to have an antagonistic relationship with his parents. Indeed, the only person he seems to like is his little sister, Helen.

Discovering the root of Krebs's problems will take careful analysis. Start with a close reading of the following passage in which the narrator comments directly on Krebs's feelings about his experiences in the war and the problems he has encountered since his return.

A distaste for everything that had happened to him in the war set in because of the lies he had told. All of the times that had been able to make him feel cool and clear inside himself when he thought of them; the times so long back when he had done the one thing, the only thing for a man to do, easily and naturally, when he might have done something else now lost their cool, valuable quality and then were lost themselves.

His lies were quite unimportant lies and consisted in attributing to himself things other men had seen, done or heard of, and stating as facts certain apocryphal incidents familiar to all soldiers. Even his lies were not sensational at the pool room. His acquaintances, who had heard detailed accounts of German women found chained to machine guns in the Argonne forest and who could not comprehend, or were barred by

> their patriotism from any interest in, any German machine gunners who
> were not chained, were not thrilled by his stories. (70)

Drawing on prevailing cultural notions and other literary works, we
might be tempted to assume that Krebs's problem reintegrating into
society stems from the violence he was forced to witness and perpetrate
in the war—especially as Hemingway takes care to note that Krebs participated in some of the most infamous battles of the war—but if we look
closely at this passage, that does not seem to be the case. Krebs thinks of
his military service as the "times so long back when he had done the one
thing, the only thing for a man to do, easily and naturally." This description suggests that something appealed to Krebs about the simplicity of
a life that entailed trying to survive and fighting a clear enemy, a life in
which there was not a dizzying array of choices but a series of necessary
actions. He could rely on gut instincts and, if he survived, know that he
had made the right choices. Even reflecting on these experiences was
in some way positive for Krebs. When he first returned home, thinking
about them had "been able to make him feel cool and clear inside himself," and they possessed a "cool, valuable quality." Krebs's descriptions of
these feelings are suggestive of confidence, peace, and perhaps pride.

Despite these positive associations, Krebs cannot immediately "get
on" with the rest of life upon return from the war. The fact that he no
doubt participated in a great deal of violence, along with his deep need
to talk about his wartime experience, suggests that he has suffered some
degree of trauma. The real problem, though, is that Krebs is prevented
from dealing with that trauma in a healthy way—telling his story to an
empathetic listener—because the citizens of his hometown have had
their fill of war stories. They have become desensitized and require more
and more excitement or horror to be enthralled. In order to be listened
to at all, Krebs has to lie, to exaggerate or claim others' experiences as his
own, and, as the narrator notes, even Krebs's "lies were not sensational
at the pool room." Telling these lies corrupts rather than validates his
memories. When we think about it this way, we can understand why, for
Krebs, lying about his experiences is worse than the experiences themselves, and we can begin to understand why some soldiers might not have
been able to deal with their trauma by talking through their memories;
because there were so many sufferers, people grew tired of these stories
and simply stopped listening.

As you prepare to write your essay on "Soldier's Home," use the close reading technique on passages that you identify as important or ones that you feel are relevant to the topic you have chosen to work on. Ask yourself why the author included a particular description or phrase. Ask why he used the precise words in the precise order that he did instead of the many other options that were available. Paying close attention to small sections of a literary work at a time can be the best way to tease out significant details. These significant details will eventually become the basis of the interpretation or argument you will present in your essay.

TOPICS AND STRATEGIES

In the sample topics below, you will find that there are numerous ways to approach writing an essay about "Soldier's Home." Once you have read through the topics, you might worry that upon choosing one, you will be leaving out too many possibilities and failing to address many significant aspects of the story. It is important to realize that you will not be able to discuss everything you think is important or interesting about the story in one essay, and you should not try to. What you should do instead is focus on one aspect or angle that seems most significant or compelling to you. Ideally, your focus on that one topic will lead you to a fresh interpretation of the story that you can present in an essay. Of course, the interpretation you create based on the topic you have chosen will undoubtedly leave other questions unanswered. This only means that there is room for other essays and other writers. Stories as rich as Hemingway's "Soldier's Home" have inspired and will continue to inspire intense and extended critical discussions. Simply think of your essay as your part in that larger, ongoing conversation. While you do not have to provide all the answers, you want to provide something fresh and provocative that will keep that conversation moving and perhaps even send it in entirely new directions.

Themes

When you are writing about a story's theme(s), you should begin by asking yourself what the story is about. What are its primary concerns? If you had to make a list of subjects that this particular story touches on, what would that list include? It is often helpful to think of typical themes to get you started, and then you can move on to themes more particular to the piece you are studying. In the case of "Soldier's Home," for example, you might find that the story addresses two themes that show up often in 20th-century American literature: alienation and family. You could certainly write an essay about the unique way that Hemingway handles either of these themes in "Soldier's Home." Looking a little harder, you might find that the story is also about trauma victims' need to talk about their experiences and the often performative nature of human beings' interactions with one another. An analysis of either of these themes would also make for an interesting and compelling essay.

Sample Topics:

1. **Alienation:** One of the first things many readers of "Soldier's Home" notice is a pervading sense of alienation and isolation. What is the cause of this alienation, and what do you think Hemingway is trying to say about it?

Reread the story, identifying and analyzing passages that seem to you to describe or comment on Krebs's alienation or isolation. Also, you will want to analyze passages that comment on Krebs's and other soldiers' reintegration into society after the war. You might start with the following:

> "Your father is worried, too," his mother went on. "He thinks you have lost your ambition, that you haven't got a definite aim in life. Charley Simmons, who is just your age, has a good job and is going to be married. The boys are all settling down; they're all determined to get somewhere; you can see that boys like Charley Simmons are on their way to being really a credit to the community." (75)

According to Krebs's mother, what roles are other young men assuming in the community? How is Krebs different from, say, Charley Simmons? Presumably, most, if not all, of these other young men have had experiences similar to Krebs's, so what might account for the differences in their postwar behaviors? Does it seem likely that Krebs will eventually reintegrate into his hometown community? Why or why not?

2. **Family:** What kind of commentary does the story ultimately make about family and its role in the recovery of one of its members?

How would you characterize Krebs's family? List all of its members and record what you know about each member. Would you say they are supportive of Krebs? Are their expectations of him realistic? Well intentioned? How do they each react to his wartime experiences and his difficulty readjusting to civilian life? Try to reconstruct the family and its dynamics in the time before the war. Do you think the family was an emotionally and psychologically healthy one before Krebs went off to war? What makes you think so? What do you make of Krebs's relationship with his sister, Helen? Would you characterize it as positive or as problematic in some way?

3. **Witnessing:** What does "Soldier's Home" have to say about the need to talk about traumatic events?

Reread the story, paying careful attention to the soldiers' tendency to talk about their experiences. To whom do they talk? How do they present their stories? What purpose does this talking seem to serve? How is the conversation different when a soldier is talking to a civilian versus when he is talking to another soldier?
   If you select this topic, you might want to do some background reading on trauma theory, which discusses the power of language and listening to deal with psychological wounds. Start with Cathy Caruth's *Trauma: Explorations in Memory* or her *Unclaimed Experience: Trauma, Narrative, History*.

4. **Social interaction as performance:** Krebs feels badly about having to tell lies about his experience in the war in order to command the attention of the townspeople and fellow soldiers. Why does he feel compelled to put on this sort of performance when he returns from the war?

Do you think that Krebs really had to tell lies about his wartime experiences? Why does he feel he needs to? Why do you think telling these lies is such a devastating thing for Krebs? As Krebs considers courting a young woman, he thinks that he "did not want to tell any more lies. It wasn't worth it" (71). Is Krebs thinking that he will have to tell lies about the war in order to court a young woman? Or is he thinking that he will have to tell other kinds of lies? Put on other kinds of acts? Locate and analyze any other types of social performance in the story, for example, the behavior of the young women whom Krebs likes to watch but whom he finds "too complicated" to try to talk to. What function does this social performance serve, and what does it say about Krebs that he finds it impossible to interact with the young women?

Character

Character analysis can be a fascinating way to approach writing an essay about a work of literature, and in the case of "Soldier's Home," you have the option of writing not only about Krebs but also about any of his family members. When writing an essay that focuses on character, you will want to analyze your character's actions and words, as well as his or her interactions with other characters. Also important to consider is the narrator's treatment of your character. Does he or she seem to be held up as a positive role model or a bad example? Perhaps the most important thing to remember when writing an essay based on a literary character is that you do not want your essay to consist merely of a catalog of character traits; ideally, you want your character analysis to help you arrive at an interpretation of the work as a whole or at least to help you reach some fresh and interesting insights about that work.

Sample Topics:

1. **Krebs:** Krebs garners very different reactions from readers, some condemning him for the weaknesses they perceive in his character and others empathizing with what they perceive as the rough situation Krebs returns to after the war. After careful evaluation, what is your estimation of this character?

   Drawing on what Hemingway reveals in the story, describe what Krebs was like before the war. What do you know about his actual wartime experiences? How is Krebs different now that he has returned from the war? Do you think these changes are permanent? How can you tell? Think about Krebs's family life as well. What effect does his familial situation have on his character and on his development into an adult? And finally, what do you make of Krebs's reaction to the young women in his town? What appeals to him about them? What discourages him from pursuing any of them? What do you think he means when he thinks: "They were such a nice pattern. He liked the pattern. It was exciting" (72). Is he a character with whom we are supposed to sympathize? Or does Hemingway intend for us to criticize the way Krebs behaves?

2. **Krebs's mother:** Analyze and evaluate the character of Krebs's mother.

   Analyze and evaluate the exchanges between Krebs and his mother and the narrator's descriptions of their interactions, including the following: "His mother would have given him breakfast in bed if he had wanted it. She often came in when he was in bed and asked him to tell her about the war, but her attention always wandered" (70). What do you make of Krebs's mother's behavior? Is it odd for her frequently to broach her adult son's bedside? Why do you think she asks Krebs about the war but then does not remain focused on his answers?

   All in all, what do Krebs's mother's motives seem to be? What do you think she wants for Krebs? Would you consider her a "good" mother? How does her behavior and the relationship she fosters with her son affect his overall development and readjustment to civilian society?

3. **Helen:** Analyze and evaluate the character of Krebs's sister, Helen.

   What does Helen represent for Krebs? Why is he able to sustain a relationship with her when he has trouble interacting with everyone else? Would you consider their attachment healthy or problematic in some way?

4. **Krebs's father:** Sometimes an absent character can play a surprisingly important role in a literary work. Although we never

actually see Krebs's father, the narrator makes several references to him. Based on these references, on the traditional role of the father in families of the 1920s, and on your own perception of the role of the father in a family unit, evaluate Krebs's father. How does his role affect his family, particularly his son?

What do you know about Krebs's father? What role does he play in the life of his family? How does Krebs seem to feel about his father? How do the other members of the family seem to feel about him? Imagine how the story might differ if he actually appeared in it and interacted directly with Krebs. How would this likely change the trajectory of Krebs's life back at home?

History and Context

You will almost always benefit from doing some background reading on the time period in which a literary work is written as well as the time period in which it was set. In the case of "Soldier's Home," this is especially true as the story is driven by nuances that you can only appreciate with the proper contextual knowledge. You might begin with some reading about World War I, including the condition of the soldiers who returned from battle and the governmental and social response to these returning soldiers. You might also be interested to learn about the general condition of American society in the 1920s. How did Americans view themselves and their relationship to the rest of the world? How were gender roles evolving? What was family life like? It is also a good idea to do some background reading on the author of a particular piece, in this case Hemingway, to develop a better sense of his circumstances and perspective. With all of this contextual knowledge in place, you will be amazed at how much richer the experience of reading the story will be when you return to it. Details that you did not notice the first time through will suddenly be meaningful, and you will be able to understand the story for what it is, an artistic depiction of or response to a particular historical and cultural moment.

Sample Topics:

1. **World War I and post-traumatic stress:** What does "Soldier's Home" ultimately have to say about the psychological and emotional effects of war on returning soldiers?

Begin with some background reading on World War I and the psychological conditions of the soldiers who returned from battle. You might try *A War of Nerves: Soldiers and Psychiatrists in the Twentieth Century* by Ben Shephard, *American Voices of World War I: Primary Source Documents, 1917–1920* by M. Marix Evans, or *World War I and the Cultures of Modernity* by Douglas Mackaman and Michael Mays. As you do your background reading, be careful to note whether your source is discussing our current understanding of these soldiers and their condition or ideas contemporary with the story, as the psychological effects of warfare were only beginning to be identified and studied at the time that Hemingway was writing "Soldier's Home."

Once you have done some research and background reading, return to "Soldier's Home," and reevaluate Krebs. Does your new knowledge about the psychological effects of battle help you better understand this character? What aspects of his character and behavior do you think can be attributed, at least in part, to his wartime experiences? Why do you think the other soldiers from Krebs's hometown seem to be adjusting better than he is? What kind of commentary do you think Hemingway is making about the psychological effects of war on returning soldiers? Is he mirroring contemporary thought on the subject, or is he presenting something new?

2. **Biographical connections:** Doing some background reading on the author of a piece of literature can often help illuminate certain aspects of the work, and that is certainly true in the case of "Soldier's Home." After some research into Hemingway's life, what new insights can you develop into the themes and meanings of the story?

Critic Steven Trout notes:

> Critical discussion of Ernest Hemingway's "Soldier's Home" has long emphasized the story's autobiographical dimension, the overt parallels between the Hemingway household in Oak Park, Illinois, and the suffocating domestic environment endured, somewhere in Oklahoma, by the returning soldier, Harold Krebs.

As a result, it has almost become customary to connect Krebs's tortured relationship with his mother to Hemingway's own turbulent family background, and to locate in the narrative's sour depiction of small-town life a reflection of Hemingway's personal dissatisfaction with his Midwestern upbringing. (5)

Read about Hemingway's childhood and his family in Carlos Baker's biography, *Ernest Hemingway: A Life Story*, then reread "Soldier's Home" with Baker's book and Trout's comments in mind. Can you expand on the similarities between Hemingway's childhood and "Soldier's Home" that Trout identifies? Or can you identify other connections between Hemingway's own life and the story "Soldier's Home"? Use your observations to draft an essay that offers an interpretation of the story based on its connections to Hemingway's own life. Remember that you do not want simply to point out similarities or differences between Hemingway's life and the story; instead, use what you find to guide you to a new interpretation of the story. For instance, if you find that Krebs's family and household do, in fact, resemble Hemingway's, try then to discover what Hemingway is saying about his family and his place in it. Why write this story about himself, if that is what it is?

3. **Relationship between government and soldiers:** What does Hemingway's "Soldier's Home" have to say about the relationship between the government and soldiers returning from duty in World War I?

According to Steven Trout,

In Our Time appeared less than two years after one of the most unsettling episodes in the history of the federal government's often uneasy relationship with returning soldiers. In 1923 a congressional investigation of the recently created Veterans' Bureau, the federal office supposedly dedicated to the just compensation and care of the 200,000 Americans wounded in the Great War, revealed an institution in actuality pledged to the bold-faced theft of tax dollars, Kafkaesque bureaucracy, and almost complete indifference toward the former soldiers it ostensibly served. (7)

Read Trout's article "'Where Do We Go from Here?': Ernest Hemingway's 'Soldier's Home' and American Veterans of World War I," in its entirety for more details on this scandal. After you have done your background reading, return to the text of "Soldier's Home." What can you glean from the story about the response of the government and society at large to returning soldiers? How might the story be commenting on society's failure to help soldiers returning from traumatic wartime experiences?

Philosophy and Ideas

"Soldier's Home" comments on both a rapidly changing American culture and the power and relevance of religion to that culture. You might use your essay to investigate what the story has to say about the fundamental changes to the very fabric of American society that were occurring in the 1920s. You might ask yourself what the story has to say about changing gender roles, definitions of family, and sacrifice versus self-indulgence, for example. Or you might focus on what the story has to say about religion and spirituality, examining Krebs and his mother and their respective reactions to religion. Why might Krebs have a different opinion about religion than his mother does? What in their respective experiences might account for this difference? Depending on your analysis of the story, you might argue that Krebs's reaction is typical of his generation in a society that, having been exposed to new scientific ideas that challenged their notion of the how the world works and having been confronted with the destruction of war, was no longer able to hold on to religion as a source of security and direction. Or you might treat Krebs not as a stand-in for an entire generation but as an individual soldier suffering a crisis of faith; you might argue, for example, that Krebs's traumatic experiences in the war have caused him to feel abandoned by God and so to forsake religion upon his return to civilian life, or that his reaction against religion is really a reaction against his mother and her efforts to infantilize and manipulate him.

Sample Topics:

1. **Changes in American culture:** American society was quickly evolving in the early decades of the 20th century. According to Robert Paul Lamb, "fundamental social constructs seemed to be everywhere disappearing in the mid 1920s" (29). He notes the "incipient sexual and gender revolution taking place" and points out that the "American family—for over a century an indispensable fortress of prevailing cultural values—was on the verge of collapse" (30–31). Lamb describes even more fundamental changes taking place in American culture as well; he writes that "a culture based on production was giving way to one based on consumption," and that "an ethos of self-denial was increasingly turning to self-indulgence, as evidenced by an alarming rise in alcoholism and drug addiction" (31). What does Hemingway's "Soldier's Home" have to say about these developments?

   You might read Lamb's article, "The Love Song of Harold Krebs: Form, Argument, and Meaning in 'Soldier's Home,'" in its entirety or peruse other sources, such as Lynn Dumenil's *The Modern Temper: American Culture and Society in the 1920s* or David M. Kennedy's *Over Here: The First World War and American Society* for more information on the changes happening in American society in the 1920s. Once you have a firm grasp on 1920s U.S. culture, return to Hemingway's "Soldier's Home." What evidence can you find there of the changes that American society was undergoing at this time? Can these changes help explain the dissonance between Krebs and his parents? What do you think Hemingway was trying to say in "Soldier's Home" about the cultural changes that were taking place? How do large-scale cultural changes affect individuals, according to the story?

2. **Religion:** What kind of commentary does "Soldier's Home" ultimately make on religion?

   Locate and analyze the references to religion in the story, including the following exchange between Krebs and his mother:

"God has some work for every one to do," his mother said. "There can be no idle hands in His Kingdom."

"I'm not in His Kingdom," Krebs said.

"We are all of us in His Kingdom."

Krebs felt embarrassed and resentful as always. (75)

Why do you think this exchange causes Krebs to feel "embarrassed and resentful"? What do you make of the "as always"? Did Krebs feel this way about religion before he went off to war, or is his attitude a reaction to his experiences?

You will want to think about the fact that Hemingway chooses to make Krebs's mother the mouthpiece of religion. What type of character is she? Is she likable, for instance? Why might Hemingway associate a character like Krebs's mother with religion?

Language, Symbols, and Imagery

Paying close attention to the tiniest of details of a literary work can sometimes lead to surprisingly large-scale revelations. For "Soldier's Home," you might start with the two photographs described in the opening passage, for example. The photo of Krebs in college is our only real glimpse into the person he was before he left for war. Thus, it makes sense to study it closely for clues as to Krebs's prewar character and personality. Hemingway follows up the description of this photograph with one of another photograph, this one taken while Krebs is overseas. The juxtaposition practically demands our attention. We must ask ourselves how is Krebs's different in the second photo? How are his conditions different? Close attention to these images can give us insight into the changes that Krebs underwent as a result of his service and perhaps help us better understand his postwar situation.

Sample Topics:

1. **Title of "Soldier's Home":** The title of a literary work can often provide a great deal of guidance as you begin to interpret a story. Stopping to think about why the author chose the precise title that he did as opposed to the many other options and variations he could have selected can be quite enlightening, particularly

in the case of "Soldier's Home." Analyze Hemingway's chosen
title for this story, and use that analysis to help you develop an
interpretation of the story.

The term *soldiers' home*, "[c]oined in the mid-19th century,
perhaps by Florence Nightingale, originally referred to a kind
of recreation hall, one presumably created through charity,"
that provided a "setting . . . not unlike the wholesome reading
rooms and recreation centers later created by the Y.M.C.A. for
American soldiers in World War I" (Trout 6). Over time, the
term came to mean something very different, however. Steven
Trout explains that

> references to a "soldiers' home," at least in the United States,
> carried a more ominous significance, especially for politi-
> cians wary of the notion that the government's obligations
> to its fighting men extended beyond their date of discharge:
> Americans now understood the term to signify a rest home
> for severely wounded veterans or a refuge for indigent former
> soldiers. (6)

Consider the rich history of the term that Hemingway used,
in a slightly modified form, as the title of this story. How do the
meanings and connotations of this term relate to Hemingway's
story? By moving the apostrophe, Hemingway has changed the
possessive from a plural to a singular. Why might this be significant? Is the title meant to carry some type of irony?

2. **Pictures:** What do the two pictures mentioned in the opening
   passage of "Soldier's Home" tell us about Krebs's development?

   Analyze the opening passage of the story, paying particular
   attention to the two pictures of Krebs that are mentioned:

   > Krebs went to the war from a Methodist college in Kansas.
   > There is a picture which shows [Krebs] among his fraternity
   > brothers, all of them wearing exactly the same height and style
   > collar. He enlisted in the Marines in 1917 and did not return to

the United States until the second division returned from the Rhine in the summer of 1919. There is a picture which shows him on the Rhine with two German girls and another corporal. Krebs and the corporal look too big for their uniforms. The German girls are not beautiful. The Rhine does not show in the picture. (69)

What does the first picture tell us about Krebs's life before the war? Contrast this picture and this vision of Krebs with the next one, the one that "shows him on the Rhine with two German girls and another corporal." What is different about Krebs here? What do you make of the fact that he looks "too big for [his] uniform"? Why does the narrator note that the "German girls are not beautiful" and that the "Rhine does not show in the picture"? Why are these things significant? What would the picture be like—what different message would it convey—if the women were glamorous and the river flowed majestically in the background?

Compare and Contrast Essays

Comparisons and contrasts can make for great idea generators and can often function as the basis for an entire essay. In the case of Hemingway's "Soldier's Home," you might compare Krebs with another of Hemingway's soldier protagonists, Nick Adams. Doing so might help you focus on some aspects of Krebs and his situation that you may have missed had you not set Krebs opposite Nick. Afterward, you might decide not to mention Nick at all in your essay, or you might decide to write an essay about Krebs and Nick, using them both to discuss Hemingway's perception of the soldier's experience and psychological and emotional difficulties readjusting successfully to civilian life.

Sample Topics:

1. **Harold Krebs and Nick Adams:** Krebs and Nick Adams are two of Hemingway's most popular fictional creations who share at least one formative experience in common: They both served as soldiers in the war. What can a comparison of these two characters tell you about Hemingway's perception of the effects of wartime experience on young men?

Read or reread "Soldier's Home" and "Big Two-Hearted River." What do you know about Krebs's and Nick's respective wartime experiences? How does each of them respond to these experiences? What are their lives like when they become postwar civilians? Describe the environment to which they return. What do you know about their respective childhood and family life? How might these factors affect them during and after their experiences in the war? Which character is more likable or sympathetic? Why?

2. **Krebs and Holden Caulfield of *The Catcher in the Rye*:** According to Cynthia Berron, "'Soldier's Home,' more than any other single work of Hemingway's, exerted the greatest influence upon [J. D.] Salinger's novel *The Catcher in the Rye*" (70). Compare and contrast these two works, particularly in regard to what they have to say about childhood and coming of age.

For Cynthia Berron, the most significant similarity between the two works is that the main characters, Holden Caulfield and Harold Krebs, when "faced with their inability to adapt to an adult world that is hypocritical and corrupt . . . seek a return to the realm of childhood" (70).

Read or reread "Soldier's Home" and *The Catcher in the Rye*. What similarities do you find between Krebs and Caulfield? What does each of them find objectionable about the adult world? Do you agree with Berron that Krebs and Holden both want to return to their "realm of childhood"? What is enticing about this realm? What about the people who surround Caulfield and Krebs? Are they trying to get these young men to mature into adults or to keep them dependent as children? Taken together, what can these two stories tell us about young men who do not wish to grow up?

Bibliography and Online Resources for "Soldier's Home"

Baker, Carlos. *Ernest Hemingway: A Life Story.* New York: Scribners, 1969.

Berron, Cynthia M. "The Catcher and the Soldier: Hemingway's 'Soldier's Home' and Salinger's *The Catcher in the Rye.*" *Hemingway Review* 2.1 (1982): 70–73.

Caruth, Cathy. *Trauma: Explorations in Memory*. Baltimore, MD: Johns Hopkins UP, 1995.

———. *Unclaimed Experience: Trauma, Narrative, and History*. Baltimore, MD: Johns Hopkins UP, 1996.

Dumenil, Lynn. *The Modern Temper: American Culture and Society in the 1920s*. New York: Hill & Wang, 1995.

Evans, Martin Marix. *American Voices of World War I: Primary Source Documents, 1917–1920*. Chicago: Fitzroy Dearborn, 2001.

Hemingway, Ernest. "Soldier's Home." *In Our Time*. New York: Scribners, 1986. 69–77.

Hemingway Resource Center. "Ernest Hemingway Frequently Asked Questions@lostgeneration.com." Available online. URL: http://www.lostgeneration.com/hemfaq.htm#soldiershome. Retrieved October 15, 2007.

Imamura, Tateo. "'Soldier's Home': Another Story of a Broken Heart." *Hemingway Review* 16.1 (1996): 102–07.

Kennedy, David M. *Over Here: The First World War and American Society*. Rev. ed. New York: Oxford UP, 2004.

Lamb, Robert Paul. "The Love Song of Harold Krebs: Form, Argument, and Meaning in 'Soldier's Home.'" *Hemingway Review* 12.2 (1995): 18–36.

Mackaman, Douglas, and Michael Mays, eds. *World War I and the Cultures of Modernity*. Jackson: UP of Mississippi, 2000.

McKenna, John J., and David M. Raabe. "Using Temperament Theory to Understand Conflict in 'Soldier's Home.'" *Studies in Short Fiction* 34.2 (1997): 203–13.

Shephard, Ben. *A War of Nerves: Soldiers and Psychiatrists in the Twentieth Century*. Cambridge, MA: Harvard UP, 2001.

Trout, Steven. "'Where Do We Go from Here?': Ernest Hemingway's 'Soldier's Home' and American Veterans of World War I." *Hemingway Review* 20.1 (2000): 5–21.

INDEX